THOMISM

and

MODERN THOUGHT

IMPRIMI POTEST:

Joseph P. Fisher, S.J.

Praep. Prov. Missourianae

IMPRIMATUR:

✠ Urban J. Vehr

Archiepiscopus Denveriensis

Die 26 Martii, 1962

THOMISM
and
MODERN THOUGHT

HARRY R. KLOCKER, S.J.

Regis College, Denver

New York

APPLETON-CENTURY-CROFTS

Division of Meredith Publishing Company

COPYRIGHT ACKNOWLEDGMENTS

Benziger Brothers Inc.: for selections from *The Philosophy of Communism* by C. J.
McFadden, copyright 1939 by Benziger Brothers Inc.

Dacre Press, A. & C. Black, Ltd.: for selections from Gabriel Marcel, *Being and Having*,
trans. by Katharine Farrer (1949).

The Bobbs-Merrill Company: for selections from George Berkeley, *A Treatise Concerning
the Principles of Human Knowledge*, edited by Colin M. Turbayne. New York, 1957
("The Library of Liberal Arts" No. 53). Reprinted by permission of the publishers, The
Bobbs-Merrill Company.

J. M. Dent & Sons, Ltd.: for selections from Immanuel Kant, *Critique of Pure Reason*,
trans. by J. M. D. Meiklejohn. Everyman's Library (1934).

Doubleday & Co., Inc.: for selections from *A Gilson Reader*, edited with an introduction
by Anton C. Pegis, copyright © 1957 by Doubleday & Co., Inc.; and for selections from
St. Thomas Aquinas, *Summa Contra Gentiles*, trans. by Anton C. Pegis (1957). Reprinted by permission of the publisher.

Dover Publications Inc.: for selections from *Philosophical Writings of Pierce*, selected
and edited by Justus Buchler; and for selections from *Language, Truth, and Logic*, by
Alfred J. Ayer ($1.25). Reprinted through permission of Dover Publications Inc., New
York 14, N. Y.

E. P. Dutton & Co., Inc.: for selections from the book, *Critique of Pure Reason*, by
Immanuel Kant. Translated by J. M. D. Meiklejohn. Everyman's Library. Reprinted by
permission of E. P. Dutton & Co., Inc.

Harper & Brothers: for selections from Gabriel Marcel, *Being and Having*. New Introduction by James Collins. New York, Harper Torchbooks, 1962.

The Harvill Press, Ltd.: for selections from Gabriel Marcel, *The Mystery of Being*,
Vols. I and II, trans. by G. Fraser and Rene Hague, copyright 1950-1951 by the Harvill
Press, Ltd.

iv

TO

My Mother and Father

PREFACE

This book is a textbook with a twofold purpose. In the first place it aims to give the student, who already possesses some knowledge of the philosophy of St. Thomas Aquinas, a basic understanding of modern, non-Thomistic systems of philosophy which are current today in Europe and America. For students trained to a greater or lesser extent in the philosophy of Aquinas, this is frequently a real need. In most colleges where Thomistic philosophy is taught the student spends most of his time in an attempt to master the Thomistic system. He takes courses in the Philosophy of Being, the Philosophy of Man, the Philosophy of God, Ethics, etc. What he learns of other systems of philosophy, he learns from a history course here or there, or from the views of adversaries which are presented out of context simply as denials of the theories he is studying. As a result, the ordinary student in the college where Thomism is taught has little awareness of systems of philosophy which are currently being taught in other colleges and universities and which are being discussed and written about both in Europe and in America. Such a student may know quite a bit about the philosophy of Aquinas, but unless he is extraordinary, he is more or less incapable of discussing other systems and other approaches to philosophy. Often he is bewildered by the complete lack of similarity between the philosophy he has studied and the philosophy he meets with and hears discussed after he leaves college.

Hence, the second purpose of this text is to show the origins of the main systems of modern philosophy and to compare them to the philosophy of St. Thomas. Since most courses in the history of modern philosophy never get very far beyond Kant, the philosophy of Kant was selected as the starting point for this text. More than any other thinker, except perhaps Descartes, Immanuel Kant has influenced the philosophy of modern times. He is, at least, the more immediate source of much Subjectivism and Idealism; and in another sense, the Experimentalism and the Sensism so prevalent in modern thinking also stems from him. The first few chapters, then, contain a presentation of Kantianism and the Idealism against which Kant wrote, but which he never succeeded in overcoming. The middle chapters deal with the pragmatic, naturalistic, and positivistic systems of modern thinking, which in their own way, owe much to the German philosopher. Existentialism is considered as the modern reaction to the Scientism and Rationalism of the previous century. At the end of each system described, a criticism is presented not only from the Thomistic viewpoint, but also from the viewpoint of evidence and the relation of the system to reality as it confronts us. The final chapters are an attempt to see reality as a whole and to show that Aquinas has at least laid the groundwork for a philosophy which most intelligently and adequately explains that reality without doing violence to experience. The last chapter points to a realm beyond the science of metaphysics which must be considered if one is to have any appreciation of reality in its totality. Hence, it is hoped that the text will lead the student not only to a basic knowledge of modern systems of philosophy, but to a greater insight into the validity and adequacy of the philosophy of St. Thomas and a fuller appreciation of Christian wisdom.

In a text which is meant to be covered in one semester, it is obvious that the treatment of the various philosophical systems discussed had to be brief. In such cases, one always does a certain amount of injustice to the philosophies under consideration. As a partial remedy for this, readings have been inserted at the end of each chapter with a view toward presenting a fuller understanding in the words of those who are most closely connected with the system of thought under discussion. The selected bibliography at the end of each chapter is also meant to be an aid to further study and understanding. Let me finally express my sincere gratitude to all those from whose teachings or writings I have drawn in one way or another. I owe special thanks to the Rev. William L. Wade, S.J. of the department of philosophy of St. Louis University for his helpful suggestions and criticism and to Patricia O'Connor,

Theresa Montoya, Mary Jean Moran, and Carol Meek for their generous help in preparing the manuscript.

Denver, Colorado
H. R. K., S. J.

CONTENTS

THOMISM

and

MODERN THOUGHT

Introduction

THE NATURE OF PHILOSOPHY

THERE IS A GREAT DEAL of discussion today about the nature of the study we call philosophy and its place in the whole area of knowledge. It is admitted in general that it is part of the tradition we term humanistic. Aristotle considered it a science in the strict sense of the word. As we shall see, later philosophers, especially modern philosophers, have been less and less willing to admit that the Aristotelian definition is the correct one. Even those who are still willing to call philosophy a science find it difficult to determine just what sort of a science it is and how it is related to the other sciences. For the present let us say simply that philosophy is a systematic study of reality and that it attempts to achieve a certain knowledge of the real which it can express in objectively valid propositions.

Such a descriptive definition, however, is not especially peculiar to philosophy. Almost the same thing could be said of some of the natural sciences. Is there any way to distinguish philosophy from these sciences? There is one way, and that is according to the method and the purpose of the various attempts to acquire knowledge. The natural sciences, for example, investigate reality in terms of its observable structure and its activity. The natural sciences are interested in processes and functions and in establishing some sort of relationship between these processes and functions. All the natural sciences take the existence of a universe in process for granted and attempt to understand this universe in terms of its processes.

Now while philosophy also makes use of experience and investigates functions and activities, it does so not to understand how these functions are related, but to reach conclusions about the nature of the reality manifested by such functions and processes. Philosophy, in other words, attempts to seek out the principles which are ultimately responsible for the real. Instead of taking the existence of things for granted, the philosopher wants to know what existence means, what matter is in terms of its realness, what motion is in its very nature, what to be a cause means. Philosophy turns its attention to being itself, to its intrinsic structure and its extrinsic source.

THE PERENNIAL PROBLEMS OF PHILOSOPHY

In its search for ultimate principles, philosophy has always looked at reality from the same basic viewpoint. Reality, to some extent at least, is certainly sensible. And philosophy has consistently inquired into the ultimate principle of this sensible section of the real. The answers have been many and varied, but the quest has always been there. Thales thought the answer was water. Others answered in terms of atomic structure. Still others went beyond mere intrinsic principles and sought the answer in terms of an extrinsic principle, which they called an efficient cause. Christian philosophers have termed this ultimate extrinsic principle God.

Another perennial problem of philosophy has been the nature and destiny of man. Man comes under consideration as a special type of being, and it can certainly be asked what it is that makes him the special type of being that he is. Again the answers have been many and varied. St. Thomas and the tradition that he followed has insisted that it is his rational soul that is ultimately responsible for man being the type of thing he is.

Thirdly, we can ask what it is that is ultimately responsible for the good life. Man has to act, and he has to act in one way or another. If his action is to lead him to a perfecting of his nature, if it is to be a source of his human development, then action must be conformed to a norm or standard that will produce the desired effect. That norm or standard is right reason, and action in accord with this norm is called moral action.

Hence ultimately it is morality which adequately leads man to the perfection of his rational nature.

Lastly, we can ask what is the ultimate principle of everything. This will be the absolutely ultimate, that which makes all that is intelligible what it is, that which makes all reality real, that which makes all beings be. This we call God. All of these questions have been considered in the history of man's thought. Some have given definite answers to all of the questions. Some have denied that answers could be found. Some have maintained a polite skepticism rather than commit themselves to an answer. But all have had to face the questions. We shall do that in the course of this book and we shall compare the answers given by various systems of modern philosophy to those given by St. Thomas Aquinas. We shall compare them and attempt to show that in the last analysis it is Thomism which provides not only the most complete answers, but also the answers which best conform to the evidence which must be considered, if we are to arrive at answers at all.

THE PROBLEM OF KNOWLEDGE

There is another problem which must be considered, because it is a problem peculiar to most modern systems of thought. That is the problem of knowledge. Today, more than at any other time, perhaps, the validity of human knowledge is questioned. A great deal of modern thought simply denies that the human mind can attain any knowledge of ultimates, not to mention knowledge of objects distinct from the thinking self. Even where knowledge of reality is admitted, it is too often limited to a knowledge of the physical universe; so that man's intellect is forever bound to his sensations. Hence the problem of human knowledge must be considered, and there must be some decision made as to its objectivity and validity.

THE PROBLEM OF GOD

If the objective validity and certainty of knowledge is a problem in modern philosophy, then obviously the conclusions which

knowledge strives to reach will be equally subject to all the difficulties and uncertainties which modern philosophers find in the
knowing process itself. Now one of the conclusions which traditional philosophy has always asserted as valid is the proposition:
God exists. To say that many systems of modern and contemporary thought no longer regard this proposition as certain is an
understatement, to say the least. To call this proposition into
question is a necessary consequence of various systems of thought
which either limit the intellect of man to a certain area of reality,
or distrust the ability of the human intellect in all areas, or deny
that intellection is in any way radically different from sensation
and imagination. It involves also a distrust of the whole metaphysical endeavor, or an outright denial that metaphysics is possible as a science. The result is either a complete skepticism or
the reduction of philosophy to an attempt to harmonize the
findings of the various natural sciences. Philosophy then becomes
a method by which the truths established by the natural sciences
are integrated in some sort of theoretical pattern. Or worse yet,
philosophy is regarded as empty speculation about areas which
natural science has not yet been able to investigate adequately.
As natural science increases, however, philosophy is bound to
decrease, until that happy day, when natural science will have
pulled away the veil from the last mystery in the universe.

Since in the space of a college text it is impossible to investigate
every problem of modern thought, this text will attempt to treat
modern philosophy primarily from the viewpoint of knowledge
of God. The aim will be, then, to indicate the basic origins of
modern and contemporary philosophy, to show how and why
the modern rejection of metaphysics and the distrust of knowledge have arisen, and how this has affected the ability of the
modern mind to arrive at any knowledge of God.

I

The Limitation
of
Intellect

KANTIAN SUBJECTIVISM

WE SHALL BEGIN our consideration, then, with the man who more than anyone else is responsible for the limitations put upon the validity of human knowledge. That man is Immanuel Kant. Kant was born in 1724 in the little town of Königsberg in East Prussia. He studied at the University of Königsberg, took his doctorate there and eventually joined the faculty.

Kant and Rationalism

Kant was trained in the rationalistic philosophy of his time. Rationalism was a system of philosophy which grew out of the thought of René Descartes and in Germany was a direct legacy from Leibniz and Christian Wolff. Basically it consisted in an a priori system deduced through a process of analyzing concepts. These concepts might have been derived from experience in the beginning, but from then on experience became completely unnecessary. Rationalists held that the human reason was completely sufficient unto itself; and, if left to itself, could logically and correctly deduce the principles of all philosophical knowledge. Fur-

5

thermore, what is deduced by such an analysis is absolutely and universally true. The Rationalists built complete systems of philosophy through such a method, and Rationalism became synonymous with metaphysics.

Now this is the way in which mathematics proceeds. A definition is arrived at based initially on some experience. Then by a strictly logical and deductive process mathematics proceeds to deduce the consequences and properties which the mind sees are necessarily contained in the definition. From the definition of a triangle the mathematician can assert that every triangle necessarily has 180 degrees. From his definition of a circle he can deduce all the properties that are necessarily connected with the concept of a circle. Such knowledge definitely has advantages. It is necessary and certain, and therefore of the highest scientific value.

Kant and Hume

This was the system of philosophizing to which Kant had been exposed. It was the type of philosophy he had accepted. Then he read Hume in German translation. David Hume, who lived from 1711-1776, had a completely different approach. He insisted that unless knowledge began in experience and remained in contact with experience, it was valueless. Yet what Hume meant by experience was always something much more subjective than objective. What the knowing subject is aware of in experience is not the thing, but rather the impressions which the thing makes upon that knowing subject. Hence, Hume divided knowledge into two elements: sense impressions and awareness of such sense impressions. There is, for example, the impression which an object—a rose— makes upon me. There is, further, my own awareness of this impression. From the very beginning Hume is dealing with his own subjective reactions to things and not with things themselves.

When he further examined these sense impressions, Hume could find in them none of the relationships and none of the principles which rationalistic philosophy had always insisted were there. There was, for instance, no impression of anything like a causal influx; there was no impression of anything corresponding to what the Rationalists called substance. Hence Hume concluded that the assertion of the existence of anything like substance, or the assertion that a causal principle was at work in the real order, were vague generalizations that went beyond any experience we can have and were, therefore, of doubtful value, to say the least. Substance, said Hume, could mean nothing else except the collection of impressions we get from a given thing. Causality could mean nothing else except the fact that some impressions are always associated in our experience. This constant connection between certain impressions is elevated to an idea of causal interdependence by our imagination. But to assert that substance exists, or that one thing is really the cause of another, is to go beyond what we have experienced. This can never be valid. For knowledge and experience are synonymous. To say we can know something which we have never experienced is the same as saying that we can know something which we have never known.

Now, while Hume's theory of knowledge marks a return—at least to a certain extent—to reality as we find it, it also succeeded in completely destroying any hope of a scientific and universal knowledge of that reality. If knowledge and experience are identical, and if all we know are the subjective impressions made upon us, then we can never really know things or the laws that govern their operations. We can, furthermore, never really know if anything exists which cannot be experienced. All knowledge is necessarily reduced to an awareness of sense impressions. Some of these impressions may be factually associated with others, but all we can know is the brute fact of such association. In my experience, the impression of fire and the impression of heat go together. They will probably be associated in my next experience. But to say that fire is the cause of heat is to assert something which I have never experienced. Association is not causality. Hume could know nothing more of the universe that what he experienced of it. And he experienced nothing which would enable the human mind to construct a certain and scientific knowledge of that universe. Hume had not only destroyed any possibility of knowing whether God exists, he had also destroyed metaphysics and all natural science.

Kant was not quite willing to give up all hope of achieving

a scientific knowledge of reality. He was convinced that science
was possible. After all, he had only to look at the marvelous
success of mathematics and physics to assure himself that the
human mind could achieve certain and universal knowledge.
Kant could never be a skeptic, and he saw that Hume's theory of
knowledge would lead to a complete skepticism. Kant did, however, give Hume credit for awakening him from his dogmatic
slumber. He saw that, if philosophy were to achieve the status
of a science, it must take account of reality and experience and
not be content to merely analyze concepts, as the Rationalists
had done. Kant's problem was now a twofold one. He had to
expose first of all the inadequacy of the rationalistic metaphysics.
And he had to determine whether metaphysics itself could ever
be raised to the level of a true and certain knowledge of the real.

Kant's Attack on Metaphysics

Accordingly Kant launched an attack against rationalistic metaphysics. This attack embraced two major points.

1. The Rationalists had failed to make a distinction between the
logical ground for a thing and the existential cause of its actuality.
The logical reason provides an explanation of the thing's structure
or essence; it cannot explain how one thing arises from another
in the real order. Take, for example, the concept of causality. If
this concept is examined in itself before we have any actual
experience of cause and effect in the real order, then the mind
can fashion for itself a possible explanation of why effects should
have causes. It can do this by reflecting on the limited nature of
conceptualized being, asking itself what is logically demanded
by such a concept of limited being and can conclude that such a
concept must implicitly involve the notion of cause. But such an
approach tells us nothing about the nature of actually existing
beings, nor does it inform us whether or not the beings which
actually exist are caused. The Rationalists, Kant saw, were content to go through such logical analyses without ever attempting
to find out if such analyses really applied to things as they are.

2. The Rationalists had also failed to distinguish between the concept of the thing and its existence. Kant saw that never from the analysis of a concept could one conclude to the existence of the object of that concept. He understood clearly that existence is never contained in the intelligibility of a thing. The concept of an existing hundred dollars is not more perfect intellectually than the concept of a possible hundred dollars. Both contain the same perfection of intelligibility as far as meaning goes. The only possible way then to go from the concept of a thing to a knowledge that the thing exists is through experience.

Kant's Problem

Yet there were difficulties. Experience might very well provide new knowledge. It could and did provide knowledge of the existential order. At the same time such knowledge was a knowledge of the purely contingent. It was a knowledge of the particular. If knowledge were to be scientific, it had to be universal, certain, and absolute. The scientist, after all, deals with conclusions that can be applied to any individual instance, with conclusions that are universally true in the particular area under the consideration of the science in question. Now while experience provided knowledge of existence and made possible the experiential advance in knowledge, it did not and apparently could not provide knowledge of the kind that is necessary for science.

On the other hand, the knowledge achieved by the analysis of concepts independent of experience was a certain and universal knowledge; hence, it met the demands to some extent, at least, of scientific knowledge. Yet such an a priori analysis of concepts failed to provide any new knowledge. In such cases the predicate of a proposition failed to add anything really to the subject. Take, for example, the proposition: The human soul is immortal. In such a proposition the predicate "immortal" merely makes more explicit what is already contained in the meaning of the subject, "soul." If I really understand what is meant by "human soul," then I also understand perfectly that such a being as the human soul must be immortal. Hence, while such knowledge is certain, universal, and absolutely true, it marks no advance in knowledge; nor does it tell me whether human souls exist or not. This is the sort of knowledge which Kant thought was proper to metaphysics. If this were the case, then obviously metaphysics provided only a knowledge of concepts. And however certain and universal such knowledge might be, it was in the end result a sterile knowledge devoid of any reference to actuality.

Kant's Solution

In his attempt, then, to overcome the skepticism of Empiricism on the one hand and the sterility of Rationalism on the other Kant set out to investigate the very conditions which made knowledge possible. He was aware that the human intellect made two basically different types of judgment. There were what he called a priori judgments—judgments in which the predicate was contained at least implicitly in the subject. Such a judgment would be, for example, all bodies occupy space. In such a judgment from the very notion of body one can conclude that a body necessarily occupies space. Such a judgment had, as a matter of fact, the universality and necessity that is characteristic of scientific knowledge. Yet at the same time such a judgment could never really increase our knowledge. It was a mere tautology in which the predicate did no more than make explicit what was already implicitly contained in the subject. On the other hand the intellect also made judgments in which the predicate was acquired from experience, as for example, this hat is red. Such judgments added something to our knowledge. These judgments he called synthetic judgments. Yet there was a difficulty here also. While such judgments did increase our knowledge, they failed to contain the necessity and universality which scientific knowledge must have. There must be another class of judgments which contained both the assertion of new knowledge and the universality and necessity demanded by science. Science was a fact. Therefore such judgments must also be a fact. Kant called them synthetic a priori judgments. His next problem was to explain how such judgments were possible.

KANT'S THEORY OF KNOWLEDGE[1]

Sense Knowledge

Sensation, as Kant saw it, was composed of a material element and a formal element. The material element was the great diversity of impressions which is constantly impinging on the senses. The senses are under constant bombardment, as it were, by a manifold of pure diversity. This pure diversity, however, would be incapable of being assimilated in terms of an experience, unless it were somehow unified. Since the diversity is not in itself unified, the unification must be provided. Such unification is the formal element in sensation, and it is a twofold one imposed on the pure diversity of the material element in sensation by man's power of sensibility itself. This first unifying factor imposed on the matter of sensation is space. It is only after the data of sensation have been localized or "spacified" that the first condition of human experience is fulfilled. But more than this is required. A unification in terms of duration must also be provided. Continuity and duration are also elements of our sensible experiences. This second principle of unification which makes sense experience possible Kant called time. Hence space and time are subjective forms of the sensibility imposing themselves on the matter of sensation, constituting a sense experience, making the pure diversity into an object for the senses.

That space and time were not something objective, associated with the material data of sensation, Kant thought was perfectly obvious. Space and time are, after all, measures of physical dimensions, and a measure exists in the one measuring rather than in the object measured. Then, too, said Kant, when one abstracts from all the qualities of sense appearances, one can proceed to the point where only space and time are left. These, then, are clearly not associated with the data of sense but are unifications imposed by the one having the sense experience. This is the first

[1] Most of the material for this section has been taken from the following works: *The Inaugural Dissertation*, trans. by J. Handyside; *The Critique of Pure Reason*, trans. by N. K. Smith; and *The Fundamental Principles of the Metaphysics of Ethics*, trans. by Thomas Kingsmill Abbott.

step in Kant's "Copernican Revolution." Instead of considering the sensing subject as passive and merely receptive of sense impressions, Kant sees the subject as formally constituting its proper sense object. No longer do the senses revolve about the sense object, but rather man's sensibility makes its object.

Subjectivity of Sensation

Since the formal element in all sensation is supplied by the sensing subject, and since it is this very imposition of the formal element which constitutes the sense object, it is obvious that this object could never be the thing in itself. Whatever such a thing in itself might be, we could simply never know. It is important to note that Kant did not deny that such things existed. Their existence is in fact implied by the causality which they exert upon us. But they can affect us only in accord with the laws and principles according to which sensation is possible. And this very possibility of sensation depends more on the sensing subject than it does on the thing in itself. Such a thing in itself may thrust itself upon us, but it can supply us only with a diversity of qualitative and quantitative modifications which must be elevated to the status of object before we can have any sensation. Kant may not have denied that things in themselves existed in their own right, but he did isolate them once and for all and make it impossible for any knowing subject ever to come into contact with them as they existed in their externality.

Intellectual Knowledge

There is, however, more to experience than sensation. If experience and sense experience were one and the same thing, Kant did not see how he could ever overcome the scepticism of Hume. He was convinced that science was possible, and, if it was, then intellectual knowledge had to complement sensation and make experience capable of providing the universality and necessity demanded by science. Such universality and necessity could never come from sensation alone. How could it? Everything in sensation is particular and individual. It is all contingent. It might just as well not have happened. Yet as a matter of fact, the knowledge which we have and which includes sense experience also includes these characteristics of universality and necessity. Where do they come from? Kant answered that they come from the intellect. For intellect is also a constituent factor in experience. It enters into experience, elevates it, imposing upon it a still higher unification in terms of the laws that make all knowledge possible. For we are constantly going beyond mere sensation and making universal and necessary statements based on the particular sensations we have. We talk in terms of necessary properties, of possibility and existence, of cause and effect. And we mean to affirm that these are universally true propositions giving us certain knowledge. Hence, it must be the proper function of intellect to provide this certainty and necessity and universality which we are aware of in our knowledge. The intellect contains within itself these pure formalities which it spontaneously imposes on sense experience and thus makes the experience an intellectual one as well. Thus the object of the senses is transformed and made also an object of intellect which regulates it according to meanings which go beyond the particularity of sensation. In other words, just as the senses impose unity upon the material element in sensation, so does the intellect impose its own special unity and intelligibility upon the already unified data of sense. These formalities which are contained in the intellect, Kant called the categories. In a way they can be called innate ideas, but the intellect is not aware of them beforehand. They are one of the elements making experience possible, explaining the characteristics which we find in our scientific knowledge, but knowable as such only by an investigation into the conditions which make knowledge possible.

It is because of the application of these categories, these pure intellectual forms on sense experience that we can speak in terms of cause and effect, substance and accident, possibility and existence. It is important to remember that the intellect is not discovering anything in the real order and asserting it. This is, as we have already seen, impossible. The intellect is interpreting sense experience coherently and scientifically. It is functioning universally because it is acting according to the laws which regulate all thought. Whether things in themselves are like that or not we shall never really know. But at least we have to think of things in this way. Causality may or may not be at work in the order of things distinct from our knowledge of them. But causality as a meaning imposed by the intellect on the data of sense insures that we will infallibly think in terms of cause and effect. This imposition of the intellectual categories did not happen at random, but was accomplished through the instrumentality of the imagination, which automatically applied the right category to the sense data at hand.

The result of such a theory was for Kant a happy one. He was now certain that he had explained the very conditions responsible for all scientific knowledge. He had found a type of knowledge between the purely a priori and the purely empirical. He had the synthetic knowledge which is demanded for all progress in science, and he had the necessity also demanded by science but previously seen as a characteristic only of a priori knowledge. This was the answer to both Rationalism and Empiricism. He called it synthetic-a priori knowledge. And he had, incidentally, the answer to another question he had posed: Why is it that after so many centuries metaphysics had made no real progress?

Effects of Kant's Theory of Knowledge

The effect on the rationalistic theory of knowledge as an analysis of concepts was, of course, disastrous. Kant was perfectly willing to admit the existence of concepts in the intellect. In fact the existence of such pure concepts, or forms, as he called them, was necessary to explain knowledge. Now these pure concepts are seen as necessarily connected with the data of sense before they can have any real meaning. In themselves they are pure intelligibilities, sheer forms which need the matter of sense in order to have any reference to experience. To analyze them in themselves is to gain at the most a knowledge of possibility, of essences; and this is a knowledge without any meaningful reference to things. It made of all rationalistic knowledge no more than an empty shell, a pure logic which, however consistent it might be in itself, was useless as knowledge of things. The theory further made all knowledge of anything beyond sense experience empty and meaningless as far as reality was concerned. All metaphysics, then, was nothing else than empty speculation on pure logical possibilities. Metaphysics had no object in experience, since metaphysics dealt with intelligibilities which transcended sense experience. But since the intellect was limited to sense experience in order to achieve valid knowledge of the real, any attempt to transcend sense experience resulted in empty speculation upon what could be considered real only in so far as it was an idea in the mind. Metaphysics had always investigated the meaning of such things as cause and effect, substance and accident, essence and existence. But these are all pure concepts existing in the mind and meant to be applied to sense experience in order to make such experience understandable. Taken apart from such experience they could not possibly give any knowledge of things in themselves, because they were not things in themselves. To speak, then, of demonstrating such truths as the immortality of the soul, the existence of God, the causal proposition was equally meaningless. These things were not given in sense experience; they transcended sense experience. And in the realm beyond such experience, if there was one, the intellect was useless. All that one can say about such propositions is that they are logically possible because they contain within themselves no logical contradiction. Whether they point to a reality beyond experience or not, it is simply impossible to tell. I cannot state that any given soul is immortal, because I get neither soul nor immortality in sense experience.

What Kant had tried to do, of course, was to get beyond the pure contingency and particularity of sense knowledge and elevate knowledge to the point where it was scientifically valid. He wanted to get beyond the Empiricism of Hume, which he felt would lead to a complete scepticism, and put knowledge on the plane of science. Yet at the same time he wanted to explain the conditions which made such knowledge possible. However, after he had made the fusion between sense knowledge and intellectual knowledge, he had, as a matter of fact, tied intellect to sense forever.

The Unity of the Self or the Ego

Now if the senses impose the unifying forms of space and time on the pure manifold of experience and the intellect in turn contributes its intelligibility and unity to the sense impressions, then there must be a principle of unity which underlies the whole process of unification. If the intellect unifies, somewhere in the background there must exist the source of the unification which is applied. This source of unity Kant called the self or the *Ego*. The whole process might be diagrammed as follows.

The Self or the Ego   *not given in experience*

The Intellect   *called reason when considering the categories in themselves*
containing
the
Categories   *called understanding when applied to sense experience*

which are applied through
the
Imagination

to

The Senses
containing
the forms
of
Space and time
which in turn
unify the diversity
of sense impressions

} *Experience*

The thing-in-itself   *not given in experience*

The Ego is not an object of experience or knowledge; neither is the thing-in-itself. The intellect, when it is functioning as regulative of sense experience, is called the understanding. When it is considering merely the pure intelligibilities which it contains, it is called the pure reason. Hence, while the ego and the pure intelligibilities are not a proper object of knowledge, they are capable of being understood, at least as the ultimate and more proximate conditions which make all proper knowledge possible.

THE PURE IDEAS: SOUL, WORLD, AND GOD

We have seen that, although the intellect is properly limited to sense experience for its valid knowledge, yet it has an innate tendency to go beyond such experience in an attempt to synthesize and unify its knowledge. That tendency is made manifest in the formulation of three ultimate ideas of unification. Those ideas are the idea of the soul, the world, and God. The idea of soul represents the unity that man is striving to achieve in terms of himself. Man would like to unify himself in terms of a principle which is the source of the unity he imposes on experience. This principle has been called the soul, and philosophers have consistently tried to prove that it is a substantial principle, that it is spiritual, immortal, simple, etc.

Soul

Kant insisted that the idea of a substantial soul was a mere expression of man's striving for unity and denied that such a principle could be actually proved to exist. The idea of soul has value only in so far as it expresses our attempt to find unity at the source of our human operations. To show this Kant considered the rationalist proof given for the existence of a substantial soul. It ran as follows:

That which cannot be thought of except as a subject does not exist otherwise than as a subject, and is, therefore, substance.
But a thinking being considered merely as such cannot be thought of except as a subject.
Therefore, a thinking being exists only as a subject; i.e., as substance.

The major premise is a definition expressing the fact that that which can never be a predicate but is only a subject of predication must exist, if it does exist, as a subject of predication. This is what is meant by a substance; for one substance can never be predicated of anything else. Now when one considers the self as a thinking being, one sees that this self cannot be predicated of anything else, that it is only a subject of predication. This is to say that the self fulfills the definition of substance; and, therefore, since it exists, it must exist as a substance. So argued the traditional Rationalists in their attempt to prove that the soul had substantial existence.

In his examination of this argument Kant concluded that the syllogism was invalid because it contained four terms. For "subject" as contained in the major premise is an objective designation for a permanently given substratum which is at the heart of the being we call man. But "subject" as contained in the minor premise is used to designate what one gets in experience—the collection of thoughts and experiences to which it is impossible to apply the category of substance, since there is no observable element of permanence in the mere consciousness of my thinking process. Hence, concluded Kant, the argument for the existence of a substantial principle in man is incapable of being proved. Now if the substantial existence of the soul cannot be proved, neither can its immortality or spirituality or simplicity.

World

One meets similar contradictions, when one considers the idea of the world. This again is an attempt to find unity at the basis of the sense experience we have of a physical universe. But to synthesize these experiences in what we call a world is capable of fulfillment along directly contradictory lines. Reason by analyzing the situation sees the need for a finite unity here. But experience, on the other hand, can always conceive another experience as possible in a series, and thus the series cannot be closed. Thus what reason proves from the one viewpoint, experience denies from another. Rationalism is directly and contradictorily opposed to Empiricism. The world can be proved to be both finite and infinite, composite and simple, contingent and necessary. Ultimately Kant resolved the last two antinomies by distinguishing between the determinism of appearances and their possibly free source, the contingency of appearances and their possibly necessary source. For, while according to appearances the law of cause and effect is inexorable, the source of such appearances may actually contain the perfection we call freedom. Since we can never know the source, we can conceive it as possibly a free source. Hence freedom remains a possibility, even though there is no such evidence given in our experience. Hence freedom, and even God, may be believed in as possible, even though whatever falls within the realm of knowledge is subject to finitude and determinism.

God—The Ontological Argument

The idea of God is also an idea of unity conceived by reason in its attempt to reach a fundamental unity of all possible objects. Having achieved the possibility of such a fundamental unity, reason then declares it to exist and calls it God. Such an approach is obviously ontological in character and as an argument for the existence of God is completely invalid. Kant's analysis of the ontological argument takes the following form. The proposition "This thing exists," is either analytic or synthetic. If analytic, then the predicate, "exists," adds nothing to the concept of the subject. If the proposition is synthetic, then it cannot be proved a priori. Yet neither can it be proved from experience; for in the world of appearances and phenomena, we experience only conditioned modes of existence. Experience can provide no way at all to distinguish between mere possibility and unconditioned existence. This makes not only the ontological argument valueless but all arguments for the existence of God.

The Cosmological Argument

When the so-called cosmological argument is considered, the same difficulties arise. This argument proceeds from the fact of contingent beings to an assertion that a necessary being exists. This necessary being is then identified with God. But the identification is hardly valid. It is necessary first to prove that this

necessary being in question is not material, that it is personal
and a creating Being. This in turn means that one must prove
a most perfect Being. Such a being will exist by virtue of its very
definition. And this is to fall back into the ontological argument.
It is interesting to note here that the later scholastic philosophers
had the same difficulty with the argument for the existence of
God based on the fact of motion. They were willing to admit
that the argument proved a first mover, but had difficulties in
identifying this first mover with God. Suarez recognized the objection, and Ockham later still insisted that the proof went only
so far as a first mover. He even admitted the possibility of many
such first movers, each the first cause in a particular series. If
this is all the further the argument leads, it is apparent that it
cannot prove by itself the existence of God.

The Great Designer

Kant lastly considered the argument based on the fact of order
in the universe. From the fact of order one can argue to the
existence of a God Who is ultimately responsible for the ordering.
But this, too, said Kant, is an invalid illation. All the argument
proves is an orderer; it by no means proves that this orderer is
God. Just as one might argue from an intricately made machine to
a machine maker, so one is accustomed to argue from an intricately ordered universe to a God. This may very well prove a
universe maker, said Kant, but there is all the difference possible
between a universe maker and a God. Plato held such a world
fashioner, which he called the demi-urge. But Plato never thought
for a moment that such a being could be identified with God.
To achieve that, said Kant, the argument from order must be sup-
plemented by the cosmological argument and that in turn by
the ontological argument. Such a proof, as we have already seen
is invalid. Consequently there are no arguments which adequately
prove the existence of a supreme being. The conclusion was a
foregone one, when we realize that every such argument must
necessarily transcend the data of sense experience. But that, too,
is to present to reason an impossible task, since by its very nature

it is limited to sense experience for any certain and valid knowledge.

Thus the final hope is destroyed that metaphysics may be a possible science. The last illusion is gone, and the critical philosophy has demonstrated once and for all that reason has definite and certain limits. Within those limits it can achieve a knowledge of appearances; outside of them, it is reduced to empty speculation about pure concepts, which as such have no relation with the real. Certain and scientific knowledge, therefore, is limited to the world of sense experience, which is to limit it to the realm of the natural sciences and mathematics. Metaphysics may express a hope or a dream or an emotional reaction, but it cannot possibly express knowledge. The position is a favorite one of modern Positivists and Naturalists, and we shall return to it later.

Kant's Theory of Morality

When he took up the question of ethics, Kant started with a fact of experience. It is evident that there is a moral law imposing itself on all individuals. Action is regulated by an "Ought." It is the task of the critical philosopher to inquire into the conditions which make this fact possible. Since the "ought" is universal, this universality demands that the ultimate principle be an a priori one. Yet since the "ought" governs action, the principle will be found in practical reason rather than in the realm of pure reason.

This reason commands without respect to circumstances or conditions. Hence it is categorical and imperative. Kant called it the Categorical Imperative. To subordinate such a law to particulars would be to make it self-contradictory. The object of this imperative is the phenomenal self, the self recognized from experience. The source is the noumenal self, the transcendental Ego, which gives the law and imposes it upon the experiential self. Hence it is the task of each individual to accept the law imposed by himself upon himself and to regulate the self he discovers in experience according to the dictates of the absolute self. Only in this way can thought, desires, sensations, inclinations be brought in line with the moral order. In this way does man become good or holy by submitting himself to the dictates of higher reason for the sake of that dictating reason. The recognition that he must do so is what Kant called duty. It is only when one acts out of sheer respect for duty, that the act can be called a truly moral act.

This also makes for the autonomy of the individual, so that the individual becomes really a law unto himself. Yet this does not mean that morality is a completely individualistic thing. For while the categorical imperative legislates for the self, it does so in such a way that the self is led beyond itself and brought into relationship with other selves. For, said Kant, one should always act so that the directive from which the act springs could at the same time become a universal law for all men. If this is impossible, then the act commanded would seem to spring rather from another source than from the imperative of practical reason.

The Postulates of Practical Reason

As we have seen earlier, reason, limited as it is to the phenomena, could not prove either the freedom of the will, the immortality of the soul or the existence of God. Yet while reason could not prove that such supra sensible realities existed, neither could it disprove them. They remained at least logical possibilities, since they contained no contradictions within themselves. It is here in the moral order that Kant is able to justify belief, at least, in these transcendental realities. For since the moral law says "ought," it also presupposes "can." And "can" becomes impossible, unless the will is free to determine itself. It is precisely this self determination that is meant by freedom. Hence, while freedom can never be proved, it is presupposed as a condition without which the moral order could not function.

Furthermore, this order directs the individual toward a state in which the phenomenal self is harmonized with the noumenal self, all desires and inclinations are made completely adequate to the moral law. This perfect adequation is not possible in this life. Hence, it demands a progress possible only on the condition of man's continued existence beyond this life. Therefore, the personal immortality, which reason could not prove, is demanded as a condition by the moral order.

Now, if nature and morality are ultimately to be harmonized, this harmonization, too, requires the condition which makes it possible. For this harmony will result in the happiness which is the reward of having observed the law. Now man did not create nature, nor can he adequately reward himself for having kept the law. Only the creator of both man and nature can do that. So that again the God Who could not be proved to exist, is postulated as the necessary condition which makes morality a possibility.

This is what Kant means by a reasonable faith. Freedom, Immortality and God were always possible—that is, non-contradictory—in the realm of pure reason. Now they are demanded by practical reason itself. They are still not objects of knowledge. But they can now be accepted as conditions of all moral living. Hence the basis of religious belief is nothing else than what is required by the moral life. And Kant saw an historical revelation as merely another expression of what he had discovered in his critique of practical reason. There is nothing in the least supernatural about such a religious belief. It is no more than an ethico-naturalistic religion based on what one is tempted to describe as a hope that beyond reason there is reason to hope.

CRITICISM OF KANT

Immanuel Kant achieved a synthesis of knowledge in terms of experience and a priori intellectual forms. This synthesis enabled him to explain how knowledge was both in contact with experience and how at the same time it could be truly scientific. Knowledge now possessed all the characteristics which were required for it to be universal, necessary, and certain. At the same time knowledge never lost its contact with experience; and, hence, there was room always for progression and completion. Thus Kant was sure that he had avoided Hume's skepticism on the one hand and the Rationalists' pure abstractionism on the other.

But Kant had also done something else. In limiting knowledge to a combination of experience and a priori forms he had also restricted knowledge forever to what could be sensibly experienced. The only knowledge of reality now possible for the human intellect was that which the natural sciences could provide, for only these dealt explicitly with sensible experience. Any knowledge which attempted to transcend such experience could only be a knowledge of pure possibilities, of what could be; it could never be a knowledge of the real. Since, according to the Rationalists, metaphysics dealt only with concepts, it was immediately evident that metaphysics could no longer be considered either scientific or valid knowledge of reality. Intellectually it was now impossible to achieve any reality except that which could be sensibly experienced.

After the Kantian critique, then, the question was: can we know there is more to reality than what can be sensibly experienced? If there is, how can we arrive at such knowledge? Is there anything in the realm of sensible experience which indicates that there must be more to reality than what we can experience?

It is obvious that, if the conclusions which Kant draws cannot be admitted, then they must be attacked at their source. If metaphysics is really possible, if the existence of God and the immortality of the soul are more than simply objects of faith, then it must be shown that knowledge is wider in range and the human intellect is capable of attaining more of the real than Kant was willing or able to admit. Hence it is that every critique of Kant must begin where he began and ask whether knowledge is as he described it or not. The basic reason which led him to the theory of knowledge which he embraced was his desire to save knowledge both from the abstractions of the Rationalists and the complete particularity and scepticism of the Empiricists. Now the test of any theory of knowledge is ultimately whether it faces all the facts involved and adequately explains them. If it explains only a few of the facts and raises greater difficulties than it answers, then such a theory of knowledge is suspect, to say the least. If it also has to force some of the facts into the theory without regard for the situation as we find it, then it is a theory doubly to be suspected. However well Kant managed to combine the best in Rationalism with the strong points of Empiricism, it is still possible to ask whether such a fusion of the abstract with

the concrete achieves anything, and whether it succeeds in conforming to the evidence and the facts at hand.

Now it is one thing to recognize that knowledge has its subjective side, that in the knowing process there is definitely an organization which takes place on the side of the knowing subject.
No one can possibly deny this. Yet it is something quite different
to insist that such subjective organization is what constitutes the
very essence of knowledge. We are not ordinarily aware of this.
At least, not before we become convinced Kantian philosophers.
In the meantime let us take a look at some of the premises that
led Kant to this final conclusion.

The Kantian Presuppositions

The two basic premises from which Kant draws his whole philosophy of the understanding come from the Rationalists on the
one hand and the Empiricists on the other. From the Empiricists
he took as a proven fact the proposition that all we know is our
sense impressions. And from the Rationalists he took the proposition as equally certain that all universality and necessity come
from the intellect. Neither proposition does he ever attempt to
prove. Each he assumes as completely certain and beyond question. He might just as easily have assumed the opposite; namely,
that there is necessity even in sense experience and that instead of
our sense impressions we know things as they are in themselves.[2]
But then there would have been no Kantian theory of knowledge.

Necessity in Contingency

At any rate, let us take his first supposition, that there is absolutely
no necessity to be found in the realm of sense experience. Upon
examination it becomes apparent that we can at least question
the assumption, and it is quite possible that examination will also
reveal that sense experience does contain some sort of necessity.
Take Socrates, for example. He is certainly contingent. He does
not necessarily exist. If Socrates sits on a chair, then the sitting

[2] *Cf.* J. Collins, *A History of Modern European Philosophy* (St. Paul,
The Bruce Publishing Co., 1954), pp. 470 ff.

itself is contingent, since it is not necessary that he sit on a chair either to exist or to exist as Socrates. Yet there is also an element of necessity here. For while Socrates is sitting on the chair, he is necessarily sitting on the chair. In Question 86 of the first part of the *Summa Theologica*, St. Thomas describes the necessity in the contingent as follows:

Contingent things can be considered in two ways: either as contingent, or as containing some element of necessity. For every contingent thing has in it something necessary. For example, that Socrates run, is in itself contingent; but the relation of running to motion is necessary, for it is necessary that Socrates move, if he runs. Now contingency arises from matter, for contingency is a potentiality to be or not to be, and potentiality belongs to matter; whereas necessity results from form, because whatever is consequent on form is of necessity in the subject. But matter is the principle of individuation. Moreover it was laid down above that the intellect of itself and directly has the universal for its object; while the object of the sense is the singular, which in a certain way is the indirect object of the intellect, as was said above. Therefore the contingent, considered as such, is known directly by sense and indirectly by the intellect; while the universal and necessary principles of contingent things are known by the intellect. Hence, if we consider knowable things in their universal principles, then all science is of necessary things. But if we consider the things themselves, thus some sciences are of necessary things, some of contingent things.[3]

Now if all this is so, and it bears out an investigation into the matter, then we have every reason to conclude that necessity is not necessarily confined to the intellect, but that it can be and is found in things. The whole realm of the contingent, as a matter of fact, is necessarily contingent and no one can do anything about that fact but accept it. It is precisely because of this element of necessity which we find in contingent things that we are able to argue to a source of such necessity, which we call a necessary being—as we shall see later, when we discuss Kant's attacks on the arguments for the existence of God. At any rate, it simply cannot be assumed that the whole of our sense experience is completely and totally contingent so that we must trace all knowledge of necessity exclusively to intellect.

[3] St. Thomas Aquinas, *Summa Theologica*, edited and annotated by Anton C. Pegis (New York, Random House, Inc., 1945), Vol. I, 86, 3.

The second assumption which Kant makes is the one which he accepts from the Empiricists, that all we ever know is our sense impressions. This assumption, too, will bear investigation, for it is certainly far from being immediately evident. The immediately evident fact seems to be, at least, that we know things, not our subjective reactions to them. Now unless we are simply driven by the force of logic applied to facts to accept such subjectivism, then it would seem a bit hasty to subscribe to it, if the facts can be just as easily explained and, perhaps, more completely and intelligently by another theory of knowledge which fits in better with our experience of what happens, when we know.

Knowledge as Representation

This second assumption is based upon a prior one; namely, that all knowledge is a representation of an object. Now depending on how we understand *representation,* will depend on how we explain the object of such knowledge.[4] In one sense we can understand a representation to be a copy of an original. A photograph is a representation of the castle we once stood before and admired. A painting is a representation of a friend of long standing. An ambassador is a representative of his country. In each of these cases the representation stands for, or substitutes for, the original. We see the photograph and we think of the castle. We look at the painting and we remember our dead or absent friend. In all these instances the representation is known directly and that which is represented is known only indirectly and by reference. Now if a concept is this sort of a representation of an original, if *it* is known and the original inferred from a knowledge of the concept, then it becomes immediately apparent that the original can never be known in itself. For how would one ever know the original? The only possible way to know what the original was like would be to compare the concept to it. But already by definition this is impossible. For knowledge is had in a concept which represents—stands for—the thing. The only possible way to compare the representation with the original would be by

[4] Frederick D. Wilhelmsen, *Man's Knowledge of Reality* (Englewood Cliffs, N.J., Prentice-Hall, Inc., 1956).

means of another concept, which now would simply stand for both the original and the first concept. This places the knower at a still farther distance from the original and each succeeding attempt to justify the real representative value of the concept leaves him still farther removed from the original. There is only one reasonable thing to do in the circumstances, and that is to settle once and for all for a knowledge of things as they affect us and to admit that we can never know them as they are in themselves. This is exactly what Kant did.

We can, however, ask if this is really the sort of representation we mean, when we call the concept representative of the object. We can start with experience, with knowledge as we are aware of it. We can face the facts and the evidence as we find it and attempt to construct a theory of knowledge, which does not do violence to the ordinary experiences we have. For it is a fact that we seem to know an object directly. Our knowledge does not seem at first glance, or even at second glance, to terminate at our concepts. It is the thing we are immediately aware of. It is the thing we speak of and point to. If, then, a theory of knowledge can be evolved which respects this immediate evidence and explains it, rather than explains it away, it would seem such a theory is to be preferred to one that rejects it.

When we say that a concept represents the thing, we do not mean that it substitutes for the thing, so that it is the concept which is known and not the thing. To speak of representation in this sense creates two major difficulties. In the first place it would follow that science deals not with things outside the soul but with things inside the soul. Science would be about ideas, not about things. Secondly, such a theory of representation would lead to the position held by some of the early Greek philosophers, who maintained that whatever seems, is true. It would follow from this that contradictories could be true simultaneously. For if the cognitive power can only judge of its subjective impression, then every such judgment will be a true judgment.

The difficulties can be avoided, however, if representation is understood in another sense; namely, as that *by which* the intellect understands and not as that which is understood.

Therefore it must be said that the intelligible species is related to the intellect as that by which it understands. Which is proved thus. Now action is twofold, as it is said in *Metaphysics* IX: one which remains in the agent (for instance to see and to understand), and another which passes into an external object (for instance, to heat and to cut). Each of these actions proceeds in virtue of some form. And just as the form from which proceeds an act tending to something external is the likeness of the object of the action, as heat in the water is the likeness of the thing heated, so the form from which proceeds an action remaining in the agent is a likeness of the object. Hence that by which the sight sees is the likeness of the visible thing; and the likeness of the thing understood, that is, the intelligible species, is the form by which the intellect understands. But since the intellect reflects upon itself, by such reflection it understands both its own act of understanding, and the species by which it understands. Thus the intelligible species is secondarily that which is understood; but that which is primarily understood is the thing, of which the species is a likeness.[5]

At first glance this may seem to be just another theory asserted in the face of the Kantian theory of knowledge. But such a theory has this definite advantage. It explains the process of knowledge without doing open violence to ordinary experience. For we certainly seem to know objects, not the subjective impressions which these objects make upon us.

Such a theory, moreover, explains how it is that we can and do come into immediate contact with things and it confirms the certainty we have from experience that a world distinct from ourselves exists. Kant affirmed, too, that the thing-in-itself really existed, but he was never able to justify such an assertion. And Fichte was just as logical as Kant, if not more so, in stating that Kant caused more difficulty than not by insisting on the existence of the thing-in-itself. Kant tried to hold on to the extramental existence of the thing-in-itself because he needed it as a cause of the impressions made upon the knowing subject. Here, too, he involves himself in difficulty. For he must assert that the causal proposition is really functioning in the world of noumena, even though all our knowledge of it is restricted to the world of phenomena. But, as Berkeley pointed out, there is no real need to insist on the external existence of the thing-in-itself to explain

[5] *Summa Theologica, op. cit.*, I, 85, 2.

the subjective impressions we have. God could just as well be making the impressions upon us. Or it is possible that we ourselves are the sole cause of such an operation. Once this is seen as a possibility, then solipsism becomes also a very real and frightening possibility.

In the face of such very real difficulties and the very real possibility that we may know the thing-in-itself, the whole Kantian theory of knowledge becomes nothing more than an a priori assertion, a pure assumption which Kant himself never attempts to prove. Since such an assumption is against common experience, it has need of real proof before one can reasonably subscribe to it.

Separation of Sense and Intellect

There are still further difficulties within the assumption itself. Kant had completely separated the faculty of sensibility from that of intellect. He did this in order to avoid reducing the intellect to a sense faculty, as the empiricists had done. It is because of such a separation that the Kantian intellect must wait for the data to be supplied by the senses, before it can impose its innate intelligibility upon them. Furthermore, he had defined intuition in such a way that only the divine intellect could be intuitive. But again no such complete separation of sense and intellect is necessary. The one can be adequately distinguished from the other without separating them. Man's sensations are specifically different from an animal's precisely because human sensation is penetrated through and through with intellection. Not only do we see a tree, but at one and the same time we know that we see a tree. Sense and intellect may be different faculties, but always it is man who sees and man who knows. The two activities are means by which man comes into contact with the thing-in-itself. We reach the real by means of an intellectualized sensation.

Nor is it true that on the sense level we are only affected by the qualities of the thing and never by the substance. The thing acts on us through its qualities. But it is the thing which acts on us, never just the qualities. The thing is present to us both substantially and accidentally, because it acts on us both substantially and accidentally. It is never just the qualities which affect us, but the qualified substance. It is precisely because of this that the senses and the intellect can refer themselves back to the whole thing and not just to the qualities. We see a red thing, not just red. We taste a sweet thing, not just sweetness. Were substance not in any way attained by the senses, it could never be attained by the intellect.[6]

Knowledge of the Real

In a Thomistic theory of knowledge it is explained how it is possible for man to come into direct contact with the thing-in-itself. It remains to be seen whether it is possible for man to know anything beyond that with which the senses make contact. For however direct our contact with the external world, unless we can go beyond the realm of sense experience, metaphysics will remain forever impossible and Kant's rejection of it will be a valid one. Unless, also, we can acquire a knowledge of supra-sensible realities, the existence of God and the soul must either be doubted, or asserted as a pure postulate, or made the object of an act of faith. Let us first consider the possibility of a knowledge which transcends the data of sense.

We have seen that in a Thomistic theory of knowledge the concept is that by which the intellect is referred to the thing. Hence the thing is the proper object of man's knowing. Granted that man can come into intellectual contact with the things of the material order, can he transcend them and come to a knowledge of that which is not material? For Aquinas such a transition is entirely possible. Man knows sensibly and intellectually the material beings with which he comes into contact. He knows their meanings—at least basically—and he asserts that these meanings exist concretized in an existing subject. He judges that material things exist, that they are real. As a result of these judgments he arrives at some understanding of what material being connotes: something sensible having existence. Once such an understanding is arrived at, there is also acquired an understanding of what is meant by material being as such. Admittedly this is not the same

[6] *Ibid.*, 45, 4 ad 1.

as being as such; it is not the being of the metaphysician; nor is it the being which the philosopher seeks ultimately to understand. But it is a step along the way.

Having arrived at an understanding of material being as something-sensible-having-existence, we can proceed to put another question. What is it that makes this sensible something be? In other words, are sensible things being because they are sensible or because of some other principle? To attribute the being of these things to their sensibility is to give a materialistic answer and to equate being with the sensible. It is to say that being is possible only on a sensible, material level and to assert that only that which is material is. There is another answer possible here. One can possibly say that the "something" is responsible for the being of the thing. That is to say that the intelligibility of the thing is what makes the thing be. This is the answer given originally by Plato to the problem of being. Being and intelligibility are in this case synonymous, and this is the position held by any of the idealistic and essentialistic systems of philosophy. There is, lastly, a third answer.

This is the answer given by an existentialistic Thomism. A material thing is real not because it is sensible, nor because it has intelligibility, but simply because it is or has existence. Consequently it is by reason of a judgment of separation that Thomism finally arrives at a knowledge of being as such. Being, then, in the strict meaning of metaphysics is that which is, and it is being precisely in so far as it is. Radically, then, it is existence which explains the reality of being, so that wherever we find existence, we find being and vice-versa. That is why St. Thomas calls existence the act of acts, the ultimate perfection which actuates all other perfections, giving them whatever reality they possess. Since man can attain existence, as he does in the judgment, he can attain being. Moreover the being thus attained is a being which is not necessarily limited to matter. It cannot yet be said that immaterial beings exist, but at least the possibility for their existence is left open. This openness to immaterial being is an openness in the order of intellect. Since the intellect can in the judgment reach existence and since existence is the act of being, the intellect can attain being. And since being is not necessarily limited to material being, the intellect can pass beyond the realm of material being to some sort of a knowledge of being wherever it may be found. Here again Kant's theory of judgment limits him to a world of mere possibilities. For a judgment for Kant was nothing else except one concept applied to or compared with another. Now existence is never connected with a concept. Hence existence could never enter into the Kantian judgment.

It becomes immediately evident also that the metaphysics which Kant criticized was not the Thomistic metaphysics. He was reacting against a Rationalism, which considered metaphysics an analysis of concepts. Judgments were all a priori, applying predicates to subjects which made these subjects more intelligible and showed more clearly what was contained in them. Such a metaphysics could lead to no knowledge of existing reality. Kant saw that clearly. But to reject Rationalism is not the same as rejecting metaphysics. Once it is evident that the human intellect can and does achieve a knowledge of being, then it becomes equally evident that the human intellect can achieve a knowledge of metaphysics. For metaphysics is the science of being in so far as it is being.

Knowledge of the Soul

Kant's subjectivistic assumptions are again only too evident, when he rejects the ability of the human intellect to come to a knowledge of soul as substance. Once he had limited the intellect to a knowledge of appearances, then any subject would necessarily remain beyond the pale of knowledge. It would make no difference whether such a subject was external to the self or the self itself. All "subject" could mean to Kant was a collection of impressions united in the experiential order. All "self" could mean was the experiential manifestation of a subject. But this subject itself could never enter into one's experience. Hence it was a foregone conclusion that Kant would deny any knowledge of the soul. Once knowledge of such a subject became impossible, then obviously no other qualities of any kind could be asserted of such an unknown and unknowable subject.

But let us admit for a moment with St. Thomas that the con-

cept is that by which we are referred to the thing. We come
into contact with things because they act upon us. As we have
seen, it is the whole thing which acts upon us, and the whole
thing, therefore, is present to us in its activity. Now any thing
can act only in accord with the nature it possesses. Therefore, too,
a knowledge of the activity of a thing will lead us infallibly to a
knowledge of the nature of that thing. It is along this line that
Aquinas leads us to an understanding of the nature of soul. To
know, for Aquinas, is to know something actual. That is why we
can know activity, because activity is an actuation of a subject.
The subject is an act in itself and is further actuated by its activity,
so that subjects themselves can become an object of knowledge.
Now the intellectual soul manifests itself as an act through its
activity and is present to itself actually in such activity. It follows,
therefore, that the intellectual soul can be an object of knowledge.

Everything is knowable so far as it is in act, and not so far as it is in
potentiality: for a thing is a being and is true, and therefore knowable,
according as it is actual. This is quite clear as regards sensible things,
for the eye does not see what is potentially, but what is actually
colored. In like manner it is clear that the intellect, so far as it knows
material things, does not know save what is in act: and hence it does
not know primary matter except as proportionate to form, as is stated
in Phys.1,7. Consequently immaterial substances are intelligible by
their own essence, according as each one is actual by its own essence.

Now the human intellect is only a potentiality in the genus of intelligible things, just as primary matter is a potentiality as regards
sensible beings; and hence it is called *possible*. Therefore in its essence
the human mind is potentially understanding. Hence it has in itself
the power to understand, but not to be understood, except as it is
made actual.

But as in this life our intellect has material and sensible things for its
proper natural object, it understands itself according as it is made
actual by the species abstracted from sensible things, through the
light of the active intellect, which not only actuates the intelligible
things themselves but also, by their instrumentality, actuates the passive intellect. Therefore the intellect knows itself not by its essence,
but by its act. This happens in two ways: in the first place singularly,
as when Socrates or Plato perceives that he has an intellectual soul
because he perceives that he understands. In the second place uni-

versally, as when we consider the nature of the human mind from knowledge of the intellectual act.

There is, however, a difference between these two kinds of knowledge, and it consists in this, that the mere presence of the mind suffices for the first; the mind itself being the principle of action whereby it perceives itself, and hence it is said to know itself by its own presence. But as regards the second kind of knowledge, the mere presence of the mind does not suffice, and there is required a careful and subtle inquiry. Hence many are ignorant of the soul's nature and many have erred about it.[7]

The intellectual soul, then, is present to itself actually in its act of thought and is consequently aware of itself as a thinking subject. The soul knows that it exists through its act of thinking as a subject of that thinking. But it is only by a careful and subtle inquiry into the nature of this activity, that we call thought, that we can come finally to a knowledge of the nature of the subject of that thinking. At any rate, the door is opened for more than a mere experiential knowledge of thought, and we can proceed from the actuality of thought and its nature to an understanding of the nature of the subject of the thought. The reason for this again is simply because the subject itself is present in its thinking and must be like the thinking which proceeds from it. From an analysis of what thinking involves we can then proceed further to a knowledge of the immateriality, spirituality, and the immortality of its subject.

Kant and the Arguments for the Existence of God

Kant reduced the arguments which could possibly prove the existence of God to three. The first he called the physico-theological argument. This proceeded from sensible experience to the assertion of the existence of a supreme cause beyond such experience. The second he called the cosmological argument, which began with any type of existence in the world and proceeded to a cause of such existence. The third, or ontological argument, abstracted from all experience and argued from the idea of God to the necessary existence of God on the basis of that idea. All

[7] *Ibid.*, 87, 1.

of the arguments he found wanting and concluded that it was simply impossible to prove that God existed.

1. THE ONTOLOGICAL ARGUMENT. This argument attempts to prove the existence of God from the idea of God. Briefly the argument states that God cannot be thought of except as existing. A merely possible God is an impossibility. Therefore God must exist. Now St. Thomas also found the argument inadequate. From the fact that I cannot think of God except as existing, it does not follow that God must exist. Kant, however, rejects the argument for a different reason. He admits that, if one thinks of God, he cannot think of Him except as existing. But he states that it is possible simply not to think of God, and then the necessity vanishes. In other words, the necessity here is a conditioned necessity, not an absolute one. Kant proceeds to question further the validity of the argument. He observes that the possibility of an existing God is a pure possibility; that is, it is simply not contradictory to suppose that God exist. But this is different from asserting real objective possibility. In order that such possibility may be asserted as actual, it must be conceived as actuable under the conditions of space and time. And since God cannot be so conceived, the existence of God contains no real or objective possibility. Furthermore, Kant recognized that existence added nothing to a concept of an essence. Hence to assert that the concept existed was asserting nothing new. From various viewpoints, then, the ontological argument was invalid. It is obvious that the Kantian objection to the argument, however invalid it may be—and it is invalid—flow from a preconceived theory of knowledge. Whatever logical difficulties he may add, the primary reason for the rejection of the argument remains the second reason given; namely, that it is impossible to conceive a non-sensible being as capable of fulfilling its possibility to exist under the conditions of space and time.

2. THE COSMOLOGICAL ARGUMENT. This argument, which begins with finite existents in the world and proceeds to argue to the existence of a necessary cause beyond the world, Kant also found invalid. In the first place it is based on the principle of causality and supposes that this principle is universally valid. Kant, however, had to restrict the principle necessarily to the

world of phenomena. Beyond experience the principle was no more than a pure concept with no object to which it could be applied. On this ground alone Kant would find the causal argument insufficient. It would take another and more adequate theory of knowledge before the causal principle could serve as a means of ascending to a first and necessary cause.

But there were other reasons as well which led Kant to reject the argument. The argument proved that an infinite series of causes was an impossibility. Yet to Kant such a series of causes did not seem to be impossible. On the supposition that the world is eternal, and Kant did not think that the opposite could be proved, there would necessarily be demanded such an infinite series of causes. Such an infinite series would extend beyond human experience, but this was no reason to say that such a series is an impossibility. Now St. Thomas, too, admits that a certain type of infinite series of causes is perfectly possible. But he makes a distinction between a series of causes accidentally ordered to each other and one in which the causes are essentially ordered to one another. In the *De Veritate*, Q. 2, a. 10, St. Thomas carefully distinguishes between the two types of causal series. Causes essentially ordered to one another are those, all of which must be actually causing here and now in order that an effect be produced. The first must actually be causing the second to move the third and so on down to the effect which is being presently experienced. If there is anywhere a break in the causal series, the whole causal action must immediately cease and there would be no final effect. If, for example, we consider a burning light bulb, the matter becomes quite clear. The bulb is actually burning because electricity is moving through a circuit. The electricity is moving through the circuit because somewhere a dynamo is turning. The dynamo is turning because it is being made to turn by water falling, and so on. Now if the series is at any place interrupted, then the electricity stops flowing and the light bulb stops burning. To suppose that such a concatenated series could be infinite would be to suppose that all this causality is coming from nowhere. Each recipient would be receiving and passing on a causal influence which had no source. This is obviously impossible. If the light bulb is burning, then there must be ultimately a source of the power which is being passed along by each of the intermediate causes. Now transfer this to the order of potency and act. If something is being actuated here and now, then there must ultimately be a pure act which is responsible for the actuation of this particular potency. Nor will any intermediate act be sufficient to explain this present actuation of this potency. For any intermediate act is act only by reason of the fact that it, too, is being actuated to actuate something else. In such a series of causes there must necessarily be a first.

Such a series of essentially ordered causes is quite different from a series of causes only accidentally ordered to one another. The latter type of causal series is made up of causes which, as a matter of fact, influence the effect, but do not necessarily do so. In other words, the effect could be had without this particular series of causes at work. In such a series there is no contradiction in stating that an infinite number of such causes is a possibility, one preceding another back in time to eternity. Thus chickens may have been laying eggs from eternity. Fathers may have been generating sons equally eternally. And so with acorns and oak trees, etc. The causal series here is mere succession of cause and effect. There is no need that all the causes be existing simultaneously in order to have this given son or that particular egg.

In efficient causes it is impossible to proceed to infinity per se, thus there cannot be an infinite number of causes that are per se required for a certain effect; for instance, that a stone be moved by a stick, the stick by the hand, and so on to infinity. But it is not impossible to proceed to infinity accidentally as regards efficient causes; for instance, if all the causes thus infinitely multiplied should have the order of only one cause, their multiplication being accidental, as an artificer acts by means of many hammers accidentally, because one after another may be broken. It is accidental, therefore, that one particular hammer acts after the action of another; and likewise it is accidental to this particular man as generator to be generated by another man; for he generates as a man and not as the son of another man. For all men generating hold one grade in efficient causes—namely, the grade of a particular generator. Hence it is not impossible for a man to be generated by man to infinity; but such a thing would be impossible if the generation of this man depended upon this man, and on an elementary body, and on the sun and so on to infinity.[8]

[8] *Ibid.*, 46, 2 ad 7.

Kant objected still further that the very concept of a completely necessary being was a contradiction. All the necessity we know is always a conditioned necessity. To conceive necessity as completely unconditioned, is an impossibility. St. Thomas would certainly admit that the necessity we experience is a relative necessity. And he would further agree that a knowledge of an unconditioned necessity is not given to us directly in our experience. But it is one thing to know such a necessity directly and another to know that there must exist such a necessity as a necessary foundation for the conditioned necessity we actually experience. Again Kant had trapped himself in the experiential order by his theory of knowledge.

Even if we grant, however, that the cosmological argument proves the need of a necessary being, it is another thing entirely, said Kant, to prove that such a being is an all perfect being, and, therefore, God. To do this one must revert to the ontological argument, and this argument has already been proved invalid. This can best be illustrated by comparing two propositions. The first is as follows:

An all perfect being is a being that necessarily exists. This proposition is the conclusion of the ontological argument, and we can agree with Kant—albeit for different reasons—that the argument is invalid. The second proposition runs thus:

A being which necessarily exists is an all perfect being. This is the conclusion of the cosmological argument and Kant insists that it is the same as the first proposition and therefore just as invalid as the first. There is, however, quite a difference in fact, even though there is a certain verbal similarity.[9] The first proposition is invalid because it asserts that from the concept of an all perfect being we can argue to the existence of that being. The second proposition is quite different. For once it is proved that there exists a being who is necessarily existing, it follows immediately that such a necessarily existing being is an uncaused pure act. Now a pure act is also an infinitely perfect being. Hence it is one and the same thing to prove that there exists a necessary being and to prove that such a being is all perfect.

3. THE PHYSICO-THEOLOGICAL ARGUMENT. This argument pro-

[9] J. Collins, *op. cit.*, p. 506.

ceeds from the fact of order in the universe to the existence of a
supreme orderer. Here again Kant found the argument insufficient.
If it proves anything, said Kant, it proves merely the existence of
a superior being, not the existence of a supreme being. It proves
a *Weltbaumeister*, not a *Weltschöpfer*. To prove that this universe maker is really the Creator of the universe, one must again
have recourse to the ontological argument. Thus one again slips
into an invalid argument. But again the objection is not well
taken. The fifth way of St. Thomas includes the design in the
universe but the argument is not precisely from design but from
the intelligent purpose which is manifested by design. To argue
just from design would, as Kant says, prove nothing else except
a superior designer. Hence, it is undoubtedly true that the usual
popular arguments from cameras and bicycles prove nothing more
than a camera maker and a bicycle maker, and then by analogy a
Great Camera Maker, etc. This is obviously not the same as to
prove an Infinite Being. But the argument used by St. Thomas is
more than just an analogy with human designers. When design
is used merely as a manifestation of intelligent purpose, then it
is an intelligent orderer to an end which is demonstrated and
ultimately an intelligent orderer who is pure act. Kant never knew
the argument as St. Thomas used it.[10] At the same time it must
be recognized that Kant saw clearly the inadequacies of the argument made use of by the Rationalists and by those who relied on
Rationalism for their apologetics.

The Moral Theory of Kant

Kant's moral theory is admittedly non-rational. Once he had restricted knowledge to the area of the sensible, it became impossible for him to construct a theory of morality on rational
grounds. So feeling and the categorical imperative had to take
over, and it is precisely here that Kant escapes the skepticism into
which his psychology threatened to plunge him. But the results
were, as E. Gilson points out, disastrous.

[10] R. L. Faricy S.J., "The Principle of the Fifth Way," *The New Scholasticism*, (April, 1957).

Here, indeed, the difficulties were appalling, since they entailed a radical antinomy between man as living in the order of nature, and man as acting in the order of morality. After all, they are bound to be the same man. For what reason, in consequence of what untold original sin, is man as a free citizen of the intelligible world condemned to live in the strictly determined world of matter? If he himself is the cause of that determination, why should his own understanding erect causal necessity as a permanent hindrance to his own free will? If we make nature to be what it is, why do we make it to be an obstacle to our own morality? As a matter of fact, this dramatic struggle in us between the law of nature and the law of morality looks a little too much like an *Epistle to the Romans* in philosophical garb. Having refused to hold metaphysical conclusions on metaphysical grounds, Kant had been necessarily dragged from metaphysics to ethics, and from ethics to theology.[11]

Kant had abdicated reason to found morality on feeling and will. Thus the universal will of each individual became the ultimate and sole standard of what was right and wrong. It is easy to see how this will should become something absolute and divine and the final source of all that was real, as it did in Johann Gottlieb Fichte.

SUMMARY

1. There are two attitudes which characterize much of modern and contemporary thought with regard to the nature and purpose of philosophy and the capacity of the human mind to arrive at truth. The first of these attitudes is one of almost complete skepticism. All that we can know is based on what we can experience, and this experience itself is nothing more than a subjective response to what we can sense. Beyond this area of what can be sensibly experienced there is nothing which can become in any way the object of our knowledge. Hence, philosophy, and especially metaphysics, is in the traditional sense, at least, a sheer impossibility. Even in the area of sensible experience, we can be sure only of the fact that we do have such experiences. To generalize about such experiences can provide us with knowledge that is probable but devoid of any certainty in the philosophical sense

[11] E. Gilson, *The Unity of Philosophical Experience* (New York, Charles Scribner's Sons, 1937), pp. 239 ff.

of the term. If there is such a thing as natural science, its function consists in providing us with conclusions which are predictive of future activity. These predictions will be indications of what we can expect to happen and will for all practical purposes be sufficient to guide our actions. They are sufficient to enable us to build our various systems of natural science upon them. The ordinary man would not dream of questioning them, or acting contrary to them. But they are not sufficient to lead to the kind of universally valid and certain knowledge that is demanded by science in the traditional sense. No absolute statements are possible. If this is true of the realm of experience, it is certainly much more true of any realm that may be supposed to exist beyond that of experience. There may be other ways to approach such a realm, through faith, for example, or through religion, but human reason can tell us nothing about it. This is the necessary result of Hume's criticism of human knowledge and the limitations he imposed upon it.

2. The second and by far the more general characteristic of modern thought is the one originating with Immanuel Kant. According to Kant, as we have seen, the human mind is capable of true scientific knowledge. This knowledge is universally valid and certain, but it is at the same time a certainty limited to the area of the experiential sciences. This certainty and universality, furthermore, are not discovered in things and their functions, but are imposed by the mind which comes into contact only with the appearances of things. Hence, for Kant, all true science is a science of appearances, and any certainty achieved by such science is rooted in the mind which seeks to interpret the data of experience. This, of course, reduces all scientific knowledge to the area of the natural sciences, for only here can data be supplied for the mind's interpretative action. Metaphysics is ruled out as a science of the "real", since it concerns itself only with pure concepts, pure possibilities, which have no necessary connection with experience. Hence, there is also ruled out any purely reasonable or scientific approach to God, to the existence and immortality of the human soul, to human freedom, etc.

3. Such concepts, however, remain purely possible; that is, they contain no contradiction in terms. Consequently, they may be ac-

cepted out of faith or religious conviction, if one chooses to do so. Added to this is the fact of a moral law—an imperative imposed on the human subject—which leads man to postulate the existence of such realities, even though there is no directly rational approach to them.

4. Thus it is that after Hume and Kant the problem of the validity of human knowledge arises and the extent to which such knowledge can be called valid. Neither Hume nor Kant was willing to concede the validity of any knowledge which transcended sensible experience. If human knowing is limited to the extent that they conceived it, then it necessarily follows that metaphysics, the existence of God, the freedom of man, the immortality of the human soul are all problems incapable of rational solution.

Criticism

1. The Kantian theory of knowledge is based on two unproved suppositions. The first of these is taken from the Empiricists and asserts that there is no necessity of any sort in the order of contingency and experience.
   The second is taken from the Rationalists and asserts that all necessity comes from the intellect. It is something imposed rather than discovered.
2. Kant is illogical in asserting the existence of the thing-in-itself, since he admits that the thing-in-itself cannot be known. Yet at the same time he is forced to admit that this unknown thing-in-itself exerts a causal influence on the knowing subject, for how else would experience of the thing-in-itself be possible?
3. The whole Kantian theory of knowledge is based on the assertion that what we know is a subjective impression of the thing rather than the thing itself. The sense impression as made intelligible by the intellect becomes that which substitutes for the thing as the object of knowledge. This, however, is not what we experience. And knowledge itself is made much more understandable, when the concept is seen as that *by which* we know and not *that which* is known.
4. Kant's criticism of the arguments for the existence of God stems logically from the theory of knowledge he has already

accepted. His rejection of the impossibility of an infinite series of causes does not take into account the distinction between accidentally and existentially ordered causes, nor does his criticism of the argument from design recognize the intelligent purpose behind the design which leads ultimately to a pure and absolute intellect. Furthermore, Kant was unable to avoid reducing all the arguments to the ontological argument, since he was never able to do anything but conceptualize a necessary Being. From the very beginning Kant's theory of knowledge cuts him off from the order of existing things. Hence, he is never able to argue, as does St. Thomas, from existing things to a necessarily existing Being. Kant is never in contact with existence, and he saw the fallacy he would commit in asserting a Supreme Existent.

5. In divorcing morality from intellect and making it consist in an imperative imposed by some unknown and unknowable Ego, Kant created far more problems than he solved. In opposing morality to reason he set up a contradiction within man himself which could only be resolved by denying either reason or morality.

SELECTED READINGS

Kant's Copernican Revolution*

We come now to metaphysics, a purely speculative science, which occupies a completely isolated position and is entirely independent of the teachings of experience. It deals with mere conceptions—not, like mathematics, with conceptions applied to intuition—and in it, reason is the pupil of itself alone. It is the oldest of the sciences, and would still survive even if all the rest were swallowed up in the abyss of an all-destroying barbarism. But it has not yet had the good fortune to attain to the sure scientific method. This will be apparent, if we apply the test which we pro-

* Immanuel Kant, *The Critique of Pure Reason*, 2nd ed., trans. by J. M. D. Meiklejohn, Everyman's Library Series (New York, E. P. Dutton & Co., Inc., 1934).

posed at the outset. We find that reason perpetually comes to a stand, when it attempts to gain a priori the perception even of those laws which the most common experience confirms. We find it compelled to retrace its steps in innumerable instances, and to abandon the path on which it had entered, because this does not lead to the desired result. We find too, that those who are engaged in metaphysical pursuits are far from being able to agree among themselves, but that, on the contrary, this science appears to furnish an arena specially adapted for the display of skill or the exercise of strength in mock-contests—a field in which no combatant ever yet succeeded in gaining an inch of ground, in which, at least, no victory was ever yet crowned with permanent possession.

This leads us to inquire why it is that, in metaphysics, the sure path of science has not hitherto been found. Shall we suppose that it is impossible to discover it? Why then should nature have visited our reason with restless aspirations after it, as if it were one of our weightiest concerns? Nay, more, how little cause should we have to place confidence in our reason, if it abandons us in a matter about which, most of all, we desire to know the truth—and not only so, but even allures us to the pursuit of vain phantoms, only to betray us in the end? Or, if the path has only hitherto been missed, what indications do we possess to guide us in a renewed investigation, and to enable us to hope for greater success than has fallen to the lot of our predecessors?

It appears to me that the examples of mathematics and natural philosophy, which, as we have seen, were brought into their present condition by a sudden revolution, are sufficiently remarkable to fix our attention on the essential circumstances of the change which has proved so advantageous to them, and to induce us to make the experiment of imitating them, so far as the analogy, which, as rational sciences, they bear to metaphysics may permit. It has hitherto been assumed that our cognition must conform to the objects; but all attempts to ascertain anything about these objects a priori, by means of conceptions, and thus to extend the range of our knowledge, have been rendered abortive by this assumption. Let us then make the experiment whether we may not be more successful in metaphysics, if we assume that the objects must conform to our cognition. This appears, at all events, to accord better with the possibility of our gaining the end we have in view, that is to say, of arriving at the cognition of objects a priori, of determining something with respect to these objects, before they are given to us. We here propose to do just what Copernicus did in attempting to explain the celestial movements. When he found that he could make no progress by assuming that all the heavenly bodies revolved round the spectator, he reversed the process, and tried the experiment of assuming that the spectator revolved, while the stars remained at rest. We may make the same experiment with regard to the intuition of objects. If the intuition must conform to the nature of the objects, I do not see how we can know anything of them a priori. If, on the other hand, the object conforms to the nature of our faculty of intuition, I can then easily conceive the possibility of such an a priori knowledge. Now as I cannot rest in the mere intuitions, but—if they are to become cognitions—must refer them, as representations, to something, as object, and must determine the latter by means of the former, here again there are two courses open to me. Either, first, I may assume that the conceptions, by which I effect this determination, conform to the object—and in this case I am reduced to the same perplexity as before; or secondly, I may assume that the objects, or, which is the same thing, that experience, in which alone as given objects they are cognized, conform to my conceptions—and then I am at no loss how to proceed. For experience itself is a mode of cognition which requires understanding. Before objects are given to me, that is, a priori, I must presuppose in myself laws of the understanding which are expressed in conceptions a priori. To these conceptions, then, all the objects of experience must necessarily conform. Now there are objects which reason thinks, and that necessarily, but which cannot be given in experience, or, at least, cannot be given so as reason thinks them. The attempt to think these objects will hereafter furnish an excellent test of the new method of thought which we have adopted, and which is based on the principle that we only cognize in things a priori that which we ourselves place in them.

Phenomena and Noumena*

But, it will be asked, what kind of a treasure is this that we propose to bequeath to posterity? What is the real value of this system of metaphysics, purified by criticism, and thereby reduced to a permanent condition? A cursory view of the present work will lead to the supposition that its use is merely negative, that it only serves to warn us against venturing, with speculative reason, beyond the limits of experience. This is, in fact, its primary use. But this, at once, assumes a positive value, when we observe that the principles with which speculative reason endeavours to transcend its limits lead inevitably, not to the extension, but to the contraction of the use of reason, inasmuch as they threaten to extend the limits of sensibility, which is their proper sphere, over the entire realm of thought and, thus, to supplant the pure (practical) use of reason. So far, then, as this criticism is occupied in confining speculative reason within its proper bounds, it is only negative; but, inasmuch as it thereby, at the same time, removes an obstacle which impedes and even threatens to destroy the use of practical reason, it possesses a positive and very important value. In order to admit this, we have only to be convinced that there is an absolutely necessary use of pure reason—the moral use—in which it inevitably transcends the limits of sensibility, without the aid of speculation, requiring only to be insured against the effects of a speculation which would involve it in contradiction with itself. To deny the positive advantage of the service which this criticism renders us would be as absurd as to maintain that the system of police is productive of no positive benefit, since its main business is to prevent the violence which citizen has to apprehend from citizen, that so each may pursue his vocation in peace and security. That space and time are only forms of sensible intuition, and hence are only conditions of the existence of things as phenomena; that, moreover, we have no conceptions of the understanding, and, consequently, no elements for the cognition of things, except in so far as a corresponding intuition can be given to these conceptions; that, accordingly, as we can have no

* *Ibid.*

cognition of an object, as a thing-in-itself, but only as an object
of sensible intuition, that is, as phenomenon—all this is proved in
the analytical part of the Critique; and from this the limitation
of all possible speculative cognition to the mere objects of experience, follows as a necessary result. At the same time, it must be
carefully borne in mind that, while we surrender the power of
cognizing, we still reserve the power of thinking objects, as things
in themselves. For, otherwise, we should require to affirm the
existence of an appearance, without something that appears—
which would be absurd. Now let us suppose, for a moment, that
we had not undertaken this criticism and, accordingly, had not
drawn the necessary distinction between things as objects of experience and things as they are in themselves. The principle of
causality, and, by consequence, the mechanism of nature as determined by causality, would then have absolute validity in relation to all things as efficient causes. I should then be unable to
assert, with regard to one and the same being, e.g., the human
soul, that its will is free, and yet, at the same time, subject to
natural necessity, that is, not free, without falling into a palpable
contradiction, for in both propositions I should take the soul in
the same signification, as a thing in general, as a thing-in-itself—as,
without previous criticism, I could not but take it. Suppose now,
on the other hand, that we have undertaken this criticism, and
have learnt that an object may be taken in two senses, first as a
phenomenon, secondly, as a thing-in-itself; and that, according
to the deduction of the conceptions of the understanding, the
principle of causality has reference only to things in the first
sense. We then see how it does not involve any contradiction to
assert, on the one hand, that the will, in the phenomenal sphere
—in visible action—is necessarily obedient to the law of nature,
and, in so far, not free; and, on the other hand, that, as belonging
to a thing-in-itself, it is not subject to that law, and, accordingly,
is free. Now, it is true that I cannot, by means of speculative
reason, and still less by empirical observation, cognize my soul as
a thing-in-itself and consequently, cannot cognize liberty as the
property of a being to which I ascribe effects in the world of
sense. For, to do so, I must cognize this being as existing, and yet
not in time, which—since I cannot support my conception by any

intuition—is impossible. At the same time, while I cannot cognize, I can quite well think freedom, that is to say, my representation of it involves at least no contradiction, if we bear in mind the critical distinction of the two modes of representation (the sensible and the intellectual) and the consequent limitation of the conceptions of the pure understanding and of the principles which flow from them. Suppose now that morality necessarily presupposed liberty, in the strictest sense, as a property of our will; suppose that reason contained certain practical, original principles a priori, which were absolutely impossible without this presupposition; and suppose, at the same time, that speculative reason had proved that liberty was incapable of being thought at all. It would then follow that the moral presupposition must give way to the speculative affirmation, the opposite of which involves an obvious contradiction, and that liberty and, with it, morality must yield to the mechanism of nature; for the negation of morality involves no contradiction, except on the presupposition of liberty. Now morality does not require the speculative cognition of liberty; it is enough that I can think it, that its conception involves no contradiction, that it does not interfere with the mechanism of nature. But even this requirement we could not satisfy, if we had not learnt the twofold sense in which things may be taken; and it is only in this way that the doctrine of morality and the doctrine of nature are confined within their proper limits. For this result, then, we are indebted to a criticism which warns us of our unavoidable ignorance with regard to things-in-themselves, and establishes the necessary limitation of our theoretical cognition to mere phenomena.

Is Metaphysics Possible?*

It is extremely advantageous to be able to bring a number of investigations under the formula of a single problem. For in this manner, we not only facilitate our own labour, inasmuch as we define it clearly to ourselves, but also render it more easy for others to decide whether we have done justice to our undertaking.

* Immanuel Kant, "Introduction" to *The Critique of Pure Reason, op. cit.*

The proper problem of pure reason, then, is contained in the question: "How are synthetical judgements a priori possible?"

That metaphysical science has hitherto remained in so vacillating a state of uncertainty and contradiction, is only to be attributed to the fact that this great problem, and perhaps even the difference between analytical and synthetical judgments, did not sooner suggest itself to philosophers. Upon the solution of the problem, or upon sufficient proof of the impossibility of synthetical knowledge a priori, depends the existence or downfall of the science of metaphysics. Among philosophers, David Hume came the nearest of all to this problem; yet it never acquired in his mind sufficient precision, nor did he regard the question in its universality. On the contrary, he stopped short at the synthetical proposition of the connection of an effect with its cause (principium causalitatis), insisting that such proposition a priori was impossible. According to his conclusions, then, all that we term metaphysical science is a mere delusion, arising from the fancied insight of reason into that which is in truth borrowed from experience, and to which habit has given the appearance of necessity. Against this assertion, destructive to all pure philosophy, he would have been guarded, if he had our problem before his eyes in its universality. For he would then have perceived that, according to his own argument, there likewise could not be any pure mathematical science, which assuredly cannot exist without synthetical proposition a priori—an absurdity from which his good understanding must have saved him.

In the solution of the above problem is at the same time comprehended the possibility of the use of pure reason in the foundation and construction of all sciences which contain theoretical knowledge a priori of objects, that is to say, the answer to the following questions:

How is pure mathematical science possible?
How is pure natural science possible?

Respecting these sciences, as they do certainly exist, it may with propriety be asked, how they are possible?—for that they must be possible is shown by the fact of their really existing. But as to metaphysics, the miserable progress it has hitherto made, and the fact that of no one system yet brought forward, as far as regards its true aim, can it be said that this science really exists, leaves any one at liberty to doubt with reason the very possibility of its existence.

Yet, in a certain sense, this kind of knowledge must unquestionably be looked upon as given; in other words, metaphysics must be considered as really existing, if not as a science, nevertheless as a natural disposition of the human mind (metaphysica naturalis). For human reason, without any instigations imputable to the mere vanity of great knowledge, unceasingly progresses, urged on by its own feeling of need, towards such questions as cannot be answered by any empirical application of reason, or principles derived therefrom; and so there has ever really existed in every man some system of metaphysics. It will always exist, so soon as reason awakes to the exercise of its power of speculation. And now the question arises: "How is metaphysics, as a natural disposition, possible?" In other words, how, from the nature of universal human reason, do those questions arise which pure reason proposes to itself, and which it is impelled by its own feeling of need to answer as well as it can?

But as in all the attempts hitherto made to answer the questions which reason is prompted by its very nature to propose to itself, for example, whether the world had a beginning, or has existed from eternity, it has always met with unavoidable contradictions, we must not rest satisfied with the mere natural disposition of the mind to metaphysics, that is, with the existence of the faculty of pure reason, whence, indeed, some sort of metaphysical system always arises; but it must be possible to arrive at certainty in regard to the question whether we know or do not know the things of which metaphysics treats. We must be able to arrive at a decision on the subjects of its questions, or on the ability or inability of reason to form any judgement respecting them; and therefore either to extend with confidence the bounds of our pure reason, or to set strictly defined and safe limits to its action. This last question, which arises out of the above universal problem, would properly run thus: "How is metaphysics possible as a science?"

The Categorical Imperative*

Everything in nature works according to laws. Rational beings alone have the faculty of acting according to the conception of laws, that is according to principles, i.e., have a will. Since the deduction of actions from principles requires reason, the will is nothing but practical reason. If reason infallibly determines the will, then the actions of such a being which are recognised as objectively necessary are subjectively necesary also, i.e., the will is a faculty to choose that only which reason independent of inclination recognises as practically necessary, i.e., as good. But if reason of itself does not sufficiently determine the will, if the latter is subject also to subjective conditions (particular impulses) which do not always coincide with the objective conditions; in a word, if the will does not in itself completely accord with reason (which is actually the case with men), then the actions which objectively are recognised as necessary are subjectively contingent, and the determination of such a will according to objective laws is obligation, that is to say, the relation of the objective laws to a will that is not thoroughly good is conceived as the determination of the will of a rational being by principles of reason, but which the will from its nature does not of necessity follow.

The conception of an objective principle, in so far as it is obligatory for a will, is called a command (of reason), and the formula of the command is called an imperative.

All imperatives are expressed by the word ought (or shall), and thereby indicate the relation of an objective law of reason to a will, which from its subjective constitution is not necessarily determined by it (an obligation). They say that something would be good to do or to forbear, but they say it to a will which does not always do a thing because it is conceived to be good to do it. That is practically good, however, which determines the will by means of the conceptions of reason, and consequently not from subjective causes, but objectively, that is on principles which are valid for every rational being as such. It is distinguished from the pleas-

* Immanuel Kant, *Fundamental Principles of the Metaphysics of Ethics*, trans. by Thomas Kingsmill Abbott, (New York, Longmans, Green & Co., 1909).

ant as that which influences the will only by means of sensation from merely subjective causes, valid only for the sense of this or that one, and not as a principle of reason, which holds for every one.

A perfectly good will would therefore be equally subject to objective laws (viz., laws of good), but could not be conceived as obliged thereby to act lawfully, because of itself from its subjective constitution it can only be determined by the conception of good. Therefore no imperatives hold for the Divine will, or in general for a holy will; ought is here out of place, because the volition is already of itself necessarily in unison with the law. Therefore imperatives are only formulae to express the relation of objective laws of all volition to the subjective imperfection of the will of this or that rational being, e.g., the human will.

Now all imperatives command either hypothetically or categorically. The former represent the practical necessity of a possible action as means to something else that is willed (or at least which one might possibly will). The categorical imperative would be that which represented an action as necessary of itself without reference to another and, i.e., as objectively necessary.

Since every practical law represents a possible action as good and, on this account, for a subject who is practically determinable by reason, necessary, all imperatives are formulae determining an action which is necessary according to the principle of a will good in some respects. If now the action is good only as a means to something else, then the imperative is hypothetical; if it is conceived as good in itself and consequently as being necessarily the principle of a will which of itself conforms to reason, then it is categorical.

Thus the imperative declares what action possible by me would be good and presents the practical rule in relation to a will which does not forthwith perform an action simply because it is good, whether because the subject does not always know that it is good, or because, even if it knows this, yet its maxims might be opposed to the objective principles of practical reason.

Accordingly the hypothetical imperative only says that the action is good for some purpose, possible or actual. In the first case it is a problematical, in the second an assertorial practical principle.

The categorical imperative which declares an action to be objectively necessary in itself without reference to any purpose, i.e., without any other end, is valid as an apodeictic (practical) principle.

BIBLIOGRAPHY

Translations of Kant's Works

Kant, Immanuel, *Critique of Practical Reason and Other Writings in Moral Philosophy*, trans. by L. W. Beck. Chicago, The University of Chicago Press, 1949.

————, *Critique of Pure Reason*, trans. by N. K. Smith. London, Macmillan & Co., Ltd., 1933.

————, *Fundamental Principles of the Metaphysics of Ethics*, trans. by Thomas Kingsmill Abbott. New York, Longmans, Green & Co., 1909.

————, *Inaugural Dissertation and Early Writings on Space*, trans. by J. Handyside. Chicago, Open Court Publishing Company, 1929.

————, *Kant's Cosmogony*, W. Hastie, ed. Glasgow, Robert Mac-Lehose & Co., Ltd., 1900.

————, *The Critique of Judgment*, trans. by James Creed Meredith. New York, Oxford University Press, 1911 and 1928. In two parts.

————, *The Critique of Pure Reason*, 2nd ed., trans. by J. M. D. Meiklejohn, Everyman's Library Series. New York, E. P. Dutton & Co., 1934.

————, *The Moral Law: Kant's Groundwork of the Metaphysic of Morals*, H. J. Paton, ed. New York, Barnes & Noble Inc., 1950.

Commentaries on Kant

Caird, E., *The Critical Philosophy of Immanuel Kant*. New York, The Macmillan Company, 1909.

England, F. E., *Kant's Conception of God*. London, George Allen & Unwin, 1929.

Jones, W. T., *Morality and Freedom in the Philosophy of Immanuel Kant*. New York, Oxford University Press, 1940.

Paton, H. J., *Kant's Metaphysic of Experience*. New York, The Macmillan Company, 1936.

————, *The Categorical Imperative: A Study in Kant's Moral Philosophy*. Chicago, Chicago University Press, 1948.

Paulsen, F., *Immanuel Kant: His Life and Doctrine*. New York, Charles Scribner's Sons, 1902.

Weldon, T. D., *Introduction to Kant's Critique of Pure Reason*. Oxford, The Clarendon Press, 1945.

The Heritage of Kant, G. T. Whitney and D. F. Bowers, eds. Princeton, N. J., Princeton University Press, 1939.

2

The Triumph
of
Mind

IDEALISM

IF KANT IS RIGHT, and if the only valid and certain knowledge
open to us is that derived from sensible experience and elevated to
the level of science by the imposition of intelligibilities contained
within our own minds, then, of course, metaphysics is nothing
more than a logical game. Neither is there any hope that we shall
ever come to a knowledge of realities which transcend such sensible
experience. The stumbling block here is experience. If experience
is necessarily connected with matter, then the human intellect is
also necessarily tied to matter. To get away from matter is to fall
into error and illusion. At least Kant thought so, as did Hume.

Yet there were thinkers before Kant who had taken an opposite
view. And they did so precisely because they were convinced that
metaphysical truth was possible for man, and they saw that such
a complete identification of knowledge with sensible experience
would not only lead to a grounding of the whole metaphysical
enterprise, but would eventually lead to complete skepticism and
materialism. It was against such skepticism and materialism that
Bishop Berkeley had written in order to safeguard such truths as
the spirituality and the immortality of the human soul and the

existence of God. Berkeley's answer to the philosophers of sense experience was simple and direct. Experience was not necessarily connected with matter. The reason he gave was a good one. Experience could not be connected with matter because there was no such thing as matter. It is obvious to everyone that if Berkeley's answer is true, there is certainly nothing more to fear from materialism.

It is paradoxical also that Kant himself became one of the main sources of much modern Idealism. It is not the Idealism of Bishop Berkeley, but it is, nevertheless, an Idealism which attempts to achieve truth and certainty not precisely by denying the existence of matter, but by ultimately absorbing matter in a higher and immaterial reality.

Immanuel Kant explicitly rejected any connection in his philosophy with the Idealism of Bishop Berkeley. Yet, as a matter of fact, he is responsible for most of the Idealism present in philosophical thought today. Idealism as a system of thought began before Kant. It continued after him irrevocably modified by what he had written. Kant, as we have seen, insisted that the object of knowledge was a subjective impression. He held that the sense object which impressed itself upon us really existed in its own right. The Idealists who followed him insisted with equal vigor that this was illogical. If the subjective impression is all we know, it is much more consistent to say that the subjective impression is all that exists. Thus most modern Idealism is based upon the Kantian theory of knowledge. It goes beyond that theory in seeking to find an ultimate intelligible explanation of the universe in terms of mind or thought. The mind which Kant so carefully limited to sense impressions succeeded in breaking the bonds which Kant had fashioned for it and escaped finally to overwhelm the very sense world in which Kant had imprisoned it.

Idealism is based on the proposition that everything is intelligible. And because everything is intelligible, everything is ultimately to be interpreted in terms of mind. This means that the ordinary mind-matter dichotomy is an unreal one. If mind is ultimately at the root of the real, then matter must finally be reduced to mind, if it is to have any meaning whatever. This, the Idealist maintains, is much more feasible and much more easily accomplished than to reduce mind to matter. Idealism is ordinarily distinguished into Subjective and Objective Idealism. The subjective type tends to state that only mind or minds exist and all else is nothing but a modification of this mind or minds. The objective Idealists will insist rather on the necessary connection of mind and object of mind. One always presupposes the other, so that, while objects may exist independently of the particular mind which thinks them, these objects can never exist apart from all mind. For the present we shall concern ourselves with the basic tenets of Subjective Idealism.

Subjective Idealism

In his book, *Types of Philosophy*, William Ernest Hocking lists the basic intuitions on which all Idealism is dependent. These are four. The first is that the real is never that which is most obvious. This is not true of any of the other sciences; nor is it true of philosophy. The physicist, for example, will insist that what the layman apprehends as a solid piece of matter is, as a matter of fact, relatively more filled with interstices than the barbed wire fence we meet in everyday experience. Chemically a piece of gold is described differently than it is in common everyday life. So too is it with reality, says the Idealist. The obvious distinction which we make between mind and matter is not nearly an exact one. Just because the distinction is so obvious, we have a real reason to distrust it and look more deeply into the nature of the real. The fact that Materialism is such an apparent explanation of things makes the materialistic philosophy least certain of any.

Secondly, the Idealist will point out that the ease with which we can imagine the non-existence of everything material is a disproof of any finality in nature. We can quite easily imagine, for example, that the room we are in does not exist, that the city we live in is not real, that the car standing outside is simply not there. No contradiction follows from such imaginative exercise. None of these things is necessary. Furthermore, we all at one time or another, engage in a certain amount of daydreaming. We fashion a world for ourselves in which we move and breathe and, perhaps, even perform heroic feats of high courage. For the time at least these worlds of our imagining assume a reality for us. They become so real that we forget and become completely oblivious to the circumstances in which we actually are. It is only some intense sensation or emotion which finally succeeds in bringing us back to the classroom or office in which we are. The argument is not that, because we are capable of such imagining, we can never know which is the real world and which is the dream world. An Idealist will admit the difference between what we call the real world and the imaginary world. But the facility with which we move out of that real world mentally proves that the mind has powers which enable it to transcend matter. Perhaps, then, matter is less real than we think it is. The more we see how little reality it has in relation to the mental world of our hopes, dreams, imaginings, feelings, and thought, the more matter comes to assume a very insignificant place in the total picture.

Thirdly, we are aware that some happenings in nature are purposeful. That is, they are directed to intelligently conceived ends. This is true of living things that can apprehend a good and strive for it. Now why do we attribute life to things? Because we find in them certain activities which indicate that they are different from the non-living. But then our judgment that certain things are not alive is based on the absence of such activity. This, however, is a negative standard. It could possibly be that some of these things are alive, but we are simply not capable of recognizing the vital activity which, as a matter of fact, they put forth. It could possibly be true that all things are alive and that, therefore, all things direct themselves intelligently to an end, that there is mind in all of nature.

On the other hand, we attribute life at times to things that we consider inanimate. We personify things, suspect things of evil intent, become angry at them, etc. We call ships "she". Poets write of the Lady Moon. Perhaps we are less wrong than we think. Or perhaps we attribute life and personality at times where we really think we have discovered it. Just as all things may be alive, at the same time I may be the only thing alive and I may be actually attributing life and personality to everything else. Soul and mind may be at the heart of everything, just as it is also possible that I am the only mind and may well be projecting my own ideas out beyond myself.

Fourthly, what is really certain, and perhaps it is the only real certainty, is the fact that I exist as a thinking self. I can call everything else into doubt, as Descartes did. I can question the existence of God and of an external world, but I find it impossible to question the existing self as a thinking self. This I am absolutely and unequivocally sure of: I think. Therefore, I know that mind exists, that my mind exists. I cannot be so certain of the existence of matter. But nothing can contravene the certainty that I have of my existing mind. Here is the last and basic certainty. This much, then, I know: mind exists. And everything else can be reduced to mind. For it is only through mind that I come into contact with the rest of the universe. And to destroy myself is, for me, to destroy the rest of the universe.

Locke and Berkeley. But how does one go about reducing everything to mind? We can follow Bishop Berkeley as he attempts to do just that in his *Principles of Human Understanding*. Berkeley had read Locke and had accepted the principle that what we know are the sensible impressions which sense objects make upon us. This theory of knowledge had led Locke into skepticism. Berkeley thought that Locke had simply not gone far enough. By pushing Locke's theory to its necessary conclusions, Berkeley hoped to avoid the scepticism into which Locke had fallen. He hoped also to achieve a certain demonstration of the immateriality and immortality of the soul and the existence of God. Now Locke had questioned the existence of substance. It is a mere name which we impose on the collections of sense impressions we have. It can hardly be anything real, since we get no knowledge of substance in any of our experiences. If this is true, then substance must be a mere term which the mind uses to explain various collections of sense data. It is these accidental qualities which we experience and nothing else. Furthermore, we can experientially analyze something in a laboratory and we never find anything but the sense qualities. Gold for the chemist is nothing else but a collection of chemical characteristics. If we dispense with substance entirely, there is absolutely no difference either as far as our knowledge of things goes or as far as practical everyday living goes. So why not dispense with it, said Berkeley.

Reality, then, consisted of nothing but various collections of accidental qualities. Now Locke had made the so-called secondary qualities of things also subjective. He considered it obvious that such qualities as color, sound, taste, odor, and tactile impressions were mere modifications of the subject sensing. This he got from the fact that various people will identify the same objective color in different ways. What tastes bitter to one, for instance, will be sweet to another. A pleasing odor will not be pleasing on a different occasion. Hence, it was obvious to Locke that the secondary qualities which are ordinarily ascribed to objects were nothing but subjective modifications of the person sensing.

SUBJECTIVITY OF PRIMARY SENSE QUALITIES. The secondary qualities might be subjective modifications of the sensing subject, but Locke also insisted that the primary qualities, such as figure, shape, size, etc., were objective. The object, in fact, consisted of such a collection of primary qualities. These were "there" and were responsible for the impressions which we call color, taste, etc. Berkeley then asked why these primary qualities should be considered any more objective than the secondary qualities. After all, we get the primary qualities only through the secondary. How do we know what shape a thing is? Only because we can see it; and we can see it because it is colored. It is the same with size and number. Unless we can perceive the secondary qualities such as color, taste, sound, etc., there is no possible way for us to get at the primary qualities of a thing. Hence there is just as much reason to say that these primary qualities are subjective as there is to say that the secondary qualities are.

Furthermore, said Berkeley, it can be proved that at least one of these sense qualities is subjective. Take distance, for example. This is something we learn. A man born blind and suddenly given sight will see things only in two dimensions. Nor will he be able to distinguish between the near and the far. If one could represent the light refraction from objects at various distances on a plane surface, they would appear to be at the same distances from one another, as we see them. But we know that in such a supposition they are all in one plane. It is obvious, therefore, that distance and perspective are subjective. Hence Berkeley had at last succeeded in reducing the complete object to a subjective idea. There was no longer any need to posit objects apart from the mind which thinks them.

Empirical Idealism

Berkeley then proceeds to push the argument still further. How, he asks, do we know that anything exists? We answer that we can see it, feel it, hear it, etc. But this means that a thing exists in so far as we perceive it. For there is no contact with the objects of the world about us except through perception. Perception is necessary in order that we can affirm that they exist. This is his famous "Esse est percipi" which expressed the necessary connection of existence with perception. The two go hand in hand and we cannot have one without the other. To insist, for instance, that an object can exist independently of perception involves one in nonsense. This is tantamount to saying that I know something exists of which I know nothing at all. It is obvious that I can know nothing of what I do not experience. Now experience is completely subjective, as he has already shown. Hence the object of such experience must be equally subjective. Again we must conclude that not only need we not go outside of the perceiving subject; we cannot, as a matter of fact, go beyond such a subject. Berkeley would not deny that a piano ceased to exist, when I left a room. But he would insist that, unless someone were perceiving it, it would not exist.

Nor do we lose anything by such a theory of reality, according to Berkeley. I shall act and react the same way, as I did formerly, when I mistakenly thought that a world of objects distinct from myself really existed. The effect will be exactly the same, if I have the idea that I am burned, as if I had been burned by something distinct from myself. The ideas which I have will all follow each other in logical sequence, so that nothing will be changed. All he has done has been to clear up once and for all what one really means when one talks about "things." Nothing is any less real as an impression on the mind than as something existing apart from the mind. Berkeley insisted that he had merely pointed out *what* was real, and had dispensed with a world which was not necessary and which could never be known anyway. It is silly, he thought, to insist on the real existence of such a world, when my ideas are completely adequate to explain what happens.

How can one possibly assert that matter exists, when the human mind can never get into contact with matter as such. To think of matter is to reduce it immediately to spirit. It is to give matter meaning, and this is the same as to say that matter is itself an idea. I never know matter. I know what I mean by matter. I know my idea of matter. To say that matter is anything else except an idea is to involve myself in the same old contradiction. It is to say that I can know something which is completely distinct from mind and which cannot possibly be reduced to an idea. This is again to say that I can have an idea of something which is not reducible to an idea. Matter is an impossibility in the face of a theory of knowledge which only knows intelligibles. And what else could any intellect possibly know? The same reasoning can be applied to the terms *objective and subjective*. Objectivity itself is a subjective idea which I have, which simply differs in meaning from another idea which I refer to as *subjective*. The distinction must be maintained within the intellect which thinks both of them. Hence in a more profound sense, *objective* is just as subjective as anything else I think of.

But what does one do about illusions and hallucinations in such a system? Does not this tend to confuse the real and the unreal, the world of dreams with that of waking? Not at all, answered Berkeley. We call real the ideas which follow one another according to a set pattern and logical sequence. The ones which do not follow such a pattern, which are not as vivid, not as logically connected, these we refer to as illusory, as fictions, as hallucinations. Thus the ordinary idea becomes the standard by which we judge and distinguish the "real" from the "unreal."

Berkeley did not conclude that only the thinking self existed. Like Descartes he argued from the presence in the mind of the idea of God to God as the necessary cause of such an idea. Furthermore, he held that other minds existed which could and did communicate with our minds. Thus the universe of Berkeley was a society of spirits with God at the head. Each mind received ideas from God and from the other existing minds. In this way he was certain that he had done away with materialism once and for all. Furthermore he had proved the existence of God and necessarily the spirituality and immortality of the soul. Hence he had defended religion and protected theism from the many attacks that are ordinarily launched against it. This is the world of subjective idealism. It is a universe of spirits in which matter and all objectivity is understandable only in terms of ideas. And ideas exist only in the mind conceiving them. The system has many difficulties and this, perhaps, is the reason why Idealism after Berkeley became more and more *objective*.

Objective Idealism

As we shall see, Subjective Idealism has its difficulties. It is precisely because of the difficulties involved in a pure Subjective Idealism that more modern Idealists have taken up the system of Objective Idealism. This sort of Idealism admits the subject—object dichotomy. It asserts that the mind which thinks, thinks something other than itself. What it continues to assert is that ultimately behind both the self and the non-self there is mind or spirit, and that it is in terms of mind or spirit that reality is to be explained. The subject cannot do without the object. But, then, neither can the object do without a mind to behold it and understand it. The object itself is, furthermore, penetrated by mind, contains mind, and is an expression of mind. The object of mind is, after all, intelligible. It contains mind.

Not only is this true of an individual object, but it is also true of nature as a whole. Nature shows activity for a purpose; there is direction to an end. And this direction is expressed in the Laws of Nature. There is obviously more at work here than mere chance or blind force. For such purposeful activity shows intelligence. Hence there must be mind immanent in nature directing it to its proper end and manifesting itself in the various activities of the universe.

THE PROBLEM OF MATTER. Here, however, a difficulty arises. If reality is ultimately mind or spirit, how is it that reality also contains that which is not spirit? Can and does reality contradict itself? Can spirit give birth to something which is the complete antithesis of itself? And if it can, why does it do so? What is this positing of something which is opposed to being at its very heart? This opposition has always been a problem of primary importance in the history of philosophy. Plato had it, and tried to solve it by relegating matter more and more to the outer darkness. The complete disjunction he made between being and nothingness was bridged by matter, which achieved a sort of half being by coming into contact with spirit or idea. Here in the realm of becoming, matter found a strange shadow existence, but Plato exiled it forever from the world of pure spirit, which was the same as the realm of being in all its fulness.

For Aristotle matter had a more subtle and, in the long run, a more adequately explained function in reality. Like Plato, Aristotle contrasted matter to idea, or form, as he called it. But this contrast was only an apparent one. More profoundly, matter was there for the good of form. Matter was potency and out of matter came all the perfections that physical beings would ever achieve. So that matter finds its perfection in form, it is elevated by form, actuated by form. The whole surge of matter is toward form and toward the good that it can achieve only in relation to form. Likewise will all material being achieve its meaning and its perfection in relation to the abstract and the non-material toward which it, too, is ordered. Hence, while Aristotle never really adequately solved the problem of the relation between the two principles, still he saw more than Plato did. And he realized that, unless matter could be given meaning in relation to form or intelligibility, it could be given no meaning whatsoever.

The attempts to reconcile the two principles, matter and spirit, have occupied the efforts of most philosophers in history; but it is only in modern times that any significant success has been achieved. Descartes certainly was instrumental in reshaping the problem, and Leibniz in his turn emphasized the superiority and all-pervasiveness of spirit. Berkeley, as we have seen, emphasized spirit to the complete denial of nonspirit. The balance which was eventually to lead to a fuller and more perfect solution was struck first by Immanuel Kant. Kant was, of course, no Idealist. But Kant put the subject-object relationship where it belonged—in the depths of the knowing subject. For Kant the object was nothing else but the impressions made upon the subject by an unknown and unknowable thing-in-itself. Subjective thought and subjective sensation were the proper objects of the knowing process. And it was this situation which the young Fichte faced, when he considered the problem which Kant had left him.

JOHANN GOTTLIEB FICHTE (1762-1814) approved thoroughly the distinction between the subject and object which Kant had set up within the consciousness of the self. But he saw no reason at all for maintaining that the thing-in-itself existed apart from the knowing subject. In fact, he declared, this was the whole difficulty with the Kantian position. Do away with the thing-in-itself and reality is much more understandable. Fichte kept the subject-object relationship, but he reduced the whole thing to the order of the thinking subject. There is a transcendental Ego which produces both the self and the non-self. For the self is aware of itself and it is also aware of that which is not itself. This dichotomy is in the experiential order, and it is out of such opposition of the self to itself that all progress in the order of mind is made possible. But then the question arose as to why the Ego should so divide itself against itself. Fichte's answer was that the essence of mind is will. Now will must express itself in action. But such action is impossible unless there is opposition, unless there is something to act on or against. Hence the fundamental mind or will divides itself against itself in the experiential order so that there can be an object upon which will can act. It is out of such action that mind perfects itself and achieves its highest glory.

Hence Fichte is similar to Berkeley in so far as he reduces the thing-in-itself to nothingness. There is only the thinking mind which expresses itself finitely in the individual selves and non-selves of everyday experience. He differs sharply from Berkeley in so far as the ultimate mind which acts is a transcendent mind which acts and thinks through the experiential selves it sets up. Hence Fichte's mind is personal only in its finite manifestations. Ultimately here the individual is lost in the impersonal, and the finite in the transcendent.

JOSEPH SCHELLING (1775-1854) raised the transcendental ego of Fichte to an absolute, and looked upon both nature and mind as manifestations of this absolute. Where Fichte had made the transcendental ego the source of the experiential ego and the non-ego, Schelling found their common source in an absolute mind. Here nature is more than just an impediment useful in bringing out the innate resources of the self. Both experiential self and nature are manifestations of Mind, each functioning in its own way to make for the final achievement of Mind as such.

GEORGE WILHELM FRIEDRICH HEGEL (1770-1831) brought to completion and systematic coherence the idealistic philosophy begun by Immanuel Kant. According to Hegel, mind and nature are not just two extrinsic manifestations of the Absolute, as Schelling had said, but they are modes of an Absolute which is inherent in and immanent to them. The Absolute is active; it is the process which takes place in history and the universe. The Absolute evolves Itself in order the better to achieve Itself. This Absolute is reason which attains its highest expression in man and is found in nature and the universe as the laws of intelligibility which are working themselves out. Reason, then, is not as Kant conceived it, a faculty of the soul. It is universal meaning and intelligibility immanent in the universe and evolving itself in the evolution of things. Here is where Hegel takes the Kantian critique and makes it into a metaphysics of all reality.

Hegel set out to develop the idealistic elements in the legacy of Kant to their ultimate. Kant, he thought, had stopped at the level of reason as a function and had regarded the ideas or categories as empty of content. But Kant had also implicitly admitted a transcendental Ego, which lay at the source of the ideas and the experience which they informed. It was on this transcendental Ego which Hegel concentrated and which he elevated to the status of Pure Idea, Absolute Spirit, all-embracing Reality. The process is a long and intricate one, and it can be presented only in rudimentary fashion here.

Kant had spoken of things-in-themselves, but contended that they were unknowable and that the human reason could deal only with their appearances. Hegel proceeded to show that the noumenal Ego was the *only* thing-in-itself and to make everything else an existential appearance of this sole reality. Everywhere in the universe he found traces of intelligibility, and does not intelligibility presuppose the presence of idea? This intelligibility is, furthermore, a progressive one; for it is an intelligibility which becomes richer and richer, until it becomes conscious of itself in man. Not only does this intelligibility achieve self consciousness, but it becomes its own object. Thus it can study itself, inquire into its own nature; and in so far as it does this, it is called Reason. But Reason itself must be ordered beyond itself; for Reason involves duality and the opposition of subject and object. Yet at the same time this duality is overcome in a still more perfect synthesis, for the Reason which opposes itself to itself is aware that Reason as subject is the same as Reason as object. This unity behind the duality in Reason is nothing else but the Pure Idea, which reconciles all diversity and even the diversity within Reason in the absolute unity of Spirit. Hence, it is by a constant ascent through the unification of opposites in ever higher and more perfect unities that absolute unity is finally reached and identified as Pure Idea or Spirit.

It can hardly be denied that Hegel had a real insight into the nature of knowledge and mind. At least he understood that knowing involved a subject and object and that this duality was overcome in the knowing process. For the subject becomes an other without ceasing to be itself. At the same time, the other is reduced to the reality of the subject, yet maintains its otherness. Now to be conscious of this, to know that I know, seemed to Hegel to be a further and still more perfect identification of the subject with itself, a unification of already existing unity. The purest and most absolute unity of all should be mind intuiting itself precisely as mind. This, too, would be the purest and most absolute reality. From another viewpoint mind would be estranged from itself in so far as it contributed itself to things as their constitutive intelligibility. Just as obviously such intelligibility would regain itself, would achieve its perfection and its highest reality, in so far as it became conscious of itself as able to do this. But to be able to do this is what it means to become a subject, a self. Consequently, in place of some unknowing and unknowable substance which Kant put at the heart of reality, Hegel substituted a substance which was completely aware of itself and identified with itself through such awareness. The perfection of such self awareness must be

absolutely unique, and all less perfect self awareness must be
merely a manifestation of the perfect self awareness. Such a manifestation would be determined, limited, finite. Yet such imperfect
manifestations of self awareness could not be really distinct from
perfect self awareness, for they would necessarily presuppose it and
be included in it.

Yet this perfect identity of being and being-known was not
something given. It was rather something to be achieved, and the
whole historical process testified to this fact. Change and development were, however, intelligibilities, and as such had to be
grounded in the Idea. Hence, there must be progression in the
Idea itself, and from this viewpoint change means progressive
reflection. From another viewpoint this reflective progression is
externalized and seen as the process going on in the physical
universe. Just as this physical universe achieved itself through
and in its physical development, so did the Idea achieve itself,
come to a more and more perfect reflective awareness of itself
through and in its reflective process. The physical process, however, as an externalization of the Idea must already be contained
ideally within the Idea. So it can be said that the external process
manifests the intrinsic perfection of the Idea gradually in history,
and the Idea itself through and in its reflection comes to an ever
more perfect realization of what it is. Thus does its being-as-self-
awareness approach ever more closely to an identification with its
being-as-such. Yet already there is complete and perfect identification here, for is not its being-as-such precisely being-aware-of-itself?

This process of self realization takes the road from being as
emptiness to being as the self-conscious self, being as Absolute
Mind. The process is described in *The Phenomenology of Mind*
and its logical justification is presented in Hegel's *Logic*, a logic
of ontology, as he calls it. Here he begins with a concept of being
which is a pure abstraction from all determination. Such a concept says "merely is." It is a concept empty of all content, an
affirmation which indiscriminately applies to everything without
difference or distinction. Such a concept Hegel saw can just as well
signify non-being as it can being. For, while on the one hand it
affirms being, at the same time it denies being. It can equally well
apply to nothing. Nothing "merely" is. There is no such thing

which can represent so empty an abstraction. Nowhere does anything "merely exist." Such a thing escapes both thought and being. For thought can only grasp the determinate, a this or a that. And being to be must be either a this or a that. Such a concept of indefinite and undetermined being involves within itself a contradiction. It both is and is not. It affirms itself and denies itself. Being and non-being shift back and forth on this level; they interpenetrate each other; they contradict each other.

Yet such contradiction at the heart of being so conceived is itself meaningful, for in both affirming itself and denying itself being tends to determine itself, and thus to resolve the contradiction within itself. The resolution of this contradiction is the first determination of being, and this Hegel calls becoming. Here is the beginning of the dialectical process which Hegel uses to explain the way in which absolute being—Absolute Mind—comes to a progressive realization of itself. There is an affirmation: a thesis—being is. At the same time there is a negation involved. For this being which is also is not. This negation is the antithesis. Out of the contradiction between thesis and antithesis comes the synthesis: becoming. Thus becoming marks the initial progress of being. It denies the denial present in being and achieves a new affirmation—the affirmation of determination within being.

It is immediately clear that the process must continue. For being thus to determine itself is to limit itself, and such limitation implies other beings. Limit is that which distinguishes, which sets bounds to being, which, then, opposes it to other beings. Such a reference to others can go on indefinitely, and from this realization comes the notion of the infinite. Being can limit itself indefinitely; it can always refer itself to another and another without end. Moreover, being is so constructed that it must keep referring itself to another; hence, it will do so infinitely. Thus, as limited, being is finite. But because limit always implies the other, being is infinite. This infinity, however, is not the true infinity. Behind the process, involved in it, embracing and embraced by both terms, being is there giving reality to all things. It transcends both the finite and the infinite. It goes out of itself only to return to itself never really managing to disengage itself from itself. It manifests itself only that in opposing itself to itself it may come to the awareness of what it already is. But it already is Spirit, Absolute Mind. Thus it is present in all things, immanent to them, externalizing itself in them, yet reducing all things back to itself, the eternal awareness of all. Thus it achieves what it already is, identifying itself more and more perfectly with itself even as it alienates itself from itself.

Hegel carries out this resolution of contradictories in all phases of his philosophy. Ultimately there will be a perfect resolution of all such opposites and all contradictories. Out of this last resolution will come the Idea, possessing full realization of itself. Here in the Idea will be contained the perfect fusion of Mind and its object. The Idea will be a perfect unity arising out of plurality, a perfect solution of apparent contradictions. Mind will have returned to itself in a perfect act of self reflection. The peak of the idealistic metaphysic is attained here with Hegel, and he remains the constant norm for all the forms of idealistic thinking which follow.

Idealism in America

Hegel was introduced to the United States in the latter half of the nineteenth century. It began with the famous St. Louis Group under Brokmeyer and Harris and spread to the eastern section of the country. As the movement spread and developed, one of its clearest and most coherent voices was that of Josiah Royce (1855-1917). In general Royce espoused the absolute position of Hegel. The position, though, had its difficulties and Royce was conscious of them. Always he had to struggle with the problem of solipsism. How in the face of reality conceived as thought could one keep from reducing everything to *my* thought? Royce attempts to keep the distinction between personal, individual thought and absolute mind by separating the partial from the whole, the finite aspect from the infinite totality. On the one level there is error, partial truth and finitude. On the other there is complete truth and infinite mind. Not only do such distinctions save individuality, but they are useful in proving from the finite level that the infinite totality exists. How could one recognize that experience is finite, unless there existed an infinite experience in relation to which one knows that one's own experience is finite? All error presupposes a truth and a truth postulates the existence of truth itself. Ultimately Royce appears to find the distinction between the finite and the infinite best expressed in the moral order. Finite selves differ from one another in the different purposes which each pursues. But these different purposes in turn demand a universal purposefulness in the light of which finite, diverse purposes are understandable. Thus this infinite purposefulness reconciles in the end all individual purposes and is a guarantee that the universe as a whole is rational. On the finite level, then, morality is nothing else but the harmony of these finite purposes with each other. Thus Royce's morality takes on a social aspect, which he considered essential to the nature of morality. Interested as he was in maintaining the distinction between the absolute mind and individual minds, Royce clearly emphasized the priority of the absolute as that which gives meaning and reality to all else. It is for this reason that he is considered basically an absolutist.

Another trend in Objective Idealism has been more pronounced since Royce. This trend emphasizes the individual and is best exemplified, perhaps, by the Idealism of Borden Parker Bowne (1847-1910). Bowne insisted that we discover an objective order, rather than create one. Yet in true Kantian fashion he also insisted that all we know of such an order is the subjective impressions which are made upon us. These subjective impressions, however, carry with them a relation to something beyond themselves. Hence it is possible to make an act of faith in the existence of an extramental world. This extramental world is nothing else but realized idea.

It is precisely here, however, according to Bowne, that Kant and his followers lost sight of the self. They were so interested in explaining how the material universe was a manifestation of idea that they forgot to investigate the self. As a result they were unable to keep it distinct from the absolute.

From now on, most of Bowne's philosophizing concerns the realm of the manifestation of the absolute rather than the absolute itself. The Hegelian position is taken for granted, but the emphasis is on the relationships existing between the finite self and its finite object. Person is defined by Bowne as a unity of consciousness.

This unity of consciousness is also what he means by substance. So that beyond the person there is no substance. This in turn leads him to conceive the material universe as a ceaselessly changing collection of qualities. Behind the person there exists, of course, the absolute, which is also present to each person. It is out of this emphasis on the person and the individual in modern and contemporary Idealism that the movement known as Personalism has developed.

The man who presents the best and most unified summary of various modern forms of Idealism is William Ernest Hocking, at present emeritus professor of Philosophy at Harvard. Hocking, too, accepts the basic Hegelian position and argues that mind is necessarily the ultimate reality and that the self and the objects opposed to the self are finally understandable only in terms of spirit. In the present order he distinguishes between self and the non-self and on this level is interested in establishing the precise point of contact between them. This point of contact he finds in the body. For the body is not the self, but it is closely connected to the self. It is through the instrumentality of the body that the self can reach out to the world of objects and these objects in turn can influence and act upon the self. There is, however, no dualistic problem here. Body is merely the external manifestation of the self, the convex side of the concave curve. Thus on this level the body manifests the self much as the self and nature as a whole manifest the ultimate reality of spirit.

Since the body is an externalization of spirit, it is obviously not contrary to spirit. Hence while the body may be subjected to the influences of nature upon it, the self can rise above both in its intrinsic nature as self. Man, then, is free. For freedom is the power of self determination and that power is within the nature of the self. Aware of the influences at work upon the body, the self can avoid or render useless such influences—at least in certain circumstances. This power of self determination demonstrates that man can act in terms of conscious meanings. For things in the universe have meaning and man is one of these things. His judgments made about the situation in which he exists must also be meaningful, since it is not consistent to state that the human mind could be essentially at variance with mind as such. Hence the yearnings for immortality are themselves meaningful, and it is certainly not impossible that a personal immortality with continued communication between minds be the ultimate destiny of man.

Hocking further sees idealistic metaphysics as a true and substantial ground for an ethics. The idealistic metaphysics recognizes man as a special value in the universe, different both from machines and brutes. Such a recognition, which engenders respect for the human person, makes possible a strictly human ethics. He finds this best expressed by Kant who saw that human beings were persons and as such could never be reduced to mere means. Such a viewpoint recognizes the basic equality of all men and thus establishes the foundation of all justice. It makes possible the honor which is due to every man and forbids that the personal principle in each should ever be subordinated to material inclination.[1]

Yet Hocking feels that he must go farther than Kant in his attempt to substantiate such an ethics. The categorical imperative is not enough. This is no more than an impulse without rational support. It is in Hegel that such a rational support for an idealistic ethics is best manifested. It is as an intelligent part of a greater whole that Hegel discovers the ethical basis of human action. For the whole is the manifestation of reason and by allying oneself with the whole one allies oneself with reason. But how does one go about making such an alliance? One must identify oneself with Reason as found in the universal institutions of mankind. Now for Hegel the institution best exemplifying the universal reason at work in the universe was the state. Yet there is a difficulty here. States can decay. They can usurp the right of the person. Hence it is better to say, as Royce did, that loyalty to causes is the best way to associate oneself with Reason. But it is still not possible to stop here. The universal must somehow be applied to the particular. It is always this man who acts. Each one of us has to do in a concrete situation what no one else can do. Hence each man must consider himself a unique being, having a view of reality granted to no other, which it is his destiny

[1] W. E. Hocking, *Types of Philosophy* (New York, Charles Scribner's Sons, 1939), p. 349.

to express. The expression of such an idea in action is finally
the obligation of each man because he is a man.[2]

In Europe Hegelian themes are again becoming popular. Not
that an absolute Idealism is finding favor, but the dialectical nature of Hegelianism is being studied. As we shall see, Sartre makes
use of Hegel's distinction between being-in-itself and being-for-
itself. Dialectical Materialism also is founded on the Hegelian
dialectic, even though the process has been turned upside down.
There has been, too, a new interest in the philosophy of history,
and the nature of spirit and religious consciousness and religious
experience is being carefully examined. Comparisons are also
being made between Hegel and contemporary German Existentialists like Jaspers and Heidegger. The whole phenomenological
movement stemming from Husserl certainly has its Hegelian elements. One finds also many discussions of logic, as Hegel understood it.[3]

This is not surprising. The complete rejection of spirit is not
easy, and mind is always there proclaiming its superiority to
matter. The human need to explain, clarify, and understand is
constantly making itself felt; and certainly Hegel had touched
upon many of the aspects of consciousness and knowledge which
all men are aware of and which invite reflection and philosophical
examination. The discussion has been for the most part limited to
consciousness and knowledge as we find it on the finite level,
but this is by no means bad. The insight is a valuable one and
can provide new philosophical truth and understanding in an
area which remains mysterious and only partially known.

CRITICISM OF SUBJECTIVE IDEALISM

The main difficulty with Berkeleyan Idealism is that it becomes
almost impossible to maintain the plurality of minds and the
God which Berkeley declared made up reality. Like Descartes, he

---

[2] *Ibid.*, pp. 335-362, *passim.*

[3] For a list of Hegelian themes discussed during the past fifty years, *cf.*
Paul Asveld, "L'Idêalisme, Allemand: Fichte, Schelling, Hegel," in R. Kliban-
sky, ed., *Philosophy in the Mid-Century* (Florence, La Nuova Italia Editrice,
1959), Vol. IV, pp. 163-174. *Cf.* also, J. Collins "Philosophy in the Nineteenth and Early Twentieth Centuries," *op. cit.*, pp. 175-186.

had argued from the idea of the perfect to the existence of the perfect as the only adequate cause. Only the perfect could be the cause of an idea of the perfect. This simply does not follow. The idea of the perfect need not itself be perfect. As a matter of fact, we have a very imperfect idea of the perfect. Such an idea is limited, finite, and inadequate. It certainly needs no perfect cause to explain it. Now once we can dispense with God as the necessary cause of the idea of God, then it becomes very easy to suspect that we are the cause of such an idea. Not only can we be the cause of the idea of God, but it is also possible to think that we are the sole cause of all the other ideas we have. Slowly but surely the terrifying idea is borne in upon us that there may very well be only one mind existing, and that is my mind. This is called Solipsism. Such a doctrine leaves one completely alone. He exists, and all else is nothing more than a projection of his mind. Practically it is impossible to live in such a situation, and we shrink from the horror which it involves.

Not only is the position practically impossible, but even theoretically there is a contradiction involved. For it is possible, perhaps, that Solipsism is the answer, that I alone exist. If this is the case, then it should be faced and borne philosophically. But such an assertion is an impossible one. To state that I alone exist is also to state that I must get over the basic notion that other things exist as well. To assert only myself, I must get out of myself to do so. Along with the notion of self goes always the notion of the non-self. To say that I am certain only that I exist is, I think, to ignore the evidence. I am equally certain that other things exist, for they are present to me, and I know myself only in knowing them. To know always involves an object. I must know something. And I cannot know myself unless I know myself as knowing something else. The knowledge of myself is a reflective knowledge, and it is achieved only when the self goes out to that which is not the self. I know that I know only when I know something that is not myself.

This knowledge of other things is, furthermore, present in us from the very dawn of consciousness. The recognition that there are material things independent of us, resisting us, forcing themselves upon our consciousness is one of the most basic facts of

our experience. Such experience is constant and inevitable. We
assert it and conform to it every waking moment of our lives. If
there are no such objects, then the only conclusion is that our
intellects have been constantly and inevitably deceiving us. If this
is true, then what hope is there that we can ever arrive at any
truth? Subjective Idealism reduces itself either to Solipsism or to a
complete skepticism about the possibility of valid knowledge.

CRITICISM OF OBJECTIVE IDEALISM

There is much in Objective Idealism that is quite consistent with
a Thomistic theory of reality. There is certainly mind at work
in the universe, and this mind is essentially different from matter.
Furthermore, the matter which we discover in the things of our
experience is made real and intelligible only by the presence within
it of intelligibility. Nature is more than matter, and I know this
to be true by the fact that I can understand it. Not only is there
intelligibility in nature, but the fact that matter itself is made into
something intelligible by being united with this intelligibility in
things is an indication that mind and not matter is what is
ultimately real. There is mind on the other side of nature, just as
there is mind on this side of nature. And nature can in all truth
be called a manifestation of mind, since the intelligibility it contains points to an understanding mind on which it ultimately
depends. The finite is an expression of the infinite, showing forth
the ways of God. I can know things because they are already
known. The universe is intelligible because it is already actually
understood. In a very real sense, then, the universe can be called
an expression of mind, and mind is ultimate in the sense that
finally everything stems from mind and is dependent on mind.

Yet the very truth which Objective Idealism possesses becomes
the ground in which excesses take root and flower into doctrines
that are finally contradictions. To say that mind is that on which
ultimately all reality depends is quite different from saying that
mind is immanent in all things. To state that nature is intelligible
is not the same as to say that nature contains a mind which is
intrinsic to it and actively working itself out in nature. To affirm
that the human mind is finite and inadequate, is not the same

thing as to say that the human intellect is a mere appearance of an absolute mind which is thinking and willing through it.

Mind and Intelligibility

The Objective Idealist position proceeds from a recognition of the intelligibility contained in nature to an assertion that, therefore, there is mind in nature. This mind may either be a world soul vivifying all of nature, or it may be Absolute Mind itself, intrinsic to the natural processes, working Itself out historically to a full and perfect realization of Itself. Neither position is tenable. In the first place, the jump from the intelligibility contained in nature to the assertion that this indicates mind in nature is an unwarranted one. Intelligibility does not mean the same thing as mind. Intelligibility indicates a passive state, an ability to be understood. Mind, on the other hand, is active. It is that which actively understands that which is intelligible. To attribute mind to nature would be to personify it, to make it capable of intrinsic reasoning powers. But there is no evidence that the natural things of the universe below man are so equipped. They are there to be understood. They do not seem in the least to be actively understanding. The only evidence that could possibly be adduced is the order to an end, the purposefulness, in nature. But this purposefulness merely indicates that things are ordered to an end, not that they actively order themselves. Such passive purposefulness does not indicate immanent mind, but rather that these things are ultimately related to an extrinsic mind.

Mind as Absolute

The Hegelian doctrine of an Absolute Mind immanent in nature, of which nature is only a finite appearance and a manifestation, has equally difficult assumptions connected with it. Nature must then be posited as a necessary foil which is needed by such a Mind actively to think Itself to a full realization of Itself. But an infinite Mind immediately present to itself is also immediately intelligible to itself. There is no need to posit any such non-self for such a self to come to a realization of itself. St. Thomas points out that

God's knowledge is first of all of Himself and that through Himself He knows all of being distinct from Himself.

God understands Himself through Himself. In proof whereof it must be known that, although in operations which pass to an external effect the object of the operation, which is taken as the term, exists outside the operator, nevertheless, in operations that remain in the operator, the object signified as the term of the operation resides in the operator; and according as it is in the operator is the operation actual. Hence the Philosopher says that the sensible in act is the sense in act, and the intelligible in act is the intellect in act. For the reason why we actually feel or know a thing is because our intellect or sense is actually informed by the sensible or intelligible species. And because of this only, it follows that sense or intellect is distinct from the sensible or intelligible object, since both are in potentiality.

Since, therefore, God has nothing in Him of potentiality, but is pure act, His intellect and its object must be altogether the same; so that He neither is without the intelligible species, as in the case with our intellect when it understands potentially, nor does the intelligible species differ from the substance of the divine intellect, as it differs in our intellect when it understands actually, but the intelligible species itself is the divine intellect itself, and thus God understands Himself through Himself.[4]

It is necessary to note here, however, that Hegel never identified Absolute Mind with God. He regarded the God of traditional theism as an inadequate substitute for Mind. The proofs which he uses are all ordered toward indicating the existence of a transcendent and immanent Mind rather than a God. In this regard he points out that Kant was never able to see the validity of such proofs, because he continually distinguished a universe of finite beings from an Infinite Being. Hence, starting with the finite, Kant was never able to transcend the finite and arrive at the Infinite.

But in Hegel's system there is no need to go from the finite to the Infinite. The Infinite is present in the finite. The finite is nothing but a temporal and spatial expression of the Infinite. In fact, to inspect the finite is to see that it really is not, that it is only the Infinite which truly is. For the Infinite to think man is at the same time for man to think the Infinite. Traditional theists

---

[4] *Summa Theologica*, I, 14, 2.

had always argued from the existence of the contingent to the existence of God. Hegel proceeds in contrary fashion. It is from a realization of the radical non-being of the contingent that he arrives at the necessary being of the Infinite. It is because of this very immanence of Infinite Mind thinking Itself in time and space that the thought of God can lead us to the actual existence of God. For what is the thought of God but God thinking Himself?

But here again the difficulties are enormous. This is to assert the existence of the Infinite at the expense of the finite. What possible being can be attributed to contingent, individual existents? Everything is absorbed by and lost to Infinite Being. The whole struggle of modern Idealism has been precisely this: to save individuality in the face of a reality which cannot be individual. This is undoubtedly why American Idealists like Borden Bowne and the Personalists insist so much on the individual. When once such an Absolute has been admitted as immanent and necessary in the finite, then, unless one insists and keeps on insisting on personality and individuality, there is every reason to suspect that the individual will simply disappear in the Absolute. This is also the fear of the earlier Hegelians like Feuerbach, who to save man made the Infinite a projection of man's desire for perfection. Marx and Engels would also reject the reduction of man and society to Mind and would use the Hegelian method to explain the reality not of mind but of matter.

Furthermore, the position of Feuerbach and the Marxists seems in this situation to be extremely well taken. It is just as easy, and perhaps more so, to assert the Absolute as a projection of the human mind as it is to assert human minds as projections of the Absolute. We are certainly much more aware and certain of the existence of our own thinking than we are of the Thinking of Absolute Mind, of which we are the mere temporal expressions. Hegel was, of course, interested in safeguarding the immanent presence of Spirit to all that which contained spirit in so far as it contained intelligibility. But this can be accomplished without losing the reality of that which is limitedly and finitely intelligible. St. Thomas asserts a God Who is Absolute and Transcendent and Who at the same time is immanently present to the finite order through His causal activity. The finite thus remains distinct from the Infinite and yet depends on the Absolute for its reality. This reality is truly the reality of the finite being. At the same time it is a reality which is ultimately intelligible only in terms of an Absolute.[5]

Objective Idealism oversimplifies the whole problem of knowledge. It is admittedly difficult to reconcile the subject of knowledge with the object of knowledge. But this dichotomy in knowledge is a fact of experience, and it is this experience which must be explained. Simply to suppress the object is not to explain what happens when we know. Idealism tacitly admits that it has not been able to suppress all objects by the very fact that it recognizes Materialism and Relativism as philosophical theories which it attempts to refute and overthrow.

Another of Idealism's favorite arguments is that consciousness is the only reality, since everything must be reduced to consciousness before it can be known. But this can be and is admitted by any Realist without having any violence done to the realistic position. To say that an object cannot be known independently of consciousness is not the same thing as to say that consciousness creates its object. Consciousness can after all be consciousness of a thing existing independently of consciousness. The fact that I only understand English, for example, does not mean that English is the only form of speech; or even that English itself is not spoken independently of my awareness of it.

Here, too, as in Subjective Idealism, Skepticism and Solipsism remain ever present difficulties. On the one hand, I can never be certain that it is really I who think; while, on the other, it is equally possible that I may be the only one thinking. Idealism as a theory does not explain knowledge as we experience it. On the contrary, it creates new and insoluble difficulties.

SUMMARY

1. Idealism in general is an insistence on the basic reality of mind or spirit as the ultimate principle constituting the real. It is, consequently, a reaction against all types of Materialism and Sensism

---

[5] J. Collins, *God in Modern Philosophy* (Chicago, Henry Regnery, Co., 1959), *cf.* chap. 7.

and attempts to safeguard the nature of metaphysical truth by showing that matter has meaning only in relation to mind. There are two basic kinds of Idealism. The first attempts to prove that only mind exists; that matter is an illusion; that reality consists of an Infinite Mind, finite minds, and ideas. This is the Idealism of Bishop Berkeley.

2. The second type of Idealism recognizes the objective reality of matter, but understands matter as a finite and temporary expression of spirit. Such an expression is necessary in so far as it aids spirit to come to a fuller and more perfect recognition of itself. This is the Idealism of Hegel and the Americans; Royce, Bowne, and Hocking.

3. Both types of Idealism are strong reactions against Materialism and Skepticism and take their stand for the existence of metaphysical truth and man's capacity to achieve it. Hence, it marks an attempt to free the human intellect from Sensism and sensible experience and from the limitations imposed on it by Hume and Kant. It is paradoxical that there were elements in the philosophies of Hume and Kant themselves which gave rise to much of what we find in modern Idealism. The difficulty here may well be that the cure is worse than the disease, for Idealism has a tendency to lose to the abstract and the absolute the very individual human intellect it is attempting to save.

Criticism

1. SUBJECTIVE IDEALISM
   a. The existence of objects independent of the mind is a fundamental and never changing human experience.
   b. Subjective Idealism leads inevitably to Solipsism.
   c. To assert only the self involves implicitly an assertion of the non-self.

2. OBJECTIVE IDEALISM
   a. The intelligibility of things does not necessarily indicate that mind is immanent to these things.
   b. Hegel's doctrine of Absolute Mind externalizing itself in

order to complete itself is itself an assertion that such a Mind is not absolute.

c. The doctrine of Absolute Mind destroys the reality of the contingent and the finite.

d. The Absolute can be explained as both immanent by its causal activity and distinct in its own proper being without doing violence either to contingency or immanence.

e. Objective Idealism oversimplifies the problem of knowledge by suppressing one of the factors—the object—which is an experiential element in all knowledge.

f. To state that an object cannot be known independently of consciousness is not the same as to say that consciousness creates its object.

g. Objective Idealism, like Subjective Idealism, leads also to Skepticism and Solipsism.

SELECTED READINGS

Of the Principles of Human Knowledge*

It is evident to anyone who takes a survey of the objects of human knowledge that they are either ideas actually imprinted on the senses, or else such as are perceived by attending to the passions and operations of the mind, or lastly, ideas formed by help of memory and imagination—either compounding, dividing, or barely representing those originally perceived in the aforesaid ways. By sight I have the ideas of light and colors, with their several degrees and variations. By touch I perceive, for example, hard and soft, heat and cold, motion and resistance, and all of these more and less either as to quantity or degree. Smelling furnishes me with odors, the palate with tastes, and hearing conveys sounds to the mind in all their variety of tone and composition. And as several of these are observed to accompany each other, they come to be marked by one name, and so to be reputed as one thing.

* From George Berkeley, A *Treatise Concerning the Principles of Human Knowledge*, intro. by Colin M. Turbayne, ed. (New York, The Liberal Arts Press, Inc., 1957).

Thus, for example, a certain color, taste, smell, figure, and consistence having been observed to go together, are accounted one distinct thing signified by the name "apple"; other collections of ideas constitute a stone, a tree, a book, and the like sensible things —which as they are pleasing or disagreeable excite the passions of love, hatred, joy, grief, and so forth.

But, besides all that endless variety of ideas of objects of knowledge, there is likewise something which knows or perceives them and exercises divers operations, as willing, imagining, remembering, about them. This perceiving, active being is what I call mind, spirit, soul, or myself. By which words I do not denote any one of my ideas, but a thing entirely distinct from them, wherein they exist or, which is the same thing, whereby they are perceived—for the existence of an idea consists in being perceived.

That neither our thoughts, nor passions, nor ideas formed by the imagination exist without the mind is what everybody will allow. And it seems no less evident that the various sensations or ideas imprinted on the sense, however blended or combined together (that is, whatever objects they compose), cannot exist otherwise than in a mind perceiving them. I think an intuitive knowledge may be obtained of this by anyone that shall attend to what is meant by the term exist when applied to sensible things. The table I write on I say exists, that is, I see and feel it; and if I were out of my study I should say it existed—meaning thereby that if I were in my study I might perceive it, or that some other spirit actually does perceive it. There was an odor, that is, it was smelled; there was a sound, that is to say, it was heard; a color or figure, and it was perceived by sight or touch. This is all that I can understand by these and the like expressions. For as to what is said of the absolute existence of unthinking things without any relation to their being perceived, that seems perfectly unintelligible. Their esse is percipi, nor is it possible that they should have any existence out of the minds or thinking things which perceive them.

It is indeed an opinion strangely prevailing amongst men that houses, mountains, rivers, and, in a word, all sensible objects have an existence, natural or real, distinct from their being perceived

by the understanding. But with how great an assurance and
acquiescence soever this principle may be entertained in the world,
yet whoever shall find in his heart to call it in question may, if
I mistake not, perceive it to involve a manifest contradiction. For
what are the forementioned objects but the things we perceive
by sense? And what do we perceive besides our own ideas or
sensations? And is it not plainly repugnant that any one of
these, or any combination of them, should exist unperceived?

If we thoroughly examine this tenet it will, perhaps, be found at
bottom to depend on the doctrine of abstract ideas. For can there
be a nicer strain of abstraction than to distinguish the existence
of sensible objects from their being perceived, so as to conceive
them existing unperceived? Light and colors, heat and cold, extension and figures—in a word, the things we see and feel—what
are they but so many sensations, notions, ideas, or impressions
on the sense? And is it possible to separate, even in thought,
any of these from perception? For my part, I might as easily
divide a thing from itself. I may, indeed, divide in my thoughts,
or conceive apart from each other, those things which, perhaps,
I never perceived by sense so divided. Thus I imagine the trunk
of a human body without the limbs, or conceive the smell of a
rose without thinking on the rose itself. So far, I will not deny,
I can abstract—if that may properly be called abstraction which
extends only to the conceiving separately such objects as it is
possible may really exist or be actually perceived asunder. But my
conceiving or imagining power does not extend beyond the possibility of real existence or perception. Hence, as it is impossible
for me to see or feel anything without an actual sensation of that
thing, so is it impossible for me to conceive in my thoughts any
sensible thing or object distinct from the sensation or perception
of it.

But, say you, though the ideas themselves do not exist without
the mind, yet there may be things like them, whereof they are
copies or resemblances, which things exist without the mind in an
unthinking substance. I answer, an idea can be like nothing but
an idea; . . . If we look but ever so little into our thoughts, we
shall find it impossible for us to conceive a likeness except only
between our ideas. Again, I ask whether those supposed originals

or external things, of which our ideas are the pictures or representations, be themselves perceivable or no? If they are, then they are ideas and we have gained our point; but if you say they are not, I appeal to anyone whether it be sense to assert a color is like something which is invisible; hard or soft, like something which is intangible; and so of the rest.

Secondly, it will be objected that there is a great difference betwixt real fire, for instance, and the idea of fire, betwixt dreaming or imagining oneself burned, and actually being so. This and the like may be urged in opposition to our tenets. To all which the answer is evident from what has been already said; and I shall only add in this place that if real fire be very different from the idea of fire, so also is the real pain that it occasions very different from the idea of the same pain, and yet nobody will pretend that real pain either is, or can possibly be, in an unperceiving thing, or without the mind, any more than its idea.

Let us examine a little the description that is here given us of matter. It neither acts, nor perceives, nor is perceived, for this is all that is meant by saying it is an inert, senseless, unknown substance; which is a definition entirely made up of negatives, excepting only the relative notion of its standing under or supporting. But then it must be observed that it supports nothing at all, and how nearly this comes to the description of a nonentity I desire may be considered. But, say you, it is the unknown occasion at the presence of which ideas are excited in us by the will of God. Now I would fain know how anything can be present to us which is neither perceivable by sense nor reflection, nor capable of producing any idea in our minds, nor is at all extended, nor has any form, nor exists in any place. The words "to be present," when thus applied, must needs be taken in some abstract and strange meaning, and which I am not able to comprehend.

The Third Kind of History—The Philosophical*

No explanation was needed of the two previous classes; their nature was self-evident. It is otherwise with this last, which cer-

* Quoted from G. W. F. Hegel, *Introduction to the Philosophy of History*, trans. by J. Sibree (London, H. G. Bohn, 1861).

tainly seems to require an exposition or justification. The most general definition that can be given is: that the philosophy of history means nothing but the thoughtful consideration of it. Thought is, indeed, essential to humanity. It is this that distinguishes us from the brutes. In sensation, cognition, and intellection; in our instincts and volitions, as far as they are truly human, thought is an invariable element. To insist upon thought in this connection with history may, however, appear unsatisfactory. In this science it would seem as if thought must be subordinate to what is given, to the realities of fact; that this is its basis and guide: while philosophy dwells in the region of self-produced ideas, without reference to actuality. Approaching history thus prepossessed, speculation might be expected to treat it as a mere passive material; and, so far from leaving it in its native truth, to force it into conformity with a tyrannous idea, and to construe it, as the phrase is, "a priori." But as it is the business of history simply to adopt into its records what is and has been, actual occurrences and transactions; and since it remains true to its character in proportion as it strictly adheres to its data, we seem to have in philosophy, a process diametrically opposed to that of the historiographer. This contradiction, and the charge consequently brought against speculation, shall be explained and confuted. We do not, however, propose to correct the innumerable special misrepresentations, trite or novel, that are current respecting the aims, the interests, and the modes of treating history, and its relation to philosophy.

The only thought which philosophy brings with it to the contemplation of history, is the simple conception of reason; that reason is the sovereign of the world; that the history of the world, therefore, presents us with a rational process. This conviction and intuition is a hypothesis in the domain of history as such. In that of philosophy it is no hypothesis. It is there proved by speculative cognition, that reason—and this term may here suffice us, without investigating the relation sustained by the universe to the divine being—is substance as well as infinite power; its own infinite material underlying all the natural and spiritual life which it originates, as also the infinite form—that which sets this material in motion. On the one hand, reason is the substance of the universe, *viz.*, that by which and in which all reality has its being and subsistence. On the other hand, it is the infinite energy of the universe; since reason is not so powerless as to be incapable of producing anything but a mere ideal, a mere intention, having its place outside reality, nobody knows where; something separate and abstract, in the heads of certain human beings. It is the infinite complex of things, their entire essence and truth. It is its own material which it commits to its own active energy to work up; or an external material of given means from which it may obtain its support, and the objects of its activity. It supplies its own nourishment, and is the object of its own operations. While it is exclusively its own basis of existence, and absolute final aim, it is also the energizing power realizing this aim; developing it not only in the phenomena of the natural, but also of the spiritual universe—the history of the world. That this "idea" or "reason" is the true, the eternal, the absolutely powerful essence; that it reveals itself in the world, and that in that world nothing else is revealed but this and its honour and glory—is the thesis which, as we have said, has been proved in philosophy, and is here regarded as demonstrated.

The inquiry into the essential destiny of reason, as far as it is considered in reference to the world, is identical with the question, what is the ultimate design of the world? And the expression implies that that design is destined to be realized. Two points of consideration suggest themselves; first, the import of this design, its abstract definition; and secondly, its realization.

It must be observed at the outset, that the phenomenon we investigate—universal history—belongs to the realm of spirit. The term "world" includes both physical and psychical nature. Physical nature also plays its part in the world's history, and attention will have to be paid to the fundamental natural relations thus involved. But spirit, and the course of its development, is our substantial object. Our task does not require us to contemplate nature as a rational system in itself, though in its own proper domain it proves itself such, but simply in its relation to spirit. On the stage on which we are observing—*i.e.*, universal history—spirit displays itself in its most concrete reality. Notwithstanding this (or rather for the very purpose of comprehending the general principles which this, its form of concrete reality, embodies) we must premise some abstract characteristics of the nature of spirit. Such an explanation, however, cannot be given here under any other form than that of bare assertion. The present is not the occasion for unfolding the idea of spirit speculatively; for whatever has a place in an introduction, must, as already observed, be taken as simply historical; something assumed as having been explained and proved elsewhere; or whose demonstration awaits the sequel of the science of history itself.

We have therefore to mention here:

(1) The abstract characteristics of the nature of spirit.
(2) What means spirit uses in order to realize its idea.
(3) Lastly, we must consider the shape which the perfect embodiment of spirit assumes—the state.

The nature of spirit may be understood by a glance at its direct opposite—matter. As the essence of matter is gravity, so, on the other hand, we may affirm that the substance, the essence of spirit is freedom. All will readily assent to the doctrine that spirit, among other properties, is also endowed with freedom; but philosophy teaches that all the qualities of spirit exist only through freedom; that all are but means for attaining freedom; that all seek and produce this and this alone. It is a result of speculative philosophy, that freedom is the sole truth of spirit. Matter possesses gravity in virtue of its tendency toward a central point. It is essentially composite; consisting of parts that exclude each other. It seeks its unity; and therefore exhibits itself as self-destructive, as verging toward its opposite. If it could attain this, it would be matter no longer, it would have perished. It strives after the realization of its idea; for in unity it exists ideally. Spirit, on the contrary, may be defined as that which has its centre in itself. It has not a unity outside itself, but has already found it; it exists in and with itself. Matter has its essence out of itself; spirit is self-contained existence. Now this is freedom, exactly. For if I am dependent, my being is referred to something else which I am not; I cannot exist independently of something external. I am free, on the contrary, when my existence depends upon myself. This self-contained existence of spirit is none other than self-consciousness, consciousness of one's own being. Two

things must be distinguished in consciousness; first, the fact that
I know; secondly, what I know. In self consciousness these are
merged in one; for spirit knows itself. It involves an appreciation
of its own nature, as also an energy enabling it to realize itself;
to make itself actually that which it is potentially. According to
this abstract definition it may be said of universal history, that it
it is the exhibition of spirit in the process of working out the knowledge of that which it is potentially. And as the germ bears in itself
the whole nature of the tree, and the taste and form of its fruit,
so do the first traces of spirit virtually contain the whole of that
history.

The result of this process is then that spirit, in rendering itself
objective and making this its being an object of thought, on the
one hand destroys the determinate form of its being, on the other
hand gains a comprehension of the universal element which it
involves, and thereby gives a new form to its inherent principle. In
virtue of this, the substantial character of the national spirit has
been altered; that is, its principle has risen into another, and in
fact a higher principle.

It is of the highest importance in apprehending and comprehending history to have and to understand the thought involved in
this transition. The individual traverses as a unity various grades
of development, and remains the same individual; in like manner
also does a people, till the spirit which it embodies reaches the
grade of universality. In this point lies the fundamental, the ideal
necessity of transition. This is the soul, the essential consideration,
of the philosophical comprehension of history.

Spirit is essentially the result of its own activity; its activity is
the transcending of immediate, simple, unreflected existence,
the negation of that existence, and the returning into itself. We
may compare it with the seed; for with this the plant begins, yet
it is also the result of the plant's entire life. But the weak side of
life is exhibited in the fact that the commencement and the result
are disjoined from each other. Thus also is it in the life of individuals and peoples. The life of a people ripens a certain fruit; its
activity aims at the complete manifestation of the principle which
it embodies. But this fruit does not fall back into the bosom of
the people that produced and matured it; on the contrary, it becomes a poison-draught to it. That poison-draught it cannot let

alone, for it has an insatiable thirst for it: the taste of the draught is its annihilation, though at the same time the rise of a new principle.

We have already discussed the final aim of this progression. The principles of the successive phases of spirit that animate the nations, in a necessitated gradation, are themselves only steps in the development of the one universal spirit, which through them elevates and completes itself to a self-comprehending totality.

While we are thus concerned exclusively with the idea of spirit, and in the history of the world regard everything as only its manifestation, we have, in traversing the past, however extensive its periods, only to do with what is present; for philosophy, as occupying itself with the true, has to do with the eternally present. Nothing in the past is lost for it, for the idea is ever present; spirit is immortal; with it there is no past, no future, but an essential now. This necessarily implies that the present form of spirit comprehends within it all earlier steps. These have indeed unfolded themselves in succession independently; but what spirit it is it has always been essentially; distinctions are only the development of this essential nature. The life of the ever present spirit is a circle of progressive embodiments, which looked at in one aspect still exist beside each other, and only as looked at from another point of view appear as past. The grades which spirit seems to have left behind it, it still possesses in the depths of its present.

BIBLIOGRAPHY

Berkeley

Calkins, M. W., *Berkeley: Essays, Principles, Dialogues, with Selections from Other Writings.* New York, Charles Scribner's Sons, 1929.

Laky, J. J., *A Study of George Berkeley's Philosophy in the Light of the Philosophy of St. Thomas Aquinas.* Washington, Catholic University of America Press, 1950.

Luce, A. A., *Berkeley's Immaterialism: A Commentary on his "Treatise Concerning the Principles of Human Knowledge."* London, Thomas Nelson & Sons, Ltd., 1945.

Fichte

Smith, W., *The Popular Works of Johann Gottlieb Fichte*, 4th ed. London, Tribner, 1889. 2 Vols.

Adamson, R., *Fichte.* Edinburgh, William Blackwood & Sons Ltd., 1881.

Schelling

Schelling, Joseph, *Of Human Freedom,* trans. by J. Gitman. Chicago, Open Court Publishing Company, 1936.
——, *The Ages of The World,* trans. by F. DeW. Bolman Jr. New York, Columbia University Press, 1942.
Watson, J., *Schelling's Transcendental Idealism,* 2nd ed. Chicago, Griggs, 1892.

Hegel

Hegel, Georg Wilhelm Friedrich, *Early Theological Writings,* trans. by T. M. Knox and R. Kroner. Chicago, University of Chicago Press, 1948.
——, *The Phenomenology of Mind,* 2nd ed., trans. by J. Baillie. New York, The Macmillan Company, 1931.
——, *Science of Logic,* trans. by W. H. Johnston and L. G. Struthers. New York, The Macmillan Company, 1929.
——, *The Philosophy of Right and the Philosophy of History,* trans. by T. M. Knox and J. Sibree. Great Books of The Western World Series, Vol. 46. Chicago, Encyclopedia Britannica Inc., 1952.
Caird, E., *Hegel.* Edinburgh, William Blackwood & Sons Ltd., 1883.
Mure, G. R. C., *An Introduction to Hegel.* Oxford, The Clarendon Press, 1940.
Stace, W. T., *The Philosophy of Hegel.* London, Macmillan & Co., Ltd., 1924.

General Studies of Idealism

Blau, J., *Men and Movements in American Philosophy.* Englewood Cliffs, N. J., Prentice-Hall, Inc., 1952.
Collins, J., *A History of Modern European Philosophy.* Milwaukee, The Bruce Publishing Company, 1954.
Hocking, W. E., *Types of Philosophy.* New York, Charles Scribner's Sons, 1939.
Hoernle, R. F. A., *Idealism as a Philosophy.* New York, George H. Doran Co., 1927.
Höffding, Harald, *Modern Philosophers.* New York, The Macmillan Company, 1920.
Muirhead, J. H., "Idealism," *Encyclopedia Britannica,* Vol. 12. Chicago, Encyclopedia Britannica Inc., 1955.
Perry, R. B., *Present Philosophical Tendencies.* New York, Longmans, Green & Co., 1912.
Royce, Josiah, *Lectures on Modern Idealism.* New Haven, Conn., Yale University Press, 1919.

3

The
New
Humanism

NATURALISM

Naturalism in Ancient Philosophy

NATURALISM AS A PHILOSOPHY has had a long and varied history.
It has its origins in ancient Greece, and it has received in the
last century a new impetus, so that it is at present once again a
flourishing system of thought. In the pre-Platonic philosophy
of Greece a philosophy of nature arose under the leadership of
Leucippus and Democritus, which, crude as it was, was, nevertheless, an attempt to explain reality in terms of natural forces at
work. For these men reality was ultimately composed of small
particles of being, all of which were completely alike in all respects.
These particles, or atoms, moved about in what was called the
Void, a large area of empty space. Hence they could agree with
Parmenides that being was all alike, everywhere similar and in all
respects the same. But instead of the one being of Parmenides,
a being in which all change and motion was necessarily an illusion, the atomists insisted that being was radically multiple. In
this way they hoped to be able to explain change as a natural
phenomenon and to avoid denying what was obviously a fact of

every day experience. Being was something given. But being was also multiple, even though the same in all of its parts. The atoms moved through the Void and, due to some external force, eventually collided with one another. This led to all sorts of accidental combinations, and it was these accidental combinations that explained the various types of beings which we meet in our everyday experience.

While the Atomists provided a crude and certainly inadequate theory of the physical world, Epicurus, who was born at Samos in 342 B.C., helped to provide a naturalistic theory of human action. He espoused the atomistic cosmology because it explained the universe without reference to gods and an afterlife. Thus men were freed from the care and anxiety that religion, he claimed, has usually bred, and were able in peace and security to work out the humanly best possible life. The ethics which Epicurus developed were based on the Greek ideal of *"Meiden agan,"* nothing in excess. Basically his ethical theory preached a harmonious development of all human faculties with the necessary modification and self control that made for the humane and cultured gentleman. The theory was as naturalistic and as this-worldly in its own sphere as was the physical theory of the Atomists in its sphere.

What is important about these early Greek attempts is not so much what was said as the attitude which lies behind the various theories. This attitude is the one which insists that reality is entirely explicable in terms of the physical universe, or, if you will, nature. Nature is a given. There is no need to ask where it all came from. It is here, and it needs to be explained in terms that are acceptable to the scientific theory of the time. It is a question not of what things are, but of how they work. Man is looked upon as simply another of nature's achievements, and his origin and destiny have meaning only in terms of the nature of which he is an integral part. There are no Platonic ideas in such a world, nor is man an alien spirit condemned for a while to a material prison house. Man is at home in nature, because that is all there is.

The attitude shows up again and again during the centuries which followed. It is not always explicitly promulgated as such. But the idea is carried forward, and by those at times who have been most other-worldly in their philosophizing. All skepticism is willing to admit at least the possibility of such a theory of reality. Descartes separated matter from spirit to such an extent that certain of his followers felt they no longer needed the material universe. Certain others felt that the material universe no longer needed spirit. Hume's skepticism questioned the validity of a knowledge which attempted to go beyond sensible experience. And Kant made such a knowledge forever void and empty. He insisted that there really existed things-in-themselves. Such things were, of course, unknowable, but their manifestations, their appearances, could be contacted and interpreted by the human mind. As has been seen, it is the function of mind to give meaning and order to the appearances which present themselves as the confused data of sensible experience. He had, furthermore, made it impossible for the mind to transcend the appearances and achieve any reasonable understanding of causes or principles which might or might not function behind the appearances. The universe had to be taken for granted and only its functions and operations were capable of being ordered and made intelligible by rational endeavor. This remains the area of Kant's greatest influence, and his impact on modern thought has always manifested itself more in terms of a subjective interpretation of the functions of a sensible reality than as an Idealism which denied the reality of the thing-in-itself.

Naturalism in the Nineteenth Century

Add to this that the scientific advances made under Newton, Copernicus, Galileo provided a knowledge of nature never before deemed possible for man, and the emphasis on natural sciences as the only certain and exact means of obtaining knowledge of reality becomes quite understandable. Then in the 19th century a scientific theory arose which opened the way for a philosophy of Naturalism which was to be applied to all areas of reality and knowledge. Charles Darwin was born in 1809, and in 1859 he published his now famous *Origin of Species*. Darwin was a biologist, and his contributions to the science of biology were of tremendous importance. Briefly, the main points of the theory he devised were as follows. He noticed that among members of the same species some were better equipped to survive than others. And in nature survival was always a problem. For nature is prodigal, and it happens that there are more members of the animal kingdom produced than there is food for their sustenance. In such a situation qualities are developed among the food seekers that enable some of them to acquire the food which is necessary. Others simply starve to death. The stronger and more savage tigers, the swifter wolves, the more hardy bears all manage to get the necessary food. Hence these survive and pass on their developed characteristics to their descendants. Here again a distinction becomes necessary. Where all are savage and all are strong, other characteristics become important, if some of the strong are to survive and others not. In this next generation, then, perhaps a certain amount of cunning develops, so that some of the strong get the food which they could not get by force. Thus the species develop new and better characteristics due to the natural exigencies of the situation. Hence it became quite easy to attribute development and progress in nature not to design or providence, but to natural selection based simply on what nature is and the way nature operates. Nor was it a far step to state, as Nietzsche did, that man is also simply a product of the natural forces at work and is just as much a part of nature as any flower or any beast.

Darwin was a biologist. His theory of natural progress and evolution was a biological one. It was left to Herbert Spencer to elevate the biological theory of Darwin into a philosophy of the cosmos. Spencer was born in 1820 and died in 1902. Between those dates he managed to apply Darwin's theory to society, to psychology and finally to all of philosophy. His *Social Statics* published in 1850 sees in society the culmination of the natural forces at work in the world. His *Psychology* published in 1855 sees mind as the highest perfection in a given area of nature. And his *Synthetic Philosophy* which he began in 1860, attempts to explain all reality in terms of the Darwinian law of evolution.

Spencer saw all knowledge as limited to the experience and content of the natural sciences. Such experience is necessarily relative and limited. It is a mere manifestation and a conditioned one of the unknowable thing, which thrusts itself upon us. We are somehow aware of this Unknowable, this Unconditioned, but such awareness leads us to religion not to knowledge. Knowledge is obtained from a consideration of experience which is subjected to the laws at work in nature. Nature itself is regarded as a self sufficient totality working itself out according to the all prevailing law of evolution.

The process was continued on the continent by Ernst Haeckel (1834-1919), a professor of zoology at the University of Jena. Haeckel proceeded to identify the "unknowable" of Spencer. He called it a constant quantity of dynamic substance underlying the variety of phenomenal manifestations. It is rather difficult to see how he could have identified this substance, since he admitted that we know only its phenomenal manifestations. According to Haeckel, there were two basic laws at work in nature: the first was the law governing the constancy of matter and force, and this law was paramount. The second was the law of evolution according to which life arises from and through psychic gradations due to irritability and reflex action, all of which culminates finally in conscious thought and purpose. Haeckel is ultimately classed as a Materialist and the nature which he explains is nothing else except dynamic material substance. Thus the cruder Atomism of the Greeks had given way to what was sometimes termed an "Energism," according to which nature and matter were ultimately interpreted in terms of energy or force. In the 19th century this theory of energy as the last physical constituent of reality was carried on by such men as Buchner, T. H. Huxley, and Ostwald. This mechanism of nature applied to the field of psychology became what was known as Behaviorism. Here mind is explained as a function of the brain, and this function is explained in terms of the Darwinian theory of evolution. Lloyd Morgan coined the word "emergence," which explained how life and mind "emerged" due to different arrangements of physical elements. The Behaviorists explained thought as physical stimulus and response, as reflexes taking place in the brain. Others more biologically inclined used the endocrine glands as the ultimate explanation of life and mind. Whatever the explanation employed all were agreed on this that there was nothing which nature and the physical universe could not explain, be it in terms of matter and force or in terms of the general law of evolution. Naturalists of the 19th century would be a little more subtle and a little more philosophical, perhaps. But before we consider them, we must first consider another form of Naturalism which is termed Positivism.

Positivism

Positivism is the critical side of Naturalism. It is interested more in the use of the scientific method and a theory of knowledge than it is in content and doctrine. Aware of the immense contributions made to knowledge by natural science, it conceives all science as the framing of laws which fit experience. Reality in itself can probably never be known, but at least it can be discussed in so far as it thrusts itself upon us in experience. Thus experience is the norm, and description rather than explanation is the method to be employed. This method is positive, not metaphysical or intuitive, and it leads to a certain and scientific knowledge of nature in its operations. One cannot go beyond nature as it manifests itself with such a method, nor does one need to. Nature is a given, a complete system. The most one can ask is, How does it function?

It was this question that Auguste Comte (1798-1857) attempted to answer on a universal level. He was aware of the great advances that the natural sciences had made, and he knew, too, that the method they employed was an empirical one based on experience and referred to experience as the last norm for validity and certainty. What Comte hoped to do was to apply this method to all of life and the world. All human living, faith, conduct, and religion were to be subjected to the positivistic method, and this method was to be the new foundation for certitude in all the areas as yet untouched by the natural sciences. Thus Positivism would generate a new science of the sciences, unifying them in one all-inclusive knowledge.

One of the realms as yet not subjected to the positivistic method was the whole area of human affairs. This was chiefly due to the fact that men had not yet fully realized that all human relations were subject to the same laws of progress and development as were other sections of nature. The reason for this was that civilization had not yet sufficiently progressed through the necessary antecedent stages. In all science and in all progress, be it historical or political, there was a necessary evolutionary law at work. This led through three various but connected levels of development. The first of these Comte characterized as the theological stage. In this stage feeling was predominant. Men tended to personify that which was mysterious and to attribute inexplicable natural happenings to the power of gods and supermen. In the second stage of development these mysterious forces are submitted to analysis, and men begin to speak in terms of causality and principles of nature. This is the metaphysical stage and is characterized by the development of the great philosophical systems. The difficulty here is that nature is explained in abstract terms, and knowledge tends to get farther and farther from the real. Hence the last stage is the highest one because it marks the return of knowledge to the concrete and to experience. This last stage Comte termed the positivistic stage, and thought that it would once and for all establish a knowledge of how nature functioned. For here instead of dealing with abstractions, men dealt with experience and from experience were able to formulate laws which governed nature in its activity. No longer would there be any need for talk of natures and essences, principles and causes, since these were meaningless in terms of concrete explanations of functions.

As a means of accomplishing his great synthesis, Comte divided all of the sciences into mathematics, astronomy, physics, chemistry, biology, and sociology. This last was to be the most concrete and complex of the sciences and was meant to unite the sciences, much as man united in himself all the functions studied by the lesser sciences. Thus sociology was conceived as the science proper to man, and man was conceived as the climax of the natural order. Not only did Comte hope to provide a science proper to man and through man a science of the other sciences, but he also gave men a new god. For now humanity was the Great Being and man was meant to worship Man. For nature was being, and it had achieved its divinity in humankind. We shall consider Positivism more at length later. For the present it is sufficient to note what the positivistic method added to the mechanistic

Materialism which had developed constantly throughout the nineteenth century.

Twentieth Century Naturalism

The rigid Mechanism of the 19th century has been looked upon by more modern Naturalists as inadequate, to say the least. At present the older version of Naturalism is considered to be merely one method which can be applied to the nature we experience. Not that Naturalism has become any less naturalistic. The basic premises of the system remain intact. Nature is still regarded as a closed system, self sustaining and self sufficient. The positivistic method of experimentation, observation, and verification is still very much in vogue. "To understand the objects and events of our experience, it certainly seems unnecessary to pass beyond those objects and events themselves, or to seek for their understanding anything more recondite or mysterious than exact observation and sustained mathematical demonstration." So writes I. Edman in his book, *Four Ways of Philosophy*, published in 1937. Hence there is still no search after the causes and natures of things that were rejected long ago. There is no need to go beyond man in order to explain man. Mind is still considered a function of nature, and, while it may no longer be susceptible of a purely mechanical explanation, it still is regarded as the highest expression of the natural process. The same substance that blooms into corn and blossoms into roses ultimately flowers into man and intelligence. "Man is developed by nature," says Edman, "and human thought is a developed process among the other processes of nature." Not only is there no need to go beyond nature, but the naturalist refuses to do so.

The naturalist assumes that nature is for practical purposes one homogenous system. . . . He assumes that it is not necessary to go beyond the discernible order of relations and objects. He makes no metaphysical generalizations or judgments. . . .

All that he means by nature is that which in experience he finds: a dynamic substance manifesting itself in action in a thousand forms which he constantly recognizes.

Nor is the rational process any different than it was.

Reason consists in a disciplined acquaintance with the habits, the growths, the forms in which this dynamic substance appears, the cycles and recurrences of ways in which it manifests itself.[1]

In the natural order of things there is nothing but the relentless working of natural law. There is no other world, no spirit as distinguished from matter. There is no divinity, unless it be nature or humanity. There is no human freedom, since man merely represents the highest stage to date of the processes of nature. We may do as we please, perhaps, but we cannot please as we please. Background, environment, training, and the natural processes take care of any illusions we may have of freedom. There may be purpose within nature, but nature taken as a whole is purposeless.

Naturalism and Morality

In such a universe is there possibly any room for moral values? Doesn't this sort of thinking return man to the jungle, where anything is permissible and the only law is the law of brute force? Naturalists do not think so. They admit that previously morality has been associated with religion, but this need not be the case. All moralities admit that they lead men to the good life, to happiness. Now what is this happiness, they ask, to which all men are to come? Since a life beyond this is already ruled out as an impossibility, the good which men seek must be a good of this world. But what is happiness in this world? Happiness means the fulfillment of desire and the exercise of one's capacity. And here we must go cautiously. Naturalism does not preach a libertinism. For man has many desires and many capacities. The harmonious development of them all is more important and makes for more happiness in the long run than does the continual satiation of this one or that. Sensual impulses are undoubtedly the strongest, but there are more facets to man than mere sensual gratification. Add to this the realization that if one such impulse becomes an obsession, the whole man is reduced to one satisfac-

[1] Irwin Edman, *Four Ways in Philosophy* (New York, Holt, Rinehart and Winston, Inc., 1937), pp. 269-270.

tion, which may eventually destroy him. The man who devotes all his energy to sex or food may very well make himself forever incapable of realizing the many other capacities which more control in this or that area would have made possible. Man himself, we are told, is a little society and must live in harmony with himself, if he is to find peace and happiness, just as various and diverse elements in the state must be disciplined and controlled, if the state is to function properly and well. The morality which is taught by Naturalism, then, is a morality founded on the knowledge that the harmonious development of all man's different faculties and capacities is essential to his well-being and his happiness. The good life is a life which makes room for all possible natural goods according to a reasonable norm and always with self-control and respect for the whole man.

But there is another problem here. Can anything really be called good in the absence of an ultimate good? Again the Naturalists think so. They point out that there are obviously things which are good in themselves, such as music, food, sex, etc. Furthermore there are things which are good as instruments: forks, bridges, pianos. An observation of nature, however, seems to indicate no all-embracing final good. Nature moves toward many and various ends. There is a flowering of possibilities in nature rather than a foreordained specification toward one ultimate end. Nature does everything and anything. It is prodigal and miserly. It points out many possibilities and it drives one at times down a single path. This is also true for man. The good life is not a prescription, but a process and a stream of constantly expanding possibilities. The ends of life are as various as they are many. There would seem to be some difficulty here in this assertion of a great variety of possibilities for the development of man, when it is equally held that man is not free, but subject to the relentless working out of natural law. However that may be, a single end is seen only as a meaningless abstraction, a fanatic exclusion of all other possibilities. Such an abstraction, because it is an abstraction, is consequently nothing and cannot possibly be an end to which man is ordered.

Nor are ideals ruled out by such a philosophy of nature. All ideals are human and therefore natural. An ideal is simply an hypothesis for action, and, like all hypotheses, it must be tested in experience. In the ethical life harmony is the over all ideal, the equilibrium of a human being living adventurously and alertly in a changing world.[2] How different this conception of ideals is from that which regards them as prescriptions from another world. Ideals are instead projections of what the human creature sees in imagination of what may be made of things as at any given junction of events they are.[3]

More recent Naturalists even speak of God and religion, not to mention the supernatural. But in true naturalistic fashion these words are mere symbols of this or that set of natural values. For Santayana, for example, God means the peak of human ideals, and the function of religion is to express human destiny in moral dimensions, in mythical and poetic images. Nor does the term, supernatural, keep any of its traditional meaning. It is not, nor can it be a participation in a higher nature. It is simply nature envisioned in its completeness and its richness, the term to which ideally, at least, nature can arrive. The same tendency to include traditional concepts is found in an article by S. Hook in his edition called *American Philosophers at Work*. Mr. Hook states that, when Naturalists deny the existence of God, they do so only in reference to our present situation. It is possible to think of God as possible, as not involving a contradiction. But in relation to reality as we know it there is no experiential evidence to suggest that God exists. To assert the existence of a being, Hook says, which has not in any way made itself capable of being experienced, is to assert existence only of that which is logically possible.

This, then, in summary is Naturalism. It is a complete system in so far as it claims to explain all that there is to be explained. Nature is given, and nature can be best explained in terms of the natural sciences. This is the only sure and certain method which leads in turn to a sure and certain knowledge. There is no evidence of anything beyond this given, nor can there be. Evolution, mechanics, natural science explain this given satisfactorily and

2 *Ibid.*, p. 293.
3 *Ibid.*, p. 295.

are constantly increasing the knowledge we can have of such a universe. Let us admit that to talk of God and spirit, of soul and immortality, is to talk of what we hope and dream of. It is to play the poet and the visionary, not the scientist nor the philosopher. This is all very well in the realm of poetry and imagery. It is a waste of time in the clearer and harsher world of scientific thought.

CRITICISM OF NATURALISM

Difficulties with the Evolution Theory

In criticizing Naturalism it is well to return to several of the cardinal points of the system. Certainly one of these points is evolution. Whether the process be explained in Darwinian terms of natural selection, or whether the more modern scientific terminology of matter and energy, modification of specific characteristics and emergence of new qualities be used, there still remains a basic problem for the evolutionist. That problem concerns the plausibility of stating that the more perfect has "emerged" from the less perfect. Looked at any way one chooses, the result still seems to indicate that we are ultimately getting something from nothing. I don't think that anyone would seriously question the fact that there has been evolution in the various strata of existing things. But the complete evolutionist will go much farther than this. He will insist that some basic world stuff has evolved through all the various stages of things as we know them, that it has passed from the inert to the active, from the non-living to the living, from the living to the sensitive and that it has finally culminated in that perfection we know as a rational human being. All of which means that, due to some happy set of circumstances, the first living thing quite suddenly rose on its hind legs, so to speak, and walked away from all the lifeless stuff about it. That somewhere further along the way one of these living things quite suddenly began to manifest signs of sensation. And that finally and much more happily this time, one of these living sensing things built a fire or invented the wheel or ate an apple with full knowledge of what it was doing.

This, of course, is a naturalistic explanation of what happened. It is also a highly imaginative and even poetic explanation of what happened. It is the naturalistic hope of what must have happened in order that Naturalists may continue to live in a cozy closed natural universe of their own making. It is an insistence that things were so because in the system which refuses to transcend nature, things have to be so. Wishing, however, has never made anything so—at least outside of the movies. And to assert that this is the way it was does not in the least prove the assertion. The difficulty remains. How is it possible for a thing to give itself what it hasn't got and which it cannot get from anything beyond itself? It is further interesting to note that these emergent transitions have happened once and never again. Far, far back in the twilight of our world the more perfect has suddenly emerged from the less perfect. But just once. And today, when scientists are doing their very best to help the process along, when all the conditions are much more favorable than they were then, the living refuses to arise out of the non-living, the sensitive never emerges from the non-sensitive, nor does the rational ever suddenly appear in the animal kingdom.

Furthermore, in the evolutionary process mind itself provides Naturalism with a special difficulty. For mind is first of all a fact of experience. It is there. In this sense, certainly, mind is a part of nature. It does mark the climax of nature, the peak of the natural perfections we find about us. The Naturalist recognizes this and then proceeds to reduce mind to simply another manifestation of matter in motion. For to the Naturalist nature is material and, therefore, everything in nature must be ultimately of the same basic stuff. The difficulty here is that mind does not act like any of the material elements from which it is supposed to have emerged. And if mind is unlike the matter which we meet in experience, then we are justified in concluding that mind is not material. Once, however, we conclude this, then we must also accept the consequences that go with such a conclusion.

Mind and Immateriality

What evidence is there that mind is different from the matter with which it is involved? As Aquinas points out, we know something about the nature of a thing from the way it acts. This is the only way we can know anything about anything. It has to manifest itself to us in some way, and it does this through its activity. And when it acts, it must act in accord with the kind of thing it is. Dogs act like dogs because they are dogs. And from their activity we know that a dog is different from a butterfly. Because a dog is a dog, he must act like a dog; and from his activity I know something about what a dog is because he projects his dogginess, as it were, in his activity. To be bitten in the leg by a dog is different from being bitten in the same leg by a mouse, because a dog can only bite me as a dog bites one. So, too, can we come to some knowledge of what mind is like from the way mind operates. We shall find in this operation of mind a projection of the very nature of mind, an extension of mind in its activity. And since mind can act only in accord with the kind of being it is, from that activity we shall necessarily find out something about the nature of mind.

Now the activity proper to mind is to know, and knowledge is basically a union of the knower with the thing known. When one knows a horse, one becomes intellectually the horse which he knows. And right from the beginning there is something peculiar about this union in knowledge. In all other unions of which we are aware, one of the elements involved in the union disappears in favor of a third and new element. When a man, for example, eats an orange, the orange ceases to be what it is and enters into the composition of the human being. Hydrogen and oxygen cease to be themselves and disappear in the new element we call water. Yet in the union which is knowledge nothing like this happens. The knower is united with the object known and yet each retains its own personal identity. I do not physically lose my being to the being of the horse which I know. I remain myself and the horse remains itself, yet both are joined and fused in the act of knowledge. The horse's being known is nothing else but my knowing the horse. There is reason here certainly to suspect that the activity produced by mind is not of the same order as the activity of the other material things we experience.

But there is more than this. Not only do we know things, but we know that we know them. I can think of a man. I can at the same time think of myself thinking of a man. In other words, the mind can reflect back completely upon itself. It can be completely present to itself in its act of being present to something else. And again this activity is peculiar to mind. The eye cannot see itself seeing. On a lower level the paint brush which is painting the wall cannot paint itself as it paints the wall. The hammer driving the nail cannot at the same time hit itself. This table at which I am typing cannot be placed on top of itself. And the reason is that the eye, the paint brush, the hammer, and the table are limited in their activities by the conditions of matter with which they are necessarily associated. These material conditions limit them to time and space and position, and these limitations accompany them always and irrevocably. Now if mind can escape from the limitations which go necessarily with matter, the reason can only be that mind itself escapes from the conditions associated with matter. And that mind does escape from such material limitations, we know from the activity which mind produces. For as a thing acts so must it be. This is saying nothing else than that mind must not be of the same order as the material things which surround it, for it acts in a way that indicates that it rises above such an order.

Note that we do not say that mind is completely and perfectly separated from matter. Knowledge begins in the senses, as Aristotle said; and knowledge is further conditioned by the well-being or deficiency of the senses which are its starting point. The brain is certainly necessary as a condition of our thinking. But granted the material conditions, then mind can function in a way which indicates clearly that it gets beyond the matter and the material conditions which were its starting point. In itself, therefore, it must be the kind of a thing which is distinct from the matter with which, as a matter of fact, it is associated. Once we recognize this, then we must also recognize that its existence does not depend on the matter with which it is joined. The existence of the matter rather depends on it, for this matter receives all of its perfection from the mind which enlivens and informs it. The death of a man, then, the corruption of his body, can have no effect on the nature of his mind. Distinct from matter by its very nature, the breakdown of the material element can have no effect on that element which exists in its own right with an existence proper to itself.

Hence it is that man, who is a part of nature, transcends the mere material side of that nature. It is here, too, that we see that there is more to nature than matter. There is the immaterial, the spiritual, here too, and we know that such is the case from the evidence which confronts us in nature. This recognition demands of us further acknowledgments. For the immaterial and the spiritual is necessarily incorruptible and immortal. So that the intellect sees that man, who transcends the material side of nature in his spiritual soul, has of necessity a destiny beyond the material. The wheel of matter will be escaped from and the end of man is at the very least a knowledge and a love of that which is eternal. This is the real completeness and enrichment toward which man surges, and it is one which he will find personally and consciously. Immortality is more than a dream and a hope. It is a certainty demanded by the evidence which we find in nature itself.

Nature and a Supreme Being

Neither is it correct to say as Mr. Hook does that there is no evidence of the existence of a Supreme Being in nature. The Infinite does not, it is true, present itself to us in an infinite experience. But this presupposes that to assert the existence of such a Being, we must necessarily experience Him as infinite. It is to assert that we must have a material manifestation of a spiritual being in so far as He is spiritual. The terms laid down make such a manifestation an impossibility to start with. But there is the other possibility that our experience of finite, limited, and material being can only be fully understood in terms of the infinite, the unlimited and the spiritual. As Aquinas writes:

Demonstration can be made in two ways: one is through the cause and is called *propter quid*, and this is to argue from what is prior absolutely. The other is through the effect, and is called a demonstration *quia*; this is to argue from what is prior relatively only to us. When an effect is better known to us than its cause, from the effect we proceed to a knowledge of the cause. And from every effect the existence of its proper cause can be demonstrated, so long as its effects are better known to us; because, since every effect depends upon its cause, if the effect exists, the cause must pre-exist. Hence, the existence of God, in so far as it is not self evident to us, can be demonstrated from those of His effects which are known to us.

And in reply to the objection that the effects in the case are not proportioned to the cause, and, consequently, from such effects nothing can be known about the cause, St. Thomas replies:

From effects not proportioned to the cause no perfect knowledge of that cause can be obtained. Yet from every effect the existence of the cause can be clearly demonstrated, and so we can demonstrate the existence of God from His effects; though from them we cannot know God perfectly, as He is in His essence.[4]

Naturalists resent being accused of assuming an a priori position in which certain areas are ruled out from the start. Where else can we start, asks Mr. Hook, but with nature as it is physically given? It is true that there is no other place to start. But this does not mean that one has to end there. And non-Naturalists find it difficult to avoid the suspicion that various types of evidence along the way are so interpreted that the Naturalist must return to his starting point. Or perhaps it is more correct to say that such evidence is so interpreted in order that the Naturalist may return to a starting point which he has already assumed is the end of his philosophical efforts. This is not to find nature a closed system, but to make it one. It is a system which rationally explains the workings of nature only to end with the irrational assertion that such rational functions have no meaning beyond themselves. This is no longer philosophy but a choice deliberately made not to ask any further questions. As such it is little more than a deliberate grounding of the whole philosophic enterprise.

4 *Summa Theologica*, edited and annotated by Anton C. Pegis (New York, Random House, 1945), vol. I, 2, 2 ad 3.

SUMMARY

1. Kant's influence has been felt not only in the idealistic philosophies which followed him, but also in those empirical systems which are much more characteristic of contemporary thought. His influence on Idealism is much less direct than it is on Empiricism. Along with him contemporary philosophers are quite willing to assume the existence of a sensible reality and to admit that this can be the only valid area of intellectual investigation. They are more and more inclined to adopt the methods of the natural sciences in carrying out this investigation because it has proved to be such a successful method.

2. Naturalism has accepted without question the Kantian limitation of intellect to the physical order of sense experience, or nature, and has asserted that there exists nothing else to be known. It strives to find in nature and in human experience a satisfying explanation of the forces at work. It regards man as the culminating factor in the evolutionary process to date; and, while it has rejected a merely mechanistic explanation of man and has admitted a distinction between matter and mind, it insists that ultimately everything is reducible to nature.

Criticism

1. The evolutionary theory is still a theory. In its complete form as asserted by Naturalism it labors under all the difficulties that follow the assertion of effects without adequate causes.
2. Mind itself manifests characteristics which indicate that it could not possibly have evolved from matter.
3. There is evidence in nature itself that there is more to reality than what is experienced. Nature exhibits itself as an effect.
4. Naturalism begins and ends with a dogmatic assertion, which it declares not to be susceptible of philosophic explanation.

SELECTED READINGS

Philosophy as Nature Understood*

All philosophers, of course, think of themselves as understanding nature, and regard their philosophies as the faithful translation into the syntax of discourse of things. "The order of ideas," said Spinoza, "and the order of nature are one." "The order of my ideas and the order of nature," each philosopher also happily assumes, "are one." Thinkers have claimed this even when they have made a system of ideas out of their desires or their hopes, or when they have read into nature an imagined world beyond it, when they have made the rhetoric of their own enthusiasms the alleged grammar of the cosmos, or identified some deep private feeling with the depths of nature itself.

But there is a tradition coming from the Greeks which has possibly a little more claim to the distinction of being simply nature understood. There is a stream of thought beginning with Democritus that has sedulously eschewed going beyond the world of phenomena, that has tried scrupulously to remain within the circle of experienced objects and events and their discoverable relations. This philosophy has tried to refrain from going to a world beyond the world, to a friend behind phenomena, to a system alleged beyond the system found, from a verifiable experience to an alleged reality beyond it. Naturalism is the name generally attached to that point of view in the history of thought which tries with intellectual modesty and moral candor to frame a systematic vision of things in terms of what critical knowledge and effective human practice reveal them to be. Philosophers so minded have called nature that circle of objects and events with which men are initially familiar, which they fruitfully explore, and which, in their lives rather than simply in the rhetoric of their words, they are constrained to respect and to understand as both the instrument and the obstacle to their desires. To be the mouthpiece of nature, and to describe without illusion man's

* Irwin Edman, *Four Ways of Philosophy* (New York, Holt Rinehart and Winston, Inc., 1937) chap. 4.

place in it, is certainly the highest ambition of a philosopher. To be such requires, in the first place, abstemiousness and courage. It requires abstention from all allegations, high and soothing, of nature's providential arrangements for man's purposes, and courage to follow the lineaments of nature in understanding, no matter what such following may mean in the abandonment of hopes and wishes. It requires an eye disciplined and steady, fixed on all things in their order and worth. It is generally conceded that no race ever succeeded in achieving all this is general outline more than did the Greeks. . . .

Naturalism until the twentieth century oscillated between emphasis on the stuff of the universe, matter, however minutely subdivided, and emphasis on operations according to mechanical regularities which could be exactly described and clearly understood in measurable quantities and through mathematical concepts. But generally speaking, mechanism has been more emphasized than materialism; not what the stuff of things is but how they operate has been studied. The system of mathematico-physical notions has yielded both practical and intellectual fruits. On the practical the whole of modern technology, industry, and transportation have been its fruits. The conception of mechanism meant the possibility of calculation; calculation meant predictability, and predictability meant control. The order of nature was not something to gape at in awe and admiration, as did Pope, or to become mystically inflamed with, as was Giordano Bruno, or resigned to, as was Spinoza. The order of nature was the order of possible operations, and to understand specific facts and their specific consequences was to be put, within limits, in control of those consequences. The whole of human progress seemed to lie within the grasp of men if they would only sufficiently explore the conditions, that is to say the mechanical relations, of the objects and events among which they lived. "Knowledge is power," Bacon had said, and three centuries of mechanical and medical triumph have confirmed his boast. By the middle of the nineteenth century the idea had widely spread (in England under the leadership of John Stuart Mill, in France stimulated by the propaganda of August Comte, the positivist) that the method of physical science applied to human affairs could be as effective in solving the problems of human relations, of government, industry, society and social institutions as it had been in the field of physical and physiological control. The method of intelligence and the mathematico-physical concept of nature seemed to go hand in hand. What had been so powerful an instrument in the control of physical things might be equally effective in human relations, social affairs and social passions. The psychologist moved from his study into the laboratory; his language and his point of view became, as they still are in many quarters today, those of the mathematically exact worker in the field of the physical sciences. Our relative incompetence in reducing the study of social affairs and human relations to mechanical terms may have profounder reasons, but the simple reason given is that we do not as yet know enough, have not explored thoroughly enough, to measure as exactly, to define as precisely, to think as tightly in social matters as in physical ones. These younger studies are of facts more complex but in no way different in kind from those with which the physical scientist deals. The hope still lingers among many that eventually everything from the movements of the stars to the movement of ideas in the mind of a philosopher may be reduced to mechanico-mathematical terms. Psychology itself, it is piously hoped, may eventually simply be a branch of physics, as astronomy is a cosmic yet special case of it. And in the laboratory we may some day—who knows?—cure men of all their psychical ills or even chemically produce men at will. . . .

The cogency of naturalism as a point of view has been lately called into question. Both the stuff of nature, matter, and the billiard-ball physics of nineteenth century mechanism have recently been called into question in the fields of the sciences themselves. Matter has dissolved into centers of force or foci of energy; matter itself is simply known by what it does; in itself it is, as Herbert Spencer said, the unknowable. The scientist turns out to be dealing with the relation of events; he never deals immediately with any gross palpable stuff called matter. The simple atoms of Democritus seem absurd to the modern biochemist. The sciences of life have moreover emphasized the habits of growth, the "tropes" of development in nature, in which an inert and dead matter, made up of static, inert and lifeless atoms, seems irrelevant. There seem, furthermore, to be elements in life and in mind not reducible to matter in motion. The phenomena of purpose, for instance, and the total reaction of an organism are not analyzable in terms of mechanical physics. The new physics itself, moreover, has reduced the whole conception of mechanism to that of a convenient system of "pointer readings." The world that the physicist used to think of as basically real turns out to be simply the "world" of laboratory measurements and mathematical deductions, marvelously fertile in practical use and fascinating to the intellectual virtuoso. But it is hardly nature itself in its absoluteness. No, the mechanical description of nature has no more right to call itself nature than a ticket of admission has a right to call itself the concert or a key to call itself a door. The identification of the reality of nature with the description of it in mechanical terms has certainly become suspect. "Nature is no system but that to which all our systems refer. . . ."

NATURALISM TRANSCENDS MECHANICAL PHYSICS. The purely mechanical ideal, however, on which earlier scientific Utopias have been based, is itself vanishing from science and scientific method. The despair of esthetic or ascetic flight, of resigned contemplation, of mechanical remaking of society, have all been posited on a set of assumptions about the nature of science and scientific method which have of late come seriously into question. Many mystics and idealists have pointed to the breakdown of the reign of mechanism in science as a sign of the correlative breakdown of naturalism as a philosophy. Nothing could be further from the facts. Naturalism is far from being dependent on the picture, almost as mythical as the theological one, of the billiard-ball physics of the nineteenth century. Naturalism is simply a faith in the unity of nature or substance, of which all life is a derivation, upon which all action is posited, and within which the structure of mechanism is seen to be simply a systematized technique of practice and of economical understanding. It is faith in causality, not in any alleged nexus of necessary causes, but in the repeatedly verified experience that facts have consequences. The structure of mechanism is something developed in the course of experimental inquiry and the development of ideas through disciplined deductive thinking. It is an order of hypothesis, suggested by observed facts, verified in the facts again at the end of experiment and deductive elaboration. The naturalist in philosophy does not assert that the relations of facts and consequences established in experimental inquiry are "reality." He does not deny or affirm the "necessity" of causal relations. He simply assumes, inferring from common experience, from the problems there found and the methods there used for solution, that nature is for practical purposes one homogeneous system. He assumes that the mechanisms disclosed or assumed in inquiry and in practice are efficacious in dealing with those problems which experience generates and those securities and enjoyments which nature thus understood may support and make possible. He assumes that it is not necessary to go beyond the discernible order of relations and objects; that these constitute one system, not of reality but of practice and of understanding. He assumes his body, other bodies, other minds, a structure he calls mechanism, and a technique of thinking he calls hypothesis, demonstration and verification. He makes no metaphysical generalizations or judgments. If the world of efficacious operations is a dream, it is a fantasy curiously steady and rewarding. If it is a madness, it is, as Santayana calls it, a "normal madness," and can be normally treated as a waking as well as a working hypothesis.

All that the naturalist means by science is a habit of mind which has proved effective in common practice, and may prove unprecedentedly fruitful in the future, the habit of experimental inquiry. All that he means by nature is that which in experience he finds: a dynamic substance manifesting itself in action in a thousand forms which he constantly recognizes. It is the life coursing within him and in others. It is the complex of materials he must and can deal with; it is the source of his problems and the field of their possible solution; it is the theater of his enjoyments, the impulsion out of which this dynamic substance appears, the cycles and recurrences of ways in which it manifests itself. Reason is not a dialectic man willfully imposes upon nature; it is his name for a sober and studious technique of reading those habits of substance, of modifying them where they are susceptible of modification, and of harmonizing his own impulses, themselves "habits" of nature, in accordance with them. The life of reason is simply life understanding its own conditions. The way of so doing is the habit of imagination in man which, become critical and circumspect, relies on observation, on clear explication of intent, on empirical verification. Dialectic, in terms of the human animal who uses it, is simply a clarification in theoretical comprehension of what is observed and desired. The error of dialecticians lies not in following the cogency of their own thinking. Their error lies in beginning in the middle; in making assumptions without first inquiring into their relevancy to the facts, and stopping before the end without finding out what reference the conclusions arrived at dialectically have to the facts open to honest observation and critical verification. . . .

An Experimentalist on Being*

Of all the great philosophies now in contention throughout the world, two of the most virile and persuasive are Thomism and experimentalism. Standing opposed to one another, these two world views periodically hurl thunderbolts of dialectic across the reaches of the intellectual community in hopes of winning more and more followers and of showing to thoughtful men how human experience can be rendered intelligible and manageable.

The polemic that ensues is, of course, difficult to follow, partly because of the widely differing premises of the two positions but in greater measure because of different syntactical grammars and terminological vocabularies used by each side. What results is a puzzling display of logic leading to contrasting conclusions, with each camp using its own terms and syntax to expound and fortify its own position.

In time, each side becomes more and more interested in the development of its own doctrine and less and less concerned with that of its opponent. Finally, the questions posed by one side are disregarded as irrelevant by the other, and dialectic withers and dies.

Maybe there is some necessity for this impasse, perhaps some

* Van Cleve Morris, "An Experimentalist Looks at Being," *The Modern Schoolman* (Jan., 1958). Cf. also R. J. Henle, "Reply," *ibid.*

epistemological and/or psychological determinism that eventually takes hold of philosophical discourse and sends the contending parties irrevocably into a condition of mutual isolation each from the other.

But on the assumption that no such determinism is at work, it may be worthy of experiment to see what one school of thought could do with a major doctrine of the other—in this case, what an experimentalist analysis would be of the Thomist's metaphysical notion of being. It is to be understood that this venture is taken with great risk, principally because of the necessity to find an easy cross-reference for two dissimilar philosophical grammars —the problem mentioned earlier. But if this semantic qualification is understood and accepted in advance, then the risk seems worth the taking.

It is well known that experimentalism has never felt the necessity to involve itself unduly in metaphysics. It may appear surprising, therefore, to find an experimentalist voluntarily venturing into this area and choosing to deal with the notion of being. In thus seeming to join battle on ground chosen by the adversary, the philosophic adventurer may appear not only a bold and reckless Quixote, tilting with a tradition of scholarship centuries old and represented by some of the greatest minds of the Western world, but also somewhat of a traitor to his own cause, venturing forth on a campaign which has no direct bearing on the major conflict and whose outcome is prejudiced in advance.

I wish at the outset to disavow both grandiose intentions in the first instance and subversive designs in the second. On the other hand, it seems to me that experimentalists' reluctance to probe the realm of metaphysics is not altogether justified. In many ways the Thomists are correct when they insist that this avoidance of metaphysics not only represents a failure to meet a major intellectual challenge but produces a void that experimentalism, if it is to be called a philosophy at all, must somehow fill. If experimentalism is to present itself for the reasonable consideration of men and as something more than a method of thinking, then it behooves it to meet and somehow deal with questions which other philosophies pose to it; and it is my feeling that the problem of being is such an issue which experimentalism has never fully dealt with.

Dewey sought, in his *Experience and Nature*, to give the metaphysical underpinnings of his position; but neither there nor elsewhere has he come squarely to grips with the problem of being as it is understood by Thomists. What, in short, does it mean to exist? The Thomists have an answer. Do the experimentalists?

It seems to me that they do; and if these modest probings in search of the answer have any legitimacy, then we may venture the hypothesis that experimentalists indeed have a notion of existence and being which is as tenable and defensible, at least to them, as that of the Thomist is to him. There is no intention, therefore, to rebut Thomism in any serious way but merely to point to the possibility that experimentalism is not without its metaphysical dimension, even though as a philosophy it has never taken the intellectual trouble to make it explicit.

We may properly commence our investigation by considering the problem of essence. The first approach we have to the "whatness" of a thing, as Thomists will agree, is its operations. We begin to understand something from the way it behaves, acts, or operates in our experience. Now, to the Thomist, these operations are only surface manifestations of an inner whatness, and they must be accounted for by some constituent which makes them what they are and not something else. What lies beneath the operations, what gives rise to them, what, in short, accounts for their being, is the essence of the thing in question. Thus we see that man has some operations which can be classified as animal and others which can be termed rational. Hence man is a rational animal. But what makes him animal and what makes him rational is his essence, which underlies both. To the Thomist it is not so accurate to say that man is a rational animal as to speak of him as an essence which possesses animality and rationality.

It is noteworthy, it seems to me, that Thomists are unable to speak of an essence in any terms other than its operations. All that can be said of an essence is (1) that it is an X which by definition is that which accounts for the operations or actions of the thing; (2) that this X receives the act of existence; and (3) that upon this receipt it forthwith sets into being the operations which we observe in our experience.

Now the experimentalist is not inclined to look beneath operations for unknown X's which account for them. He sees in this intellectual step the genesis of a host of difficulties which have plagued philosophy for more than two thousand years. He is content, for good or ill, to accept the operations of things as they are; he accepts the existence of operations; and this is as far as he feels warranted to go. The experimentalist holds that a thing is its operations and nothing more, and in so doing he of course departs not only from St. Thomas but from Aristotle himself. To speak of any thing is to speak of its actions, its behavior, its motions and operations. And when we speak of existence we speak of the existence of these operations, not the existence of some inert, motionless thing (essence) which has actions. We see, then, that an existing essence is to the experimentalist an existing cluster of operations and that a being, in this primal condition, is not an essence existing so much as operations existing. . . .

What can we say of the existence of operations? A clarification of the term itself may be of help. To the experimentalist an operation is relational; it refers to what occurs between aspects of reality, rather than to aspects of reality themselves. Indeed, reality is redefined here; for what relates "things" to experimentalists, are their relationships to other "things." A leaf is green; its greenness constitutes one of its operations. But this operation does not come into existence until it is conceived in relational terms, until there is an organism to see the greenness, attach meaning to it, and thus respond in some way to it. A leaf is also edible, and edibility is one of its operations; but this operation refers to a relationship between the leaf and something else—an eating organism—and does not come into existence until the organism carries through its operation of eating the leaf. . . .

In some ways, therefore, we can begin to see—and this is our second note on operations—that the ontological existent here under scrutiny, an operation, is not a thing in the substantive sense but an event. Something is happening, transpiring; and our use of the substantive term "something" again reveals that the word in common parlance refers to events as well as to inert "things." Properly considered, things are really events taking place, not isolated and independent essences exercising the act of existence. A "thing" to conclude, is a cluster of operations, and operations are events transpiring, occurrences happening; and in the transpiring and happening the events and occurrences can be said to be existing.

To be seen in all of this are the underlying reasons for the experimentalist's insistence on the principle of continuity. The very concept of operations signifies a connection between things —a seeking organism with something seen, an eating organism with something eaten, a breathing organism with air. What constitutes reality, in the experimentalist sense, is what connects things rather than what separates and distinguishes them. Man is not separated from nature; he is one with it. His animal operations of nutrition, reproduction, and growth represent relationships with his environment; and his rational processes are of the very same order. The operation of knowing is merely another and higher operation performed by a natural organism; it represents another connection, another type of linkage, another mode of relationship existing in the world.

Thus we can say that a real world, a world of relationships, very probably existed prior to man but that knowledge of this world did not. It was not until an organism constituted in part by the operation of knowing arrived on the scene that knowledge could arise. It is for this reason that experimentalists insist that truth, as a product of knowledge, dates from man's arrival. There was no truth before his emergence because there was no process of knowing which could lead to it. Moreover, truth itself is in this sense simply another name for functional knowledge, knowledge that is usable in the organism's interaction with his environment.

The experimentalist's epistemology is therefore conceived in terms of verification, the making of truth, rather than, in the case of the Thomist, in terms of discovery, the finding of antecedent truth. When Columbus discovered America he added something to reality. It is correct to say that the continent was there before he sailed, and the Thomist would be inclined to say that he did not add anything to the world; and its post-Columbian refinement represented a new relationship added into the world, an increment of functionally usable knowledge coming into existence in our universe. Truth, so conceived, is made, not found out. . . .

BIBLIOGRAPHY

Expositions of Naturalism

Blau, J. L., *Men and Movements in American Philosophy*. Englewood Cliffs, N. J., Prentice-Hall, Inc., 1952.

Buechner, L., *Force and Matter*. New York, Truth Seeker Company, Inc., 1950.

Cowte, A., *A General View of Positivism*, trans. by J. H. Bridges. London, Tribner, 1865.

Dewey, John, *Reconstruction in Philosophy*. Boston, Mass., Beacon Press, 1948.

Dewey, John, *Experience and Nature*. New York, W. W. Norton & Company, Inc., 1929.

Edman, Irwin, *Four Ways in Philosophy*. New York, Holt, Rinehart and Winston, Inc., 1937.

Haeckel, Ernest, *The Riddle of the Universe*. New York, Harper & Brothers, 1899.

Huxley, Thomas Henry, *Lay Sermons, Addresses and Reviews*. New York, E. P. Dutton & Co., Inc., 1913.

Ostwald, Wilhelm, *Natural Philosophy*, trans. by T. Seltzer. New York, Holt, Rinehart and Winston, Inc., 1910.

Perry, R. B., *Philosophy of the Recent Past*. New York, Charles Scribner's Sons, 1926.

Russell, Bertrand, *What I Believe*. New York, E. P. Dutton & Co., Inc., 1926.

Sellars, Roy Wood, *Evolutionary Naturalism*. Chicago, Open Court Publishing Company, 1922.

Spencer, Herbert, *Data of Ethics*. New York, D. Appleton and Company, 1884.

Spencer, Herbert, *First Principles*. Akron, Ohio, Werner Company, 1864.

Watson, John, *Psychology from the Viewpoint of a Behaviorist*. Philadelphia, J. B. Lippincott Co., 1929.

Werkmeister, W. H., *A History of Philosophical Ideas in America*. New York, The Ronald Press Company, 1949.

Commentaries on Naturalism

Brennan, R. E., O. P., *Thomisic Psychology*. New York, The Macmillan Company, 1941.

Howison, G. H., *The Limits of Evolution*. New York, The Macmillan Company, 1904.

Klubertanz, G. P., S.J., *The Philosophy of Human Nature*. New York, Appleton-Century-Crofts, Inc., 1953.

Lodge, Oliver, *Life and Matter: Criticism of Haeckel's Riddle of the Universe*. New York, G. P. Putnam's Sons, 1905.

Reith, Herman, C. S. C., *An Introduction to Philosophical Psychology*. Englewood Cliffs, New Jersey, Prentice-Hall, Inc., 1957.

Ward, James, *Naturalism and Agnosticism*. New York, The Macmillan Company, 1903. 2 vols.

4

The Search for a
Norm of Meaning

PRAGMATISM

NATURALISM, AS WE HAVE SEEN, is willing to limit the knowledge of man to the physical universe of our experience because, as a matter of fact, that is all there is for us to know. This knowledge, achieved by means of the method of natural science, is exact and conclusive. All other propositions which deal with a supposed reality beyond the scope of natural phenomena are necessarily illusory, or wishful thinking, or by their very nature poetic and emotional. The supra sensible is simply ruled out as having any reality independent of the subjective feelings of the knowing agent.

Such rejection of the supra sensible has not always been so definite in the history of philosophical thought. The limitation of man's ability to reach certainty has been accompanied more commonly with a skepticism in regard to the validity of the claim that a knowledge of the supra sensible is possible. Such a skepticism is as old as the history of philosophy itself. There were the sophists in ancient Greece who were willing to defend either side of an argument, and the Roman world had its Sextus Empiricus just as St. Augustine had to deal in his own day with the Academics. And in the middle ages there was a William of

Ockham to question the certitude of demonstrations of spiritual realities that previously had gone unquestioned.

There is no one who is not aware of Descartes' systematic doubt in his quest to find an indubitable starting point from which demonstrations of the non-empirical could take their departure. It was this precise starting point—the certainty of the thinker as a thinking subject—that cast in doubt the whole reality of a material universe. In British Empiricism there were Locke and Hume to push this skepticism deeper and deeper into the possibility of knowledge of this material universe and to question the very existence of substance, of secondary sense qualities and of the causal relations themselves which knit this universe together. We have already studied the result of this on the philosophy of George Berkeley, and his assertion that only in a complete Idealism could certainty be achieved and the essentially spiritual nature of the universe be saved. It was Immanuel Kant who tried to escape both from the Idealism of Berkeley and the skepticism of Hume by combining the two spheres in a system of knowledge which related the spiritual and the necessary to the material and the contingent through the mediation of the intellect. Yet it was this very conjunction of both elements that resulted in ruling out of our knowledge any certainty with regard to the spiritual in itself or the material thing in itself.

Yet the reaction of Naturalism—the denial of the existence of the supra sensible—has not been the ordinary reaction. It was not, for example, the reaction of Kant, who, in his categorical imperative, found reasonable grounds to postulate the existence of God and the immortality of the soul. Here a more or less reasonable faith substituted for the impossibility of certain knowledge, much as it had substituted for William of Ockham with regard to the existence and the immortality of the soul. Locke and Hume were themselves men of belief in the realities they were unable to demonstrate, and Catholic Fideism and Traditionalism[1] are his-

[1] Both Fideism and Traditionalism were attempts within the Church to safeguard the faith against the attacks of extreme Rationalism, on the one hand, and Scepticism on the other. Both doctrines insisted on the incapability of human reason to achieve certitude in the natural order. Hence, human reason necessarily had to commit itself to some sort of supra-rational norm.

torical movements testifying to the impact made on Catholic philosophy and theology by the challenges of skepticism and more modern science.

There is still another reaction, and this one has been called characteristically American. It is the reaction of Pragmatism.

Basically, Pragmatism accepts the Kantian limitation of the intellect to the phenomena of the material world. Yet it is willing to make judgments about things in themselves and about realities which transcend sensible experience. The necessity for such judgments in a world of activity is easily apparent, and where the intellect cannot reach such conclusions on its own, there is another power in man which enables him to do so. Hence instead of falling back upon faith, Pragmatism relies on the will and on the need to act. It is this need to act which ultimately becomes the decisive factor in settling questions, which intellectually admit of no solution. In the end truth is a question of utility and value, and it is this which is set up as a norm, not only for truth and error, but for good and evil as well.

Origins of Pragmatism—Peirce

The founder of American Pragmatism is usually regarded as Charles Sanders Peirce, a professor at Harvard University, who in 1878 published an article in the *Popular Science Monthly* entitled, "How to Make Our Ideas Clear." In this article thought is described as a mere means to belief, whatever other effects it may accidentally produce.

Thought is only one such system, for its sole motive, idea and function is to produce belief, and whatever does not concern that purpose belongs to some other system of relations. The action of thinking may incidentally have other results; it may serve to amuse us, for example, and among dilettanti it is not rare to find those who have so per-

---

For the Fideists this norm was authority, and this authority was to be found in revelation. The Traditionalists found the norm in a primitive revelation given to the human race and passed on to each generation through tradition. The doctrines of the Fideists and the Traditionalists were condemned at various times by the Church, and the Vatican Council defined that human reason could come to a true and certain knowledge of such natural truths as the existence of God, that this God is personal, etc.

verted thought to the purposes of pleasure that it seems to vex them to think that the questions upon which they delight to exercise it may ever get finally settled.

But the soul and meaning of thought, abstracted from the other elements which accompany it, though it may be voluntarily thwarted, can never be made to direct itself toward anything but the production of belief. Thought in action has for its only possible motive the attainment of thought at rest; and whatever does not refer to belief is no part of the thought itself.[2]

Belief, that toward which thought tends, has three characteristics: first, it is something we are aware of; second, it appeases the irritation of doubt; third, it involves in our nature the establishment of a habit of action. Thus beliefs are ordered to action and different beliefs are distinguished by the diverse actions to which they lead. From the very beginning of the essay the reader is made aware that action is the all important thing, and that intellectual propositions are to be eventually judged on what they produce in practice.

This, according to Peirce, is the only possible way an idea can be judged. Our idea of anything is our idea of its sensible effects. We cannot picture electricity, but we know what electricity does. What, for instance, do we know of weight, except that it is something which makes bodies fall to the ground? For the same reason Peirce thinks that it is foolish for Catholics and Protestants to disagree on the manner in which Christ is present in the Eucharist, as long as it produces the same effects both here and hereafter. Hence it follows that, as long as two ideas have the same effects, they have the same meaning. From this viewpoint it would eventually make no difference whether the universe is ruled by God or by matter, since everything would still continue to act in the same way.

Pragmatism for Peirce was a method, not a philosophy, and, as a matter of fact, he wrote on metaphysics, ethics and epistemology. All of these areas he thought could be clarified by the application of the pragmatic method. Yet the method itself has metaphysical and epistemological implications, and it is no wonder that modern

2 *Philosophical Writings of Peirce*, Justus Buchler, ed. (New York, Dover Publications, Inc., 1955), p. 28.

Empiricists and Positivists have found in Peirce a fertile source for their Positivism. Yet he himself was always quite careful to distinguish his pragmatic method from philosophy itself. Pragmatism is meant to make philosophy clear, and philosophically Peirce considered himself some sort of a Scotistic Realist. This Realism achieves clarity and meaningfulness in so far as it can be reduced to and judged by the results to which it leads. John Dewey expresses this function of the pragmatic method in an article entitled "The Development of American Pragmatism."

Peirce developed the theory that the rational purport of a word or other expression lies exclusively in its conceivable bearing upon the conduct of life; so that, since obviously nothing which might not result from experiment can have any direct bearing upon conduct, if one can define accurately all the conceivable experimental phenomena which the affirmation or denial of a concept would imply, one will have therein a complete definition of the concept.[3]

Progress of Pragmatism—James

The Pragmatism of Peirce was further developed and clarified by another Harvard professor, William James (1842-1930). He had been well educated in science and had graduated from Harvard with a medical degree. Philosophically his background was an empirical one in the tradition of Locke, Berkeley, Hume, and Mill. His philosophical security was shaken, however, by the Materialism and the Agnosticism into which Empiricism had fallen, and the biblical controversies at the turn of the twentieth century became of great interest to him. This and the failure of his health caused him to turn again to an examination of the meaning of life. Materialism offered him nothing in the spiritual realm, and his father's affiliation, Transcendentalism, could not provide him with the assurance his scientifically trained mind looked for.

His examination of philosophy led him to divide philosophers into two types, the tough-minded and the tender-minded. The tough-minded are the more scientific and empirical, while the

---

[3] Cf. Studies in the History of Ideas, Vol. II (New York, Columbia University Press, 1925).

tender-minded are inclined to be rationalistic, religious and romantic. The following classification is famous:[4]

THE TENDER-MINDED	THE TOUGH-MINDED
Rationalistic (*going by principles*)	Empiricist (*going by facts*)
Intellectualistic	Sensationalistic
Idealistic	Materialistic
Optimistic	Pessimistic
Religious	Irreligious
Free-Willist	Fatalistic
Monistic	Pluralistic
Dogmatical	Skeptical

James thought he had found in Pragmatism a system that would adequately embody the best in both types of mentality. It remains religious like the rationalistic philosophies, and at the same time it maintains intimacy with the facts like the empiricalistic systems. In 1907 James published a lecture entitled "What Pragmatism Means." In it he laid down the basic tents of the pragmatic method, as he understood it.

Pragmatism as Method

According to James, Pragmatism is basically a method of settling disputes that might otherwise be endless. For centuries philosophers have argued over such questions as: Is the world one or many? Is the soul immortal or not? Is there a universal principle of causality at work in the universe? No satisfactory answer has ever been given to these and similar questions. But, if we resort to the pragmatic method, we simply try to interpret each action by tracing its respective practical consequences. Thus, if there is any meaning to the question about which we are disputing, it will come out in such a tracing of its practical consequences. If not, then, obviously, the practical results will be the same.

It is astonishing to see how many philosophical disputes collapse into insignificance the moment you subject them to this simple test. . . . There can be no difference . . . in abstract truth that doesn't express

[4] William James, "The Dilemma in Philosophy," in *Pragmatism* (New York, Longmans, Green & Co., Inc., 1908), p. 12.

itself in a difference in concrete fact, imposed on somebody, somehow, somewhere, and somewhen. The function of philosophy ought to be to find out what definite difference it will make to you and me, at definite instants of our life, if this world-formula or that world-formula be the true one.[5]

Thus for James, too, Pragmatism is a method and not a theory of reality. It is an attitude which looks away from first principles, categories, and supposed "necessities" to last things, to fruits, consequences, and facts. Up to this point James is saying practically the same thing as Peirce. But in his theory of truth he widens and broadens the theory of Peirce. For Peirce, a proposition had meaning in so far as it resulted in meaningful consequences. James went farther. Such practically coherent results not only gave a proposition meaning, they also made the proposition true. Thus according to him, our ideas become true in so far as they help us get into satisfactory relationship with other parts of our experience. Purely objective truth is nowhere to be found. Practically, however, anything is true which stands up under the test of practical benefit. Thus metaphysical speculations can be judged only in relation to future consequences. Where there are no such consequences, there can obviously be no judgment as to the truth or falsity of the proposition in question. This comes very close to making truth depend on usefulness or expediency, and it is not very far from the insistence of the logical positivist that a true proposition is one which can be verified in experience.

Truth as Process

In an attempt to prove the theory, James pointed out that action alone is the only way we can come to a belief that we possess concepts in common. Thus two people can argue from now till eternity about the meaning of green. The only possible way to find out if they both mean the same thing is to ask each one the color of the lawn on which he is walking, or to put both of them in a car before a stop light and find out if both will start when the light changes from red to green. Thus sensation alone terminates dis-

[5] William James, "What Pragmatism Means," in *Pragmatism* (New York, Longmans, Green & Co., Inc., 1908), pp. 49-50.

cussion. This test is to be applied to all controverted questions, theological as well as philosophical.

The truth is not a stagnant property inherent in an idea, but is something which happens to an idea. The idea becomes true, is made true by events. Truth is a process, the process in which an idea is verified. This verification takes place in action. Now since all action is aimed at achieving some good, truth seems to be equated with what is beneficial to the person seeking some satisfaction. The true, then, is the useful, the beneficial, the expedient. It is very hard to see how this keeps truth from being anything but purely and personally relative.

In an article entitled "Humanism and Truth" James formulates the following points in an attempt to make his theory of truth coherent and to avoid such a complete Relativism.

1. An experience, perceptual or conceptual, must conform to reality in order to be true.
2. By 'reality' humanism means nothing more than the other conceptual or perceptual experiences with which a given present experience may find itself in point of fact mixed up.
3. By 'conforming' humanism means taking account of in such a way as to gain any intellectually and practically satisfactory result.
4. To 'take account of' and 'to be satisfactory' are terms that admit of no definition, so many are the ways in which these requirements can practically be worked out.
5. Vaguely and in general, we take account of a reality by preserving it in as unmodified a form as possible. But to be then satisfactory, it must not contradict other realities outside of it which claim also to be preserved. That we must preserve all the experience we can and minimize contradiction in what we preserve is about all that can be said in advance.
6. The truth which the conforming experience embodies may be a positive addition to the previous reality, and later judgments may have to conform to it. Yet, virtually at least, it may have been true previously. Pragmatically, virtual and actual truth mean the same thing: the possibility of only one answer, when once the question is raised.[6]

Thus James hopes to avoid a theory of truth that is purely and personally relative by injecting a theory of coherence into ex-

[6] William James, *The Meaning of Truth* (New York, Longmans, Green & Co., 1909), pp. 100-101.

perience. This coherence would include not only all the facts of personal experience, but also all the experiences of others involved in the personal experience of each one. In this way he hopes to maintain some sort of equilibrium of experiences, each fact of which would cohere with all the other facts, before it could be accepted as true. Since no one can ever possibly know all the facts, it is obvious that no theory of absolute truth will ever be possible. Any newly discovered fact might very easily change the whole picture overnight. And every newly discovered fact must be made to fit coherently into the present fact picture, before it can possibly be accepted. The truth situation is like Penelope's fabric, easily unweavable and never able to be completed. It is a delicate skein suspended on the one side by a past that tomorrow may prove to be completely unreliable, and on the other side by a future that is never attainable.

Radical Empiricism

In his later years James drifted more and more toward what he called a "Radical Empiricism." In his preface to *The Meaning of Truth*, he describes this Empiricism as follows: this Radical Empiricism consists first of a postulate, then of a statement of fact, and lastly of a generalized conclusion. The postulate is that the only things that shall be debatable among philosophers shall be things definable in terms drawn from experience. The statement of fact is that the relations between things, conjunctive as well as disjunctive, are just as much matter of direct personal experience, neither more so nor less so, than the things themselves. The general conclusion is that therefore the parts of experience hold together from next to next by relations that are themselves parts of experience. The directly apprehended universe needs no extraneous transempirical connective support, but possesses in its own right a concatenated or continuous structure. Thus knowledge and the object of knowledge are both reduced to the flux of experience, and this Radical Empiricism includes the pragmatic method in determining the value of any experience. By adhering to these two principles it is discovered that thoughts and things are absolutely homogeneous as to their material, and their opposition is only one of relation and function. There is no thought-stuff different from thing-stuff. The same piece of pure experience can stand now for a fact of consciousness, now for a physical reality, according as it is taken in one context or another. Nor does it help to seek the subject of these varied experiences in an effort to distinguish one from another. For such a subject would be discoverable only in the effects produced and would be definable in terms of these results alone. Since subject and object are all portrayed and found in the same experience, the only conclusion that Radical Empiricism can reach is that they are both ultimately the same. Reality is synonymous with the flux of experience, and how real it all is depends on how useful or how beneficial it all is. Thus Radical Empiricism is somehow kept from being a pure Materialism by some sort of a will to believe that it is not the same. This is a Materialism that is not tough-minded enough to say so plainly.

Pragmatism Expanded—Dewey

It was left to John Dewey (1859-1952) to take up the teachings of Peirce and James and apply them to history, sociology, politics, and education. For Dewey, too, Pragmatism is principally a method— the method of natural science. Yet it is a method which must be applied to the situation as we find it. Philosophy enjoys no superior position from which it can look down upon a reality from which it has abstracted. This was the thought of such philosophers as Bacon, Descartes, and Kant. And this was also their greatest error. The philosopher is part of his time and milieu, and he cannot possibly philosophize accurately, if he attempts to step out of it.[7]

Bacon, Descartes, and Kant each thought with fervor that he was founding philosophy anew because he was placing it securely upon an exclusive intellectual basis, exclusive, that is, of everything but intellect. The movement of time has revealed the illusion; it exhibits as the work of philosophy the old and ever new undertaking of adjusting that body of traditions which constitute the actual mind of man to scientific tendencies and political aspirations which are novel and

[7] John Dewey, *Philosophy and Civilization* (New York, Minton Balch & Co., 1929), pp. 3-4.

compatible with received authorities. Philosophers are parts of history, caught in its movement; creators, perhaps in some measure of its future, but also assuredly creatures of its past.[8]

Philosophy must grow out of the experience of the philosopher and this experience is had in the political, scientific, cultural, and historical situation in which he finds himself. This experience is of the real and constitutes the real, and it is only in it and in relation to it that philosophy has any meaning at all. This, as Dewey sees it, is precisely the contribution of Pragmatism and he considers it one of the major philosophical triumphs in history.

It is not too much to say, therefore, that for the first time there is made possible an empirical theory of ideas free from the burden imposed alike by sensationalism and a priori rationalism. This accomplishment is, I make bold to say, one of the three or four outstanding feats of intellectual history. For it emancipates us from the supposed need of always harking to what has already been given, something had by alleged direct or indirect knowledge in the past, for the test of the value of ideas. A test of the nature of ideas in terms of operations to be performed and the test of the validity of the ideas by the consequences of these operations established connectivity with concrete experience. At the same time, by the emancipation of thinking from the necessity of testing its conclusions solely by reference to antecedent existence it makes clear the originative possibilities of thinking.[9]

The situation in which this experience takes place is the naturalistic one of the nineteenth century. It accepts the Darwinian theory of evolution and regards mind and man as climactic processes emerging out of the universal dynamism of nature. And this experience itself is part of nature and cannot be rightly distinguished from nature. Dr. Piatt in his article, "Dewey's Logical Theory," writes as follows of the connection between nature and experience.

Experience and nature are not separate entities conjoined or added together; experience is rather the forms which nature assumes in interactions of nonorganic and organic events including human events. Much of the difficulty in understanding Dewey would be obviated, if

[8] John Dewey The Quest for Certainty (New York, Minton, Balch & Co., 1929), p. 114. Reprinted by permission of G. P. Putnam's Sons from The Quest for Certainty by John Dewey. Copyright 1929 by John Dewey, © 1957 by Roberta L. Dewey.
[9] Ibid.

more attention were paid to his naturalism and less to his empiricism. Instrumental and experimental logic is naturalistic, not a logic of a separate world of thought but a logic of natural events which are functioning on a meaning level. By the same token, naturalistic metaphysics may appropriately be regarded as instrumental and experimental because thinking behavior only actualizes and utilizes to better advantage the instrumental and experimental potentialities of natural events.[10]

Pragmatism Joined to Naturalism

It is here in what he means by experience that the Naturalism which is conjoined to Dewey's Pragmatism becomes clear. For nature is experience and experience is nature. Reality is a series of events acting and reacting on one another. Thus "to be" comes to mean the same thing as "to act," and this interaction takes place on the purely physical level, on the level of living things and on the level of knowledge. There is no need any longer for substances or causes. There are just complicated relationships to constitute the framework of the real. Reality is what it does. It is something happening, transpiring. A "thing" is a cluster of operations. A modern Experimentalist makes this clear in a recently published article.

Now the experimentalist is not inclined to look beneath operations for unknown X's which account for them. He sees in this intellectual step the genesis of a host of difficulties which have plagued philosophy for more than two thousand years. He is content, for good or ill, to accept the operations of things as they are; he accepts the existence of operations; and this is as far as he feels warranted to go. The experimentalist holds that a thing *is* its operations and nothing more, and in so doing he of course departs not only from St. Thomas but from Aristotle himself. To speak of any thing is to speak of its actions, its behavior, its motions and operations. And when we speak of existence, we speak of the existence of these operations. . . .[11]

In such a context truth must consist solely in a relative consistency, forever variable, necessarily verifiable in experience before

[10] *The Library of Living Philosophers,* P.A. Schilpp, ed. (Evanston, Ill., Northwestern University Press, 1939).

[11] Van Cleve Morris, "An Experimentalist Looks at Being," *The Modern Schoolman* (Jan. 1958), p. 127. *Cf.* also A. J. Reich, "Substance, Language, and Symbolic Logic," *The Modern Schoolman* (March, 1958).

it can have any meaning whatsoever. Meaning itself can be meaningful only in reference to the situation in which it arises and to which it must again be referred. Causation cannot possibly mean the action of an agent on a patient. There are no agents and no patients. There are only events having matter as a character, and out of these events spring other events, which we characterize as life and mind. It is no wonder that Dewey could say "effects" are more adequate indications of nature than are "causes." They would have to be since they contain more than any of the causes from which they evolved.

Pragmatism and Religion

In the field of religion and its relation to the pragmatic method Dewey shows again his close connection with the postulates of Naturalism, so that it is not surprising that he is much more dogmatic about the nature of religious belief than James ever was. James, as we have seen, was quite content to allow a religious belief to stand, provided it was of practical consequence in the life of the individual who held it. Thus a religious dogma could be pragmatically verified—at least for the individual—in terms of the effects it produced experientially. Dewey is quite unwilling to go that far. In his *Essays in Experimental Logic* he asks the following question:

Does Mr. James employ the pragmatic method to discover the value in terms of consequences in life of some formula which has its logical content already fixed; or does he employ it to criticize and revise and, ultimately, to constitute the meaning of that formula? If it is the first, there is danger that the pragmatic method will be employed only to vivify, if not validate, doctrines which in themselves are pieces of rationalistic metaphysics, not inherently pragmatic. In the last there is danger that some readers will think old notions are being confirmed, when in truth they are being translated into new and consistent notions.[12]

It is easy to see Mr. Dewey's difficulty. He does not want to say simply that any religious idea can be made to have value in the pragmatic order. This would be to admit that even the most out-

[12] John Dewey, *Essays in Experimental Logic* (Chicago, University of Chicago Press, 1916), p. 313.

moded dogmatic notions could be saved by Pragmatism, even though they are no longer scientifically tenable. Science, in Dewey's view, had done much to eradicate many false religious notions and had reduced them to the realm of myth, superstition, fear and ignorance—where they belong. These ideas should never be able to be verified and given meaning, especially by a philosophy which prides itself on its scientific method and scientific accuracy. Hence, he claims that, whatever good such pragmatic verification of these ideas would accomplish, would in the long run be overcome by the harm they would do. People might even tend to return to such notions as objectively valid ones, and then no self-respecting Pragmatist would be able to face the contradiction spawned by Pragmatism. It is one thing to recognize that such superstitions and blind fears are part of the experience of all men. It is quite another to be willing to dignify these ideas by granting that they may have useful or beneficial consequences in the realm of experience.

Now it is one thing to say that the world is such that men approach certain objects with awe, worship, piety, sacrifice and prayer, and that this is a fact which a theory of existence must reckon with as truly as with the facts of science. But it is a different thing to say that religious experience gives evidence of the reality of its own objects, or that the consciousness of an obligation proves the validity of its special object, or the general fact of duty carries within itself any deliverance as to its source in reality. . . .
Injunctions and prohibitions which are empirically unescapable, may be called categorical imperatives, and their existence may be quite as significant for a just theory of nature as is the law of gravitation. But what sort of objects beyond themselves they give evidence of, whether tribal taboos, a Kantian thing-in-itself, God, a political sovereign, or a network of social customs evolved in the effort to satisfy needs, is a question to be settled by the denotative method, by finding and pointing to the things in the concrete contexts in which they present themselves.[13]

Thus Dewey would acknowledge religion and the notion of God as a fact of experience, but he would want to distinguish carefully between the "scientific" interpretation of such a fact

[13] John Dewey, "Experience and Nature," in John L. Childs, *American Pragmatism and Education* (New York, Holt, Rinehart and Winston, Inc., 1956), pp. 323-324.

and the ordinary connotations which the fact had for most people. However such a notion might be helpful or beneficial in the life of the ordinary person, such utility should never be allowed to lead to a mistaken idea of what God and religion mean. What, then, is the real meaning of such terms? And here again Dewey's Naturalism comes to the fore. Certainly what the terms cannot mean is something beyond the realm of nature and experience. There is idealism in nature; there is inspiration for those who look to see it; there are goals toward which man may strive. The reasonable pursuit of such goals and the ability to allow inspiration to direct human activity, all this is part of what religion means. And the same is true of God. To speak of God as a person, Who directs the activity of a finite world, Who leads all things which He has created to their proper ends, is to speak of a God Who simply cannot exist. Were God of such a nature, then there is no reason why there should be pain and evil in the work of His creation. From the experiential and naturalistic viewpoint God is simply a symbolic representation of the end and goal of human striving. He is something created and projected by man who seeks for unity and purpose and symbolizes the hope to find that purpose as the term of his activities. Thus God and religion are made true by man, just as man makes true his thoughts and ideas in so far as he brings them to realization.

It is the task of Pragmatism, thought Dewey, to replace faith in the supernaturalism of traditional religion with faith in the religious possibilities of ordinary human experience. For Pragmatism is the method of intelligence, and there is such a thing as faith in intelligence. This sort of faith can also take on religious qualities. It demands devotion to the methods and processes by which truth is discovered. These methods are, of course, the methods of science, and a man's religious qualities will then be judged by the intensity of his devotion to science. Added to this is the value of the democratic principle of the worth and dignity of the human personality. When men realize that they and the community to which they belong must develop from within and must take full responsibility themselves for their decisions, that they can no longer rely on the traditional God in the heavens to rescue them from their mistakes and failures, then at last there will be hope for the success of the human community on earth. Thus the realm of morality and religion will finally be seen not as something distinct from everyday human living, but an integral part of it, emerging out of nature and renovating the nature from which it has arisen.

The ideal ends to which we attach our faith are not shadowy and wavering. They assume concrete form in our understanding of our relations to one another and the values contained in these relations. We who now live are parts of a humanity that has interacted with nature. The things in civilization which we most prize are not of ourselves. They exist by grace of the doings and sufferings of the continuous human community in which we are a link.[14]

Pragmatism and its various offshoots—Instrumentalism and Experimentalism—has taken on ever increasing importance on the American philosophical scene. It has linked itself to science and is ever hopeful of making the same gigantic strides that science has made in the last fifty years. It appeals to many both because it is a method which promises to give accurate and precise results closely allied to and verifiable in experience and because it claims it is able to avoid the abstractions and deadening influences of Rationalism and Idealism. Thus, too, it is able to limit knowledge to an area where certainty can be achieved, even if it is only a relative certainty which further experience may make untenable the next moment. Along with the reference to factual situations it can also preserve an openminded attitude that is ever ready to accept the fruits and consequences of experiment and investigation. It puts religion on a natural and scientific plane and seeks to do away forever with illusion and wishful thinking.

LOGICAL POSITIVISM

Origins

In the early 1920's a movement began at the University of Vienna which has and still is exercising a distinct influence on modern philosophy. The movement grew out of a seminar at the university

[14] John Dewey, *A Common Faith* (New Haven, Conn., Yale University Press, 1934), p. 87.

and included such men as Carnap, Wittgenstein, Neurath, Frank, Schlick, and Reichenbach. In 1939 Wittgenstein went to the University of Cambridge in England, and the movement spread in the British Isles so that it aligned itself with British Analysis and today includes such names as those of Ayer, Ryle and Wisdom. The movement has also been felt in America, since many of the members of the original Vienna Circle migrated to the United States when Hitler came to power.

Relation to Natural Sciences

It is in many ways a difficult movement to characterize clearly. This is due to the fact that it is still a young movement, and its complete platform has by no means been established. Leading writers in the field are still rejecting today what they wrote yesterday and there is also a great deal of disagreement among those who style themselves Logical Empiricists. In general, however, it can be said that the proponents of the system are all agreed that natural science holds the key to knowledge, and there is a general assumption that the only possible method by which knowledge can be acquired is the method of natural science. This is certainly understandable considering the gigantic strides that science has made in the last one hundred years. The contribution of science is all the more impressive when it is compared to that made by philosophy in an equal amount of time. The answer could certainly lie in the precise, accurate, empirical method which science employs. If this method could be applied to and by philosophy, there seems reason to hope that philosophy will also come into its own.

Rejection of Aristotelian Logic

Furthermore, what has seemed to hold philosophy back has been the sterile abstractionism of the Rationalists and Idealists. Add to this the supposed discovery that Aristotelian logic has been shown to be inadequate, and it becomes immediately apparent that a new method must be devised before philosophy will reach its full capacities. Hence it is that most Logical Empiricists, following the lead of Wittgenstein and Bertrand Russell, are interested in developing a new mathematical logic to replace the antiquated Aristotelian version. It can be seen at once that Logical Empiricism bears a distinct resemblance in many ways to Pragmatism and Naturalism. What it adds is a distinct emphasis on mathematical logic and logical analysis of language. This far, at least, most logical empiricists would agree.

. . . all Logical Positivists could still agree that they (a) hold Humean views on causality and induction; (b) insist on the tautological nature of logical and mathematical truths; (c) conceive of philosophy as a logical analysis, i.e., as a clarification of the language we speak in every day life; and (d) that such analysis leads to the rejection of metaphysics in the sense that, e.g., the points at dispute among the traditional forms of idealism, realism and phenomenalism could not even be stated or, at least not be stated in their original intent, in a properly clarified language.[15]

The authors of a recently published history of philosophy view the movement as follows:

Viewed historically, logical empiricism appears as a serious effort to construct a theory of meaning and a theory of knowledge that reconcile the valid elements of rationalism and empiricism and subscribe to the principles of logic and the procedures of the natural sciences. To this great task it brought especially the technical equipment of mathematical logic and a knowledge of the procedures of experimental and theoretical physics uncommon to philosophers to say nothing of an unusal ability in philosophical analysis.[16]

It would seem that Immanuel Kant had failed. Furthermore we learn from Rudolf Carnap that the function of such logical analysis is to analyze all knowledge, all assertions of science and of everyday life in order to make clear the sense of each such assertion and the connections between them.[17]

[15] Gustav Bergman, "Logical Positivism," in Vergilius Ferm, ed., *A History of Philosophical Systems* (New York, Philosophical Library, Inc., 1950), p. 472.

[16] B. A. G. Fuller, *A History of Philosophy*, 3rd ed., rev. by S. M. McMurrin (New York, Holt, Rinehart and Winston, Inc., 1955). *Cf.* introduction to the section on logical positivism.

[17] R. Carnap, *Philosophy and Logical Syntax* (London, Kegan Paul, Trench, Truebner & Co., Ltd., 1935), pp. 9-10.

Analysis of Language

What exactly does this analysis of language entail? Briefly, it comes to this. All propositions are divided into analytic and synthetic propositions. Synthetic propositions are those derived from experience and which can be referred to experience for their verification. Such propositions, however, may refer either indirectly or directly to experience. Hence they must be analyzed and those referring only indirectly to experience must be reduced to other sentences, "protocol sentences," which can and do refer directly to experience. An ultimate experiential proposition would be one which could be further explained only by pointing. To elucidate the point and to make clear the confusions often contained in everyday language, Carnap proposed a series of propositions. A proposition which has a real object and which refers immediately to the data of experience is one like this: "The rose is red." This is clear. But take a proposition like this: "The rose is a thing." Now it might seem at first sight that such a proposition is empirical, but the predicate, "thing", is one of those vague and confused terms so characteristic of the metaphysicians. It is not in the least explicit enough to suggest any direct reference. Hence, while people might think that the proposition is empirical, as a matter of fact, it is not. There is no real object here. The proposition is really a proposition about terms and not about real objects at all. What the proposition really means to say is this: The word, "rose", is a thing word. Hence upon analysis it becomes clear that what was apparently a proposition about a real object was really about words. A further example may make the position somewhat clearer. If I say, "Mr. A visited Africa," I have made a statement which has a real, existing object to which the proposition can be referred. Now, suppose I say, "This book treats of Africa." Again it seems that the proposition has a real objective reference. But, if one looks more closely, it becomes clear that "Africa" in the first proposition is not the same as "Africa" in the second proposition. This book certainly has nothing to do with the land that Mr. A visited. What I should say is that in this book is contained the word, "Africa." For that is what the book treats of, not the dark continent itself.

One must be on his guard, therefore, lest he mistake a pseudo-object proposition for a real object proposition. Yet this is what most of us do all the time, according to Carnap, and it is the function of Logical Empiricism to protect us from such loose and confusing modes of speech. Only those propositions which can be actually or possibly referred to a real object are propositions worthy of empirical science. Only these have real meaning. The others may have meaning in so far as one term is predicated of or opposed to another term, but they can have no objective reference. They are meaningful on a linguistic level only.

Besides such real-object-propositions—and these are the propositions formed by the empirical sciences—Logical Empiricists also admit the existence of analytic propositions. These are the propositions formed by mathematics and logic. Such propositions may be formally meaningful, but they have no real object, because, as a matter of fact, they are tautologies. The predicate merely makes explicit what is already implicitly contained in the subject. Where, then, do metaphysical propositions fit in? They are not tautologies. Every metaphysician claims that he is saying something about a real object. Yet neither can the object, about which he is talking, be found in the realm of experience. Thus a metaphysical proposition cannot be empirically verified. The only conclusion is that the metaphysician is saying nothing at all. Such propositions are meaningless.

I will call metaphysical all those propositions which claim to represent knowledge about something which is over or beyond all experience, e.g., about the real essence of things, about things in themselves, the Absolute, and such like.

Now let us examine this kind of proposition from the viewpoint of verifiability. It is easy to realize that such propositions are not verifiable. From the proposition: "The principle of the world is water" we are not able to deduce any proposition asserting any perceptions or feelings or experiences whatever which may be expected for the future. Therefore the proposition, "The principle of the world is water," asserts nothing at all.

Metaphysicians cannot avoid making their propositions non-verifiable, because if they made them verifiable, the decision about the truth or falsehood of their doctrines would depend upon experience and therefore belong to the region of empirical science. This consequence they wish to avoid, because they pretend to teach knowledge which is of a higher level than that of empirical science. Thus they are compelled to cut out all connection between their propositions and experience; and precisely by this procedure they deprive them of any sense.[18]

To say, however, that such propositions are meaningless is not to deny that they have their function. They are expressive, as laughter is or as is lyric poetry. They manifest hopes or desires or certain feelings. From such a viewpoint it may even be desirable to have such propositions. That, however, is not the point here. Philosophically speaking they make no sense. There is only one task proper to philosophy, and that is to provide a method of logical analysis. As Wittgenstein put it:

The object of philosophy is the logical clarification of thoughts. Philosophy is not a theory but an activity. A philosophic work consists essentially of elucidations. The result of philosophy is not a number of philosophical propositions; but to make propositions clear. Philosophy should make clear and delimit sharply the thoughts which otherwise are, as it were, opaque and blurred.[19]

Another way to say this is to say that science is the pursuit of truth, while philosophy is the pursuit of meaning. Thus the philosopher is consigned to make meaningful statements about scientific facts.

Attitudes Toward Metaphysics

It might be well to pause here for a moment and consider the various attitudes toward metaphysics as expressed by Naturalists, Pragmatists, Logical Empiricists, and Kant himself. The Naturalist states that metaphysics is meaningless simply because there is nothing beyond the empirical order. There is simply nothing about which one can be a metaphysician. The Pragmatist regards metaphysics as wearisome, theoretical dispute which can never be satisfactorily solved. There may be such a realm of metaphysical realities beyond the world of everyday experience, but man can know nothing about it with certainty. Whatever meaningfulness

[18] *Ibid.*, pp. 15-18.
[19] L. Wittgenstein, *Tractatus Logico-Philosophicus* (London, George Routledge & Sons, Ltd., 1922), 4.112.

such truths or realities possess is to be determined solely by their workability in the business of living. Kant had rejected metaphysics as consisting of empty concepts, formally meaningful, but objectively sterile. The human intellect because of its very structure was unable to transcend the phenomena.

Now the Logical Empiricist is not saying exactly the same thing, although there are, of course, similarities. The theory of knowledge from which the Logical Empiricist operates is not the same as that proposed by Kant. There are no synthetic a priori judgments in Logical Empiricism. The human intellect does not enter necessarily and essentially into the construction of the object as it does in Kant. The theory is much more nominalistic. A universal concept is a term which the intellect constructs to refer indefinitely to many things. It is simply a word whose object reference is vague. The whole function of philosophy as we have seen, is to analyze and verify by direct reference to experience. The reason why metaphysics is impossible is not because the intellect cannot reach such a realm, but because such so called metaphysical concepts can have no reference to sense experience. They are meaningless precisely because there can be no experiential verification of their truth or falsity. Hence for a Logical Empiricist it is neither true nor false to say: The soul of man is immortal. Upon analysis one finds that the statement should never have been made.

The Verifiability Principle

In such a system ordered toward the discovery of meaning through logical analysis the principle of the verification of meaning plays a necessarily important part. Hence Logical Empiricists attach a great deal of importance to verification and the meaning of verification. "The meaning of a proposition," writes Moritz Schlick, "is the method of its verification." And somewhat less strictly, "Verifiability means the possibility of verification."[20]

Now something may be possible in two ways, continues Schlick. We call something empirically possible, when it does not contra-

[20] Moritz Schlick "The Meaning of Verification," in J.L. Jarrett, Jr., and S.M. McMurrin, eds., *Readings in Contemporary Philosophy* (New York, Holt, Rinehart and Winston, Inc., 1954).

dict the laws of nature. The difficulty here is that we can never gain a complete knowledge of the laws of nature. We can never be completely certain at any given time that we are aware of all the laws at work in producing a certain natural phenomenon. In this case there is only one thing to do. We have to fall back upon past experience. But past experience is also incomplete. Hence we can have no real certainty that any given proposition is empirically possible. This is the sort of process the scientist uses in an attempt to determine whether a proposition is true or not. And while he may never achieve certainty, he can come at least to a statement which is highly predictable of future activity and which for the time being gives him something to work with. But before a proposition can be submitted to such a test, it must already have meaning. How, then, do we know if a proposition is meaningful or not?

There must be another criterion of possibility in order to determine the meaningfulness of a proposition. And this second kind of possibility Schlick terms logical possibility. "That is logically possible," he writes, "which can be described."[21] Now that is describable which can be found in experience and which can be submitted to the grammar and syntax of our language. Hence, if some proposition cannot be so described, then it is meaningless and should never have been enunciated. Whatever, then, cannot be found in experience is indescribable and necessarily meaningless. There are questions which should never have been asked and there are propositions which analysis shows should never have been formulated. Metaphysics is simply a great mistake.

The result of our considerations is this: Verifiability which is the sufficient and necessary condition of meaning, is a possibility of the logical order; it is created by constructing the sentence in accordance with the rules by which its terms are defined. The only case in which verification is logically impossible is the case where you have made it impossible by not setting any rules for its verification. Grammatical rules are not found anywhere in nature, but are made by man and are, in principle, arbitrary; so you cannot give meaning to a sentence by discovering a method of verifying it, but only by stipulating how it shall be done. Thus logical possibility or impossibility of verification is always self imposed. If we utter a sentence without meaning

[21] *Ibid.*

it is always our own fault. "The tremendous philosophic importance of this last remark will be realized when we consider that what we said about the meaning of assertions applies also to the meaning of questions. There are, of course, many questions which can never be answered by human beings. But the impossibility of finding the answer may be of two different kinds. If it is merely empirical in the sense defined, if it is due to the chance circumstances to which our human existence is confined, there may be reason to lament our fate and the weakness of our physical and mental powers, but the problem could never be said to be absolutely insoluble, and there would always be some hope, at least for future generations. . . .

"But what about those questions for which it is logically impossible to find an answer? Such problems would remain insoluble under all imaginable circumstances; they would confront us with a definite hopeless *Ignorabimus*; and it is of the greatest importance for the philosopher to know whether there are any such issues. Now it is easy to see from what has been said before that this calamity could happen only if the question itself had no meaning. It would not be a genuine question at all, but a mere row of words with a question mark at the end. We must say that a question is meaningful, if we can understand it, i.e., if we are able to decide for any given proposition whether, if true, it would be an answer to our question. And if this is so, the actual decision could only be prevented by empirical circumstances, which means that it would not be logically impossible. Hence no meaningful problem can be insoluble in principle. If in any case we find an answer to be logically impossible we know that we really have not been asking anything, but what sounded like a question was actually a nonsensical combination of words. A genuine question is one for which an answer is logically possible. This is one of the most characteristic results of our empiricism. It means that in principle there are no limits to our knowledge. The boundaries which must be acknowledged are of an empirical nature and, therefore, never ultimate; they can be pushed back further and further; there is no unfathomable mystery in the world.[22]

Ethical Norms and the Existence of God

With such a criterion of meaningfulness already laid down one can be pardoned for doubting at the outset whether propositions expressing ethical norms can possibly have any meaning. And no one will be surprised to read that such statements can have no meaning at all, as the Logical Positivist understands meaning. An

[22] Moritz Schlick, "Meaning and Verification," *Philosophical Review*, (1936).

ethical statement may well be considered an expression of emotion, a command to act as one would like people to act, but it can never be considered a meaningful statement, if by that one means a statement that has actual reference to experiential fact. In fact, anyone who still thinks that such statements express an objective situation is hopelessly of a pre-scientific type of mentality, says H. Feigl.

The quest for certainty, here in the field of morals just as elsewhere, may lead to emotionally soothing or edifying results. But the acceptance of an absolute authority or extramundane sanction for morality, like the belief in an absolute source of factual truth manifests a not fully liberated, pre-scientific type of mind. A completely grown-up mankind will have to shoulder the responsibility for its outlook and conduct; and in the spirit of empirical and naturalistic humanism it will acknowledge no other procedure than the experimental and no other standards than those prescribed by human nature and by our own insights into the possibilities of improving human nature.[23]

Thus the statement, It is wrong to commit wilful murder, is either a command not to act in a certain way, or it is an emotional-motivational appeal not to act that way. An ethical imperative like the Golden Rule, Feigl tells us again in the same context, simply means: Would that everybody behaved towards his fellowmen as he expects them to behave toward him!

"What objective or factual reference could possibly be contained in the statement, 'It is wrong to kill'?" asks A. J. Ayer.[24] Let us take an example: Here is a man, who out of jealousy kills an old friend of the family. He does it at night in the rain with a shotgun. These are the facts at hand. They are the facts which the police will consider and which both lawyers at the trial will try to interpret one way or another. What does it add to the actual situation to say that it was right or wrong to commit such an act of murder? Obviously it adds nothing at all. The facts remain exactly the same, whether a moral judgment is made about them

---

[23] Herbert Feigl, "Meanings in Ethical Discourse," *Twentieth Century Philosophy*, Dagobert D. Runes, ed. (New York, Philosophical Library, Inc., 1947).
[24] A. J. Ayer, *Philosophical Essays* (New York, St Martin's Press, Inc., 1954). *Cf.* the essay, "Analysis of Moral Judgements."

or not. It is clear that the moral judgment made in such a situation is meaningless, when looked at in this light. There is nothing in the order of factual experience to which it can be referred. At the most it can only be a subjective expression of distaste to say that the act was morally wrong. Or it can be interpreted as a command not to act in such a way, which command would be based on one's disinclination to be a like subject of such an act on another dark and rainy night.

In his article entitled "A Critique of Theology," A. J. Ayer begins by noting that among philosophers, at least, it is generally conceded that the traditional proofs for the existence of God in the ordinary theological sense are of no value. The basic reason for the deficiency of these arguments is that any argument is only as strong as the premises from which it proceeds. But the conclusion of any argument pretending to demonstrate the existence of God is a conclusion drawn from premises which are only probable. Therefore, it follows that such a conclusion can be only probable. This, Ayer claims, is obvious enough. If the premises are based on experience, they are subject to all the uncertainties and probabilities of all such experiential assertions. As we have already seen, experience is boundless, and any future experience may well produce facts which change the whole picture of past experience. We can never have a thoroughly complete experience. Hence the assertions we make based on the limited experience open to us are necessarily limited and relative and, therefore, only probable. Neither do we gain anything in the way of certainty by fleeing to a priori propositions. These are tautologies, and consequently lack all capacity to assert anything meaningful of the real order.

Let us look for a moment at one of the traditional arguments advanced to demonstrate the existence of God. It is asserted that finality exists in nature. The argument then proceeds to demonstrate the necessary existence of an ultimate final cause to explain the fact of order in nature. This final cause is then termed God. Briefly put, the argument states that God exists because order exists in nature. But then, states Ayer, the proposition: *God exists* means nothing more than this: *Order exists in nature*. As dubious as the second proposition is, even if we grant its truth, the first proposition, *God exists*, can mean no more than what is signified by the second. The only experiential reference the second proposition can have is a supposed order of events in experience. This is also the only experiential reference the first proposition can have. Therefore, it is obvious that the two propositions have exactly the same meaning. If one wants to say that God exists and means no more than this by the statement, Ayer sees no real difficulty with the statement. But it hardly enables one to state that what he means by God is the traditional supra-sensible being of traditional theism. To mean more than what can be experientially verified by any statement is to go into metaphysics. And by this time it should be clear that metaphysics is meaningless.

The position taken here by Logical Empiricism is quite different both from Agnosticism and Atheism. The Agnostic is willing to grant that such a being as God may exist. He simply isn't able to prove such a statement, nor is he able to disprove it. Hence philosophical Agnosticism may go hand in hand with faith in the existence of such a divine being. Atheism, on the other hand, claims that it can disprove positively the proposition, *God exists*. It asserts that it can demonstrate the metaphysical impossibility of the existence of a God. Logical Positivism takes neither position. It simply asserts that the statement, *God exists*, is without any significance. It may be an expression of emotion, it may be wishful thinking, it may be lyrical poetry, but philosophically such a proposition is without meaning.

The difficulty here, of course, is the theory of knowledge already assumed by Logical Positivism. Where propositions are meaningful only when they can ultimately be referred to direct experience, then any proposition which cannot be so referred can have no possible significance. In a logic in which all terms are necessarily univocal such a proposition as *God Exists* can mean only what the premise means on which it is based. But the premise is meaningful only in terms of concrete experience. Therefore, the so-called conclusion is either meaningless, or it is asserting the identical thing asserted by the premise in different words. Even the traditional metaphysicians admit that all we know about God is acquired from sense experience. What other meaning can God have for the human mind, then, except what that mind discovers in sense experience?

If one allows that it is impossible to define God in intelligible terms, then one is allowing that it is impossible both for a sentence to be significant and to be about God.[25]

Recent Developments in Analytic Philosophy

As was previously mentioned, Logical Empiricism is still in a state of transition both in this country and in Great Britain. British philosophers, and especially those at Oxford, have rejected the logical atomism of Russell and the early Wittgenstein. The present tendency is to deny that sentences and propositions can be reduced to basic facts in the real order. The clarification of language has itself become the end rather than the means to an end. Meaning has more and more come to refer to linguistic usage. It is no longer conceived as pointing beyond itself, but as referring simply to the function that terms have in a proposition. Thus metaphysics, as an explanation of the real—even if that real is only experienceable—has come to be regarded as completely impossible. Language and thought are synonymous, and philosophy consists only in clarifying thought by clarifying the way terms are used.

It is interesting to note in this regard what has happened to the verification principle. Due to an ever increasing pressure on the part of its adversaries, the verification principle is no longer regarded as a universal criterion. The principle originally stated that no proposition is true, unless it can be verified in experience. The modification was soon made that "experience" here meant conceivable experience rather than actual experience. More recently still it has been denied that the principle could ever have been universal, since this would immediately give it a metaphysical status. Hence the principle can refer only to individual propositions taken singly, and even then verification can only mean determining the meaning of the terms employed. This meaning in turn can be decided not by referring these terms to

[25] A. J. Ayer, "Critique of Theology," in J. L. Jarrett, Jr., and S. M. McMurrin, *op. cit.*

something beyond the proposition, but by understanding their function within the proposition itself.

This development has shifted the discussions somewhat, of course. If language is not meant to express anything about reality, but is to derive its meaningfulness from its own intrinsic relationships, then these relationships were bound to be the object of main interest. Here, of course, new problems began to arise. Wittgenstein in his later works took the position that what he had said or written was no longer meaningful in the old sense of the term. What did "meaningful" mean then? There were those who asked whether meaning could really be communicated. Hence the problem of Solipsism has been and remains a real one in contemporary analytic philosophy.[26]

CRITICISM OF PRAGMATISM

Experiential Verification of Values

No one would deny that the appeal to experience is a valuable one, at least in certain cases. Certainly both Aristotle and St. Thomas realized the importance and even the necessity of sense experience in regard to knowledge. Each made it the indispensable starting point of any philosophical or scientific knowledge. And certainly where verification in sense experience is possible, such reference to the experiential order is both important and necessary. This is the method employed constantly by the natural sciences, and it has produced an exactitude which is the glory of those sciences. Pragmatism, however, seems to proceed on two unverified assumptions. The first is that this method of the natural sciences can be applied to and employed by a theory that deals primarily with values. The Pragmatist states that a concept or theory will be true and will be meaningful in so far as this concept or theory is proved workable or beneficial. This is obviously an attempt to include the norm of utility in the verifica-

---

[26] For a clear discussion of the origin and present status of analytic philosophy, cf. J. O. Urmson, *Philosophical Analysis* (Oxford, The Clarendon Press, 1958).

tion process. And this is immediately to go beyond the goals determined by the method of the natural sciences. The scientist is not as such interested in the utility or workability of his theories. He is not interested in what good such theories may produce. In fact, there may be and often are bad effects as well as good. The scientist is indifferent to both. His verification process considers only whether the theory fits the facts of experience or not. But the Pragmatist would go further. He wants to include the concept of value, and he makes this concept the ultimate criterion of truth and meaning. One can very well ask here by what objective reference to experience can the value of a certain concept or proposition be determined?

Assumption of Kantian Theory of Knowledge

The second assumption which the Pragmatist makes is that the Kantian theory of knowledge is true. For like Kant the Pragmatist professes to know only the appearances of things. He deals with phenomena and functions, and professes a complete inability to transcend the appearances in his knowledge of things. Hence the tendency is toward Sensism and Subjectivism. And this Subjectivism is manifested in the whole theory of utility and workability which Pragmatism sets up as the criterion of truth. For it is clear that the norm of utility and workability will very possibly differ from individual to individual, from society to society. What the Agnostic considers beneficial will not seem so to the Rationalist. What is workable in a communistic society may very well be considered impossible to a democratic one. The best that can result from such a theory is a complete Relativism which must ultimately be unable to decide any question except in terms of the individual or of a given social system.

Inadequate Criterion of Truth

Let us take a further look at this pragmatic criterion of truth. We might very well ask, What of propositions which are discovered to be neither practically advantageous nor disadvantageous? Consider a proposition like this: The king of Ethiopia

carries an ivory sceptre. Certainly the proposition is either true or
false. Yet what benefit or utility is there for the ordinary American citizen in the verification of such a proposition? Yet obviously
the proposition has meaning. It seems very difficult to say that the
meaningfulness involved is determined by the workability of the
proposition. It seems that in regard to such inconsequential truths
the criterion proposed by the Pragmatist is of little or no value in
determining the meaning or truth of the proposition.

We can further inquire as to how often a proposition must be
referred to experience before one can decide whether it is true
or not. Certainly there are scientific propositions, which are held
as true today, which for centuries could not meet the test of
experience. Were they false up to the time of their experiential
verification? Was it not true that the planet Jupiter was in orbit
around the sun, before astronomists were able to plot accurately
its course and verify its position in the heavens? Or take the
formula developed by Einstein in 1906, $E = mc^2$. It was not until
the 1930's that the formula was actually verified by means of the
bombardment of the atom. Yet mathematically it was considered
not only meaningful but true long before that.

Then, if we consider the ideas that actually are verifiable in
experience, what of those that are both beneficial and deleterious?
The idea of immortality has its compensating features. It can
make life more interesting and give it deeper meaning than otherwise it would have. But it also includes the possibility of an
unhappy eternity. Fear, doubt, and disturbance are also contained
in it. Is its utility and advantageousness, then, merely a matter of
emphasis? And can the person who concentrates on the en-
nobling and useful side of the idea entirely ignore the darker
consequences which it also entails? It would seem that one who
accepts the idea as true does so for other reasons than merely
practical and experiential ones. Or take the proposition, study is
good. Certainly various reasons both for and against the truth
of the proposition can be adduced. Experientially, too, the proposition can be verified both ways. Along with the progress in knowledge, the perfection of intelligence, the gaining of respect from
one's colleagues go also the time consuming effort, the lack of
sleep, the missing of other enjoyable activities, etc. Again the

meaningfulness and truth of such a proposition seem to require a standard of judgment which goes beyond mere usefulness or experience. And, of course, there is always the problem of the perfect imitation. How is one to judge which is the true picture, which the imitation, when both give the same satisfaction?

Truth and Consistency

The consistency theory of truth espoused by Pragmatism also has its difficulties. According to this theory each truth must be judged in accord with all the other truths of experience. It must be consistent with all else, before it can be accepted as meaningful and true. But experience is constantly providing us with new truths and new meanings. A complete experience is an impossible term, which no man can ever reach. Hence truth, too, becomes an impossible term which no one can ever attain in its plenitude. Truth, then, is necessarily relative; it necessarily looks toward new experience and consequently toward the possibility of having to restate itself, reform itself, renew some facts of itself and reject others. There is no truth of our experience which does not stand in danger of being revised or even rejected tomorrow. But is this really true? If it is, then the Pragmatist is in the rather awkward position of stating that it is unchangeably true that all truth is changeable. But, if that is true, then it is also true that not all truth is changeable. But even in the order of everyday experience, we find some truths that we know are not changeable in relation to future experience. There are all sorts of these. It is true, for example, that the sun rose this morning. No future experience will ever change that fact of experience. It is true that I am sitting here typing this manuscript at present. Future facts will not modify or alter that in any way. There are literally thousands of such propositions that we can formulate which are unalterably true, which no further experience will in any way modify. That there are some inadequate truths possessed by us, which will be modified by future experience, means simply that human insight is neither exhaustive nor complete in all cases. But to deny that it can never reach certain knowledge of any part of reality at any time is certainly going beyond the evidence at hand.

Pragmatism furthermore seems to state that all true beliefs are good in the sense of being advantageous. This would seem to follow, if the truth of a belief is determined by its beneficial effects. But to say that a true belief is good, indicates a preformulated theory of what is good. Is this theory of what is good derived from experience or not? If it is not, then the whole theory of truth is based upon a rationalistic assumption of the meaning of good. If it is gotten from experience, then it hardly seems an adequate norm. For certainly there are truths which are not practically beneficial. Suffering can in certain cases be good, even when such suffering is to all intents and purposes practically useless. Again there are beliefs which are held as true which impose rigid discipline and self denial on those who accept them. Consider the belief that it is good to defend one's country in time of war. The acceptance of such a belief quite often imposes the sacrifice of all that a given individual may regard as good, so that there are no apparent experiential advantages at all. Is such a belief true or not? We can ask the question in another way. If a belief is true in so far as it works, or is good, is it also true to say that what works is necessarily right? If pragmatism agrees to this, then might will very well turn out to be right, and we can justify any conqueror who ever rode the face of the earth.

Inadequate Concept of Religion

With regard to religion, Pragmatism—especially the Pragmatism of John Dewey—chooses to regard religion as a complex of fears, hopes, and dreams. It regards God as a projection of man's idealism and religious ceremonies and rites as a mere human expression of some sense of the mysterious and unknown. Religion in modern times seems to Dewey to be little more than a sophisticated version of a more primitive form of dance and incantation ceremony practiced in the torch lit villages of savage peoples. But this is hardly what any intelligent person means by religion. As we have previously seen, there is evidence in nature itself of something that is not merely of the same order of the physical things which surround us. No Naturalist or Pragmatist has ever succeeded in explaining mind in naturalistic or pragmatic terms. The only possible explanation is in terms of the lyric leap called emergent evolution, and we have already seen what heavy difficulties are involved in such a pseudo explanation. The evidence for spirit is in the world of physical nature, and the attempt to ignore it or reduce it to matter is nothing else but a forcing of evidence into preconceived and preassumed positions. Causality is a fact of experience, and it is totally explicable only in terms of an ultimate and absolute cause.

Once we realize this, then the realization also comes that it is perfectly possible for such a cause to have revealed truths which men are incapable of attaining by their natural powers. The question then is whether or not such a revelation has actually taken place. And the evidence for the historicity and validity of such a revelation is there for all men of good will to read. The evidence is more weighty and more clear than is the evidence for many an historical incident which the same people accept without question. This is not the place to enter into an historical justification of the claims made for a supernatural revelation, but the evidence is such that it can hardly be brushed aside as a mere expression of human hopes and fears. In the light of such a revelation religion becomes a highly reasonable and intelligent act of man. To assent intellectually to truths which are given to man by an infallible first cause can hardly be called mere wishful thinking. And when these truths are compared to those attained by the noblest minds in history without the help of revelation, they are seen not only to conform to what is considered best in human thought, not only to prescribe norms and standards of action which are completely noble and perfective of human nature, but also to surpass by far the purely human gropings of natural philosophy. It is intelligent to assent to the proposition that God necessarily exists. It is intelligent to accept the evidence that the soul is spiritual and therefore immortal. And it is the complement and perfection of intelligence to recognize and embrace a final truth, which is none-the-less true for having been revealed to man by the first truth. Reason made perfect by revelation is man's highest achievement on this earth. It requires no rejection of evidence, no forcing of evidence into a preconceived system, but, on the contrary, explains the available evidence better than it could otherwise be explained. The assent of religious faith is the highest and most intelligent act that man is capable of, that act in which he most perfectly finds his humanity and most perfectly realizes on this earth the dignity and perfection of his being.

CRITICISM OF LOGICAL EMPIRICISM

Logical Empiricism is basically a radical Sensism attempting to reach certain knowledge by using what it considers the only possible method, the method of natural science. It has a Kantian background in so far as it recognizes along with Kant the inadequacy of purely a priori judgments and turns to experience as the ultimate touchstone of all certain knowledge. It does, however, reject the Kantian synthetic a priori solution to the problem of knowledge and tries to explain and clarify the meaning and the truth of propositions by means of linguistic analysis. In a sense this is its strongest point. No one would deny that such an analytical method can and does clarify meanings. On the other hand the method itself is also Logical Empiricism's greatest weakness. One can ask whether philosophical propositions can really be reduced to ordinary language. Has not a philosophical terminology been built up precisely because ordinary language was found to be inadequate to carry the burden of exact philosophical thought? To attempt to clarify at least some philosophical propositions by reducing them to everyday language is, as F. Copleston remarks, akin to making the village postman the ultimate norm of philosophical meanings.[27] One can also doubt that a univocal mathematical logic is adequate to solve the difficulties. It would seem that reality is richer than that. And the language which expresses our contact with the real has, if not all, at least some of the complexities of that reality. There are univocal terms, of course. But it is difficult to see how all terms can be univocal. And to dismiss analogy as vagueness and confusion is also to dismiss from consideration some of the more complex problems which reality presents and which it is the job of the philosopher to solve.

[27] F. Copleston, S.J., *Contemporary Philosophy* (Westminster, Md., The Newman Press, 1956).

Neither does it seem that Logical Empiricism is simply able to dismiss the difficulty. Many of the terms which Empiricists use remain analogous. To cite just one instance. When the Logical Positivist states that a metaphysical proposition is a poetic statement and nothing more, certainly he is using the word, poetic, in an analogous sense. It should be sufficiently clear that a statement like "the causal proposition is universally valid" can hardly be called poetry in the same sense that "Margaret, are you grieving over Goldengrove unleaving" is called poetry.

Knowledge vs. Predictability

Secondly, when a Logical Empiricist speaks of determining the meaning of a statement by linguistic analysis and discovering its truth through verification in experience, he seems to be speaking primarily of statements which can be shown to be meaningful and true in order that they may be predictive of future events. But predictability is not the only thing at stake here. It is true that many of the propositions formulated by the natural sciences are predictive propositions. The scientist who has discovered the proportions of hydrogen and oxygen necessary to form water can also predict that, when these same proportions are used in the future, water will again result. But there is more to science, and especially to philosophical science, than predictability. Both scientist and philosopher are looking for explanations of how things got to be what they are here and now and why they operate as they do. Explanation means something different, of course, in each area. For the philosopher explanation means an understanding of the real in terms of its ontological content and structure. It strives to express the radical intelligibility of things with regard to the ultimate principles both intrinsic and extrinsic, which constitute them in being. It is not the same with explanation as it is understood in the natural sciences. In this area being is supposed, but it is not the explanation of the being of the thing which is the goal. The scientist seeks to explain the events and characteristics which he can observe and to reduce these events to a coherent and intelligible system. His concern is much more with the phenomena and their inter-relationships than it is with essences or substances in the philosophical sense. This explanation of how events take place, of how the phenomena are related, may take two forms. It may, first of all, be an ontological explanation in the sense that through observation and experiment the scientist is able to isolate the real factor or factors that are responsible for the events in question. In this instance ontological means something measurable and observable, which is seen as radically responsible for the activity with which the scientific investigation began. In this case the real is a quantified real capable of being known through the methods proper to natural science. There may be something more radical behind the quantity, but to the scientist this can only be some unknown X. Neither is he really concerned with this.

On the other hand, scientific investigation may very well lead to the realization that there are elements in reality which are at the source of the observable happenings, but which themselves cannot be isolated by experiment nor brought into the realm of the observable. The scientist knows they are there, but he cannot know what their reality is like. Hence, he constructs a sign or a symbol which stands for such realities, and it is this symbol which he then uses in place of the reality itself. This knowledge is called a constructural knowledge as opposed to an ontological knowledge, as above described. Such constructs play a large part in modern science, and it is a part which becomes increasingly important as the science in question becomes more and more mathematicized. Such symbols remain grounded in the real, although they do not really express the reality itself. Nevertheless, they do express some intelligible grasp of the constancy behind observable happenings and to this extent they express the universality with which science deals.

There are, of course, other views of the nature of scientific explanation.[28] Some of these are not as realistic as the one dis-

---

[28] For a more complete discussion of this whole problem, the student is referred to the following works: J. Maritain, *The Degrees of Knowledge*, new translation under the supervision of Gerald B. Phelan (London, Geoffrey Bles, Ltd., 1959), pp. 21-70, 136-201. C. E. M. Joad, *Guide to Thought* (London, Faber and Faber, Ltd., 1944). Sir J. Jeans, *The New Background of Science* (London, Cambridge University Press, 1934). A. C. Crombie, *Robert Grosseteste and the Origins of Experimental Science* (Oxford, The

cussed above. According to them a scientific theory is simply an attempt to correlate scientific concepts, which are already abstractions from things. Such correlations are considered valid, if they maintain an internal consistency. It is this logical consistency in which science is interested and not in any thing-in-itself. Some scientists, like Eddington and Jeans, will further maintain that the very meaning of the terms used is derived from their function in the theory and not from any objective reality. This seems to be true of mathematics and of mathematical-physics, where the notions and concepts used have meaning and validity only with reference to the system which embraces them. In these instances a given theory could not be proved to be the one which explains the real as it is. Any evidence might turn up tomorrow which would invalidate the theory and no longer make it internally consistent. There is also the possibility that different theories, which are mutually contradictory, might be equally valid in explaining the situation under consideration. Such a theory, then, is possible in so far as it contains no internal contradictions or inconsistencies and enables the scientist to work with it and to express it in mathematical formulas.

Yet even here it seems that explanation involves much more than mere predictability. There is a search for meaning and intelligibility, and it is not denied that such intelligibility is ultimately grounded in the real. The scientist may pay no attention to this real; he may think it is not able to be apprehended as it is; he may deal only with his own intellectual formulations and their inter-relationships; but he will also realize that beyond the formulations and the abstract intelligibilities and mathematical symbols there is a reality, which he cannot get at scientifically. What the nature of such a reality may be is not his to ask. But this does not mean that no one can ask the question and attempt to find an answer. Now the very asking of such a question is obviously going to lead one into metaphysics, and the Logical Positivist has already outlawed such excursions into what is considered a no man's land of meaningless and barbarous entangle-

Clarendon Press, 1953). A. S. Eddington, *The Nature of the Physical World* (London, Cambridge University Press, 1929). J. O. Wisdom, *Foundations of Inference in Natural Science* (London, Methuen and Co., Ltd., 1952).

ments. But it is well to note that the metaphysics against which
the Logical Empiricists rebelled was the idealistic and rationalistic
metaphysics of Hegel, Spinoza, and Berkeley. There is a distinction and a vital one that must be made between Rationalistic
Idealism and a metaphysics which brings one into contact with
the real. Yet from this sort, too, the Logical Empiricist has already
cut himself off. There is implicit in much of the theorizing about
knowledge the Kantian assumption that the human mind can only
know *sense data*. This so-called sense data is nothing else but
the subjective impressions which things make upon the observer.
In fact, for many Logical Empiricists things themselves are only
various collections of sense data. Along with the rejection of the
Kantian a priori synthetic judgments there is also a rejection
of any real knowledge of things and even of the things themselves. Knowledge, in turn, is limited to a subjective Sensism
which one is then forced to express in simple and univocal terms
so that discourse may be made meaningful. But then one might
reasonably ask by what right knowledge is so limited by the
Logical Empiricist? Surely, there is the suspicion here that one is
throwing out the baby with the bathwater; for it seems that all
metaphysics is denounced because of the difficulties in rationalistic
and idealistic metaphysics. The case for the inadequacy of metaphysics is itself inadequate.

One could object in much the same way to the charge that
the problems of metaphysics are pseudo-problems. Questions such
as, Is there a necessary first cause? Is the soul immortal? Is the
causal proposition universally valid?, seem to be valid enough
and have seemed so to many people for a considerable time. One
does not solve a problem simply by denying that the problem
exists nor does the so-called solution have a great deal of value
when it stems from a theory of knowledge which takes for granted
that all propositions which transcend sense experience are meaningless. The question which C. E. M. Joad asks in his *Critique
of Logical Positivism* is very much in place here. What precise
metaphysical problems has Logical Positivism solved? What have
linguistic analysis and the empirical method accomplished in
actually convincing people that the metaphysical questions which
they ask and have been asked for centuries are meaningless?

Again it would seem that the Logical Empiricist dismisses the problem rather than offers a solution.

The Verification Principle

We have already seen what an important place the verifiability principle holds in the teachings of Logical Empiricism. There is a sense, certainly, in which such empirical verification has a necessary function in philosophy. According to both Aristotle and St. Thomas all knowledge starts with experience of sensible being. Existing sensible effects are starting points and necessary reference points in which the conclusions drawn from them and about them are grounded. The proposition, a necessary Being exists, is verifiable in the sense that it is the only possible explanation of why contingent, sensible beings exist. The proposition, the human soul is spiritual and immortal, is grounded in and verified by certain experienceable activities, which otherwise are inexplicable. It is quite clear, however, that this is not what Logical Empiricists mean when they state that a proposition has no meaning, unless it can be verified in sense experience. The proposition, God exists, or The soul is immortal, can have meaning only if somehow one can conceive possible sensible circumstances in which the exact propositions can be empirically verified. And since by definition and agreement such verification is impossible, the propositions can at the most be accepted as poetry or emotion.

But there are difficulties here, also. How can sense experience, which after all is the only possible form of knowledge open to man, possibly state that there is nothing beyond sense experience? What does sense experience know but sense experience? The answer is clearly—nothing. What can sensation proclaim about what is or is not possibly beyond the reach of sensation? The answer again is—nothing. Nor can the principle itself be verified. If one makes the statement: Only that which can be verified sensibly is true, how is one able to determine that the statement itself is true? Certainly such a universal statement cannot be verified in sense experience. The statement itself is a metaphysical statement and quite incapable of experiential verification. It is another of the pure assumptions of Logical Empiricism.

Need for Analogy

Furthermore, as has been already pointed out, the situation is not helped especially by reducing ethical statements and statements about God to poetry and expressions of emotion. If it is merely an expression of emotion or of wishful thinking to say that lying is morally evil, then this is certainly to use the word emotional in an analogous sense. It is certainly not emotional in the same way that a cry of pain or grief is. Nor, as we have seen, do people mean the same thing when they say that God exists, or that a necessary Being exists, as they do when they say that contingent beings exist. The first statement explains the second and it is not nor is it meant to be identical with the second. It is true, as Professor Ayer points out, that our propositions are formed from direct experience with sensible objects, but this does not mean that such propositions cannot refer to anything beyond the sensible. All that it means is that they cannot refer univocally to anything not material and sensible. Here again the refusal of the Logical Empiricist to admit anything like analogy in the predication of terms necessarily restricts him to the sensible order. St. Thomas is able to avoid the difficulty precisely because he recognizes that, while the names we use are taken from sensible experience, at the same time they can be predicated of that which transcends the sensible. For the sensible object can only possesss such perfection as signified by the name sensibly. The non-sensible and immaterial will possess the same perfection but also in accord with its non-sensible and immaterial nature. In the *Summa Theologica*, Aquinas asks whether God can be known by us in this life. He writes:

Our knowledge begins from sense. Hence our natural knowledge can go as far as it can be led by sensible things. But our intellect cannot be lead by sense so far as to see the essence of God; because sensible creatures are effects of God which do not equal the power of God, their cause. Hence from the knowledge of sensible things the whole power of God cannot be known; nor therefore can His essence be seen. But because they are His effects and depend on their cause, we can be led by them so far as to know of God whether He exists, and to know of Him what must necessarily belong to Him, as the first cause of all things, exceeding all things caused by Him.[29]

And again in the following question, article 2, he states:

. . . these names signify the divine substance and are predicated substantially of God, although they fall short of representing Him. Which is proved thus. For these names express God, so far as our intellects know Him. Now since our intellect knows God from creatures, it knows Him as far as creatures represent Him. But it was shown above that God prepossesses in Himself all the perfections of creatures, being Himself absolutely and universally perfect. Hence every creature represents Him, and is like Him, as far as it possesses some perfection: yet not so far as to represent Him as something of the same species or genus, but as the excelling source of whose form the effects fall short, although they derive some kind of likeness thereto, even as the forms of inferior bodies represent the power of the sun. . . .

Therefore the aforsesaid names signify the divine substance, but in an imperfect manner, even as creatures represent it imperfectly. So when we say, God is good, the meaning is not, God is the cause of goodness, or, God is not evil; but the meaning is, Whatever good we attribute to creatures pre-exists in God, and in a higher way. Hence it does not follow that God is good because He causes goodness; but, rather, on the contrary, He causes goodness in things because He is good. As Augustine says, Because He is good, we are.[30]

Logical Empiricism has arbitrarily narrowed the field of the knowable. It has further arbitrarily limited the means and the method by which knowledge can be acquired. There is no knowledge which is not scientific knowledge, and by science is meant natural empirical science. As we have seen, these statements themselves transcend the possibility of verification in the realm of empirical science. As a philosophy, therefore, it is necessarily inadequate. Logical Empiricism destroys philosophy by reducing it to a mere method, useful, perhaps, for clarifying the statements of science but forever incapable of any insights proper to itself.

[29] St. Thomas Aquinas, *Summa Theologica*, Anton C. Pegis, ed. (New York, Random House, Inc., 1945), I 12, 12.
[30] *Ibid.*

SUMMARY

Pragmatism

Pragmatism is for the most part just as this-worldly as Naturalism, although here and there—notably in Peirce and James—one finds a willingness to accept the possibility of a reality which transcends mere sensible experience. The only key at hand, however, to an understanding of such a reality—if there be one —is that of the pragmatic method. This is basically a norm of expediency and usefulness in practice, so that ideas are given meaningfulness and truth depending on how they affect the daily working out of one's hopes and ideals.

Logical Positivism

Logical Positivism hopes to show through an analysis of language and the principle of verifiability that metaphysics and ethics has all been a great mistake, based solely on confusions in the use of language. The aim of philosophy is simply to clarify what is confused and obscure. And what has been confused and obscure up to now is language. Metaphysics has fed on this confusion. To eliminate the confusion, therefore, is necessarily to eliminate metaphysics. The means to accomplish this are linguistic analysis and the scientific method.

Criticism

1. PRAGMATISM
   a. The appeal to experience can be a valid one, but it can never be the only criterion of truth.
   b. Pragmatism proceeds from two unverified assumptions: the method of the natural sciences is capable of judging values; the Kantian theory of knowledge is correct.
   c. There are propositions which are true or false which cannot be pragmatically verified.

d. There are other propositions which were true before they were pragmatically verified.

e. Total consistency is inadequate as a norm of truth because there are truths we are certain of before they are related to the whole body of truth. In some cases such total consistency is impossible to discover, but this merely points to the limitations of the human intellect, not to its inability to acquire any truth.

f. Pragmatism presupposes a speculative theory of what "good" means.

g. Pragmatism ignores the rational basis found in experience for asserting the existence of God and the meaningfulness of of religion.

2. LOGICAL POSITIVISM

a. Linguistic analysis can be helpful at times in clarifying meanings, but it can also obscure meanings by reducing to confused language the terminology built up by philosophy to achieve more exact expression and understanding.

b. The Logical Positivist rejects analogy, yet continues to use terms analogously in his explanations.

c. Logical Positivism tends to reduce all science to propositions which are predictive of future events. There is more to science than this.

d. The verifiability principle is itself a metaphysical statement about the nature of true knowledge and cannot itself be verified experientially.

SELECTED READINGS

What Pragmatism Means*

The pragmatic method is primarily a method of settling metaphysical disputes that otherwise might be interminable. Is the world one or many?—fated or free?—material or spiritual?—here

* William James, "What Pragmatism Means," in *Problems in American Civilization*, (Boston, D. C. Heath & Co., 1957).

are notions either of which may or may not hold good of the
world; and disputes over such notions are unending. The pragmatic method in such cases is to try to interpret each notion by
tracing its respective practical consequences. What difference
would it practically make to anyone if this notion rather than that
notion were true: If no practical difference whatever can be traced,
then the alternatives mean practically the same thing, and all dispute is idle. Whenever a dispute is serious, we ought to be able
to show some practical difference that must follow from one side
or the other's being right. . . .

Pragmatism represents a perfectly familiar attitude in philosophy, the empiricist attitude, but it represents it, as it seems to
me, both in a more radical and in a less objectionable form than
it has ever yet assumed. A pragmatist turns his back resolutely and
once for all upon a lot of inveterate habits dear to professional
philosophers. He turns away from abstraction and insufficiency,
from verbal solution, from bad a priori reasons, from fixed principles, closed systems, and pretended absolutes and origins. He
turns towards concreteness and adequacy, towards facts, towards
action, and towards power. That means the empiricist temper reg-
nant and the rationalist temper sincerely given up. It means the
open air and possibilities of nature, as against dogma, artificiality,
and the pretense of finality in truth.

At the same time it does not stand for any special results.
It is a method only. But the general triumph of that method
would mean an enormous change in what I called in my last
lecture the 'temperament' of philosophy. Teachers of the ultra-
rationalistic type would be frozen out, much as the courtier type
is frozen out in republics, as the ultramontane type of priest is
frozen out in protestant lands. Truth, for him, becomes a class-
name for all sorts of definite working-values in experience. For
the rationalist it remains a pure abstraction, to the bare name
of which we must defer. When the pragmatist undertakes to
show in detail just why we must defer, the rationalist is unable to
recognize the concretes from which his own abstraction is taken.
He accuses us of denying truth; whereas we have only sought to
trace exactly why people follow it and always ought to follow it.
Your typical ultra-abstractionist fairly shudders at concreteness:

other things equal, he positively prefers the pale and spectral. If the two universes were offered, he would always choose the skinny outline rather than the rich thicket of reality. It is so much purer, clearer, nobler. . . .

Metaphysics has usually followed a very primitive kind of quest. You know how men have always hankered after unlawful magic, and you know what a great part in magic words have always played. If you have his name, or the formula of incantation that binds him you can control the spirit, genie, afrite, or whatever the power may be. Solomon knew the names of all the spirits, and having their names, he held them subject to his will. So the universe has always appeared to the natural mind as a kind of enigma, of which the key must be sought in the shape of some illuminating or power-bringing word or name. That word names the universe's principle, and to possess it is after a fashion to possess the universe itself. 'God,' 'Matter,' 'Reason,' 'the Absolute,' 'Energy,' are so many solving names. You can rest when you have them. You are at the end of your metaphysical quest.

But if you follow the pragmatic method, you cannot look on any such word as closing your quest. You must bring out of each word its practical cash value, set it at work within the stream of your experience. It appears less as a solution, then, than as a program for more work, and more particularly as an indication of the ways in which existing realities may be changed.

Theories thus become instruments, not answers to enigmas, in which we can rest. We don't lie back upon them, we move forward, and, on occasion, make nature over again by their aid. Pragmatism unstiffens all our theories, limbers them up and sets each one at work. Being nothing essentially new, it harmonizes with many ancient philosophic tendencies. It agrees with nominalism, for instance, in always appealing to particulars; with utilitarianism in emphasizing practical aspects; with positivism in its disdain for verbal solutions, useless questions and metaphysical abstractions. . . .

See the exquisite contrast of the types of mind! The pragmatist clings to facts and concreteness, observes truth at its work in particular cases, and generalizes.

Pragmatism and Religion*

According to pragmatism, man is a civilizational as well as a biological creature. He both inherits and learns his human nature. The customs, institutions, and traditions of each social group breed habits, outlook, tastes, and attitudes in their immature members which become one with their very being. Human creatures are as social in their natures as the intellectual and moral meanings which flow from their minds, and create their objects of allegiance and devotion. Cultures, moreover, are products of group experiences that have been influenced by factors of time and place and life circumstance. Pragmatists regard culture as one of the fundamental factors in all educational activity. They consider that a program of organized education tends to become an intrusion and an impertinence whenever it seeks to shape the development of the young—without due regard for the patterns of the particular culture and history of which they are a part. They hold that our young, by virtue of their membership in our culture, will necessarily grow up to become Americans; the opportunity of education is to share in the determination of the kind of Americans they shall become.

As we have emphasized, American culture has its distinctive traits, but it is nevertheless an inherent part of Western civilization. The fact that this civilization of the West has often been designated as "Christian" is an evidence of the central place that religion has long held in it. The legends, the symbols, the holy personages, the holy places, the holy days, the music, the paintings, the architecture, the literature, the rituals, the myths, and the faith associated with the Hebraic-Christian tradition are a primary part of the social heritage of Western man. Much of the wisdom that we of the Western world have accumulated from all we have done and undergone is preserved in this religious tradition, and its moral ideals constitute the norms by which we measure the good in human conduct. We shall continue to refine, to revise, and to expand this religious inheritance, but there is small

* John L. Childs, *American Pragmatism and Education* (New York, Holt, Rinehart and Winston, Inc., 1956).

likelihood that we shall ever repudiate it wholesale. In one form or another, we shall continue to transmit the pattern of this inheritance to our young.

The problem, however, of the way in which this tradition shall be communicated to the young is an important one for public education in our country. The fact is that religion in Western civilization is more than an esthetic adornment, or a record of certain phases of human experience, or a venerable form of human association, aspiration, and worship. It is also a system of belief about the origin and the nature of the world, and the origin, the nature, the duties, and the destiny of man. Although many of these beliefs were developed in a prescientific and in a predemocratic period, they are alleged to have a supernatural origin, and hence an authority and a relevance that are of enduring worth. In the life of Western man, these theological beliefs have been intimately associated with the ethic of human brotherhood, and some consider this connection is so inherent that the democratic morality of regard for the worth and dignity of each human being could not survive were this historic framework of religious belief to disintegrate. The perennial philosophic task for those who thus believe that the moral welfare of mankind depends upon the continued acceptance of this system of religious belief is to show how all developments in scientific thought and in human perspective can be harmonized with the essential doctrines of this traditional pattern.

Pragmatism, as a movement in philosophy committed to empirical procedures, signifies a break with this classical conception of the problem and the function of philosophy. It refuses to accept the burden of the apologetic role—a role which so easily degenerates into a form of special pleading and partisan propaganda. In one of his early papers, Peirce pointed out that philosophic thought becomes a "sham" when it is a predetermined "conclusion which determines what the reasoning shall be," and not "the reasoning which determines what the conclusion shall be." He had a deep aversion for any system of thought which pretended to have a regard for truth and which at the same time was willing to block or pervert the process of inquiry in order to maintain the authority of inherited doctrines.

Dewey shared this faith of Peirce in the value of untrammeled inquiry. He found nothing spiritual in any movement which seeks to support traditional beliefs by the restriction of inquiry and the distortion or the suppression of evidence. He was confident that whatever was of worth in our religious heritage could adapt itself to knowledge as it is progressively developed through scientific research. Dewey stated that he had not been able "to attach much importance to religion as a philosophic problem" because this so easily results in a "subordination of candid philosophic thinking to the alleged but factitious needs of some special set of convictions." He also declared that he had "enough faith in the depth of the religious tendencies of men to believe that they will adapt themselves to any required intellectual change." He was convinced that "the great intellectual transformation" which was taking place in Western life called for more drastic reconstruction in religious outlook than many of the contemporary leaders of institutionalized religion were prepared to undertake. He led in the effort to develop an interpretation of religion that would be in harmony with the morality inherent in experimental practice and democratic living.

William James shared the pragmatic view that empirical procedures should be relied upon in all domains of human experience, and he sought to utilize the method of pragmatism in order to develop an empirical interpretation of the nature and the significance of religious experience. His effort to determine the concrete human import of traditional religious beliefs and attitudes aroused wide interest. As we indicated in an earlier discussion, his view of the way in which pragmatic principles and tests could be used to discover the value for human conduct of traditional religious outlooks and doctrines diverged in certain important respects from that of Peirce and Dewey. . . .

Meaning and Verification*

The dividing line between logical possibility and impossibility of verification is absolutely sharp and distinct; there is not a

* Moritz Schlick "Meaning and Verification," *Philosophical Review* (1936).

gradual transition between meaning and nonsense. For either you have given the grammatical rules for verification, or you have not; tertium non datur.

Empirical possibility is determined by the laws of nature, but meaning and verifiability are entirely independent of them. Everything that I can describe or define is logically possible—and definitions are in no way bound up with natural laws. The proposition "Rivers flow uphill" is meaningful, but happens to be false because the fact it describes is physically impossible. It will not deprive a proposition of its meaning if the conditions which I stipulate for its verification are incompatible with the laws of nature; I may prescribe conditions, for instance, which could be fulfilled only if the velocity of light were greater than it actually is, or if the Law of Conservation of Energy did not hold, and so forth.

An opponent of our view might find a dangerous paradox or even a contradiction in the preceding explanations, because on the one hand we insisted so strongly on what has been called the "empirical-meaning requirement," and on the other hand we assert most emphatically that meaning and verifiability do not depend on any empirical conditions whatever, but are determined by purely logical possibilities. The opponent will object: if meaning is a matter of experience, how can it be a matter of definition and logic?

In reality there is no contradiction or difficulty. The word "experience" is ambiguous. Firstly, it may be a name of any so-called "immediate data"—which is a comparatively modern use of the word—and secondly we can use it in the sense in which we speak, e.g., of an "experienced traveller," meaning a man who has not only seen a great deal but also knows how to profit from it for his actions. It is in this second sense (by the way, the sense the word has in Hume's and Kant's philosophy) that verifiability must be declared to be independent of experience. The possibility of verification does not rest on any "experiential truth," on a law of nature or any other true general proposition, but is determined solely by our definitions, as we have explained, and through them verifiability is linked to experience in the first sense of the word. No rule of expression presupposes any law or regularity in the world (which is the condition of "experience" as Hume and Kant use the word), but it does presuppose data and situations, to which names can be attached. The rules of language are rules of the application of language; so there must be something to which it can be applied. Expressibility and verifiability are one and the same thing. There is no antagonism between logic and experience. Not only can the logician be an empiricist at the same time; he must be one if he wants to understand what he himself is doing.

No more difficulty than in the case of the other side of the moon will be found in discussing, as another significant example, the question of "immortality," which Professor Lewis calls, and which is usually called, a metaphysical problem. I take it for granted that "immortality" is not supposed to signify never-ending life (for that might possibly be meaningless on account of infinity being involved), but that we are concerned with the question of survival after "death." I think we may agree with Professor Lewis when he says about this hypothesis: "Our understanding of what would verify it has no lack of clarity." In fact, I can easily imagine, e.g., witnessing the funeral of my own body and continuing to exist without a body, for nothing is easier than to describe a world which differs from our ordinary world only in the complete absence of all data which I would call parts of my own body.

We must conclude that immortality, in the sense defined, should not be regarded as a "metaphysical problem" but is an empirical hypothesis, because it possesses logical verifiability. It could be verified by following the prescription: "Wait until you die!" Professor Lewis seems to hold that this method is not satisfactory from the point of view of science. He says:

"The hypothesis of immortality is unverifiable in an obvious sense. . . . If it be maintained that only what is scientifically verifiable has meaning, then this conception is a case in point. It could hardly be verified by science; and there is no observation or experiment which science could make, the negative result of which would disprove it."

I fancy that in these sentences the private method of verification is rejected as being unscientific because it would apply only to the individual case of the experiencing person himself, whereas a scientific statement should be capable of a general proof, open to any careful observer. But I see no reason why even this should be declared to be impossible. On the contrary, it is easy to describe experiences such that the hypothesis of an invisible existence of human beings after their bodily death would be the most acceptable explanation of the phenomena observed. These phenomena, it is true, would have to be of a much more convincing nature than the ridiculous happenings alleged to have occurred in meetings of the occultists—but I think there cannot be the slightest doubt as to the possibility (in the logical sense) of phenomena which would form a scientific justification of the hypothesis of survival after death, and would permit an investigation by scientific methods of that form of life. To be sure, the hypothesis could never be established as absolutely true, but it shares this fate with all hypotheses. If it should be urged that the souls of the deceased might inhabit some super-celestial space where they would not be accessible to our perception, and that therefore the truth or falsity of the assertion could never be tested, the reply would be that if the words "super-celestial space" are to have any meaning at all, that space must be defined in such a way that the impossibility of reaching it or of perceiving anything in it would be merely empirical, so that some means of overcoming the difficulties could at least be described, although it might be beyond human power to put them into use.

Thus our conclusion stands. The hypothesis of immortality is an empirical statement which owes its meaning to its verifiability, and it has no meaning beyond the possibility of verification. If it must be admitted that science could make no experiment the negative result of which would disprove it, this is true only in the same sense in which it is true for many other hypotheses of similar structure—especially those that have sprung up from other motives than the knowledge of a great many facts of experience which must be regarded as giving a high probability to the hypothesis.

Meanings in Ethical Discourse*

A little reflection suffices to show that the meaning of the term "ethics" is highly ambiguous and that it designates at least

* Herbert Feigl, "Meanings in Ethical Discourse," *Twentieth Century Philosophy*, Dagobert D. Runes, ed. (New York, Philosophical Library Inc., 1947).

five different types of endeavor: (1) Moral "vision," *i.e.*, the recognition, discovery, or "good" way of life or of an uppermost standard of moral evaluation; (2) Moral exhortation, education, and propaganda; (3) Empirical studies of actual moral evaluations, either descriptive or explanatory; (4) The technology of the "good" life—a branch of applied science concerned with the discernment and perfecting of means (instrumental values) in view of certain ends (terminal values); (5) The logical analysis of ethical terms and sentences—either by the casuistic Socratic method or by the elaboration of a hypothetico-deductive system of ethical norms. The five-fold division just outlined is itself a result of the Socratic type of approach. (Quite analogous distinctions apply to aesthetics.)

Ethical norms or imperatives as discovered or intuited in (1), proclaimed and advocated in (2), factually studied in (3), practically implemented in (4), and subjected to a meaning analysis in (5) may be reconstructed as sentences referring to a possible (usually not actualized) state of affairs and expressed with an emotional-motivational appeal. In the use of such terms as "ought," "should," "right," "good," "duty," etc., lies the irreducibly directive component of moral value-judgments. An ethical imperative like the Golden Rule simply means: "Would that everybody behaved toward his fellow men as he expects them to behave toward him." This sentence, having its accent in the emotive appeal, could not possibly be deduced from a knowledge of facts only; it is neither true nor false. It is rather an invitation (suggestion, request, exhortation, or command) to make the contained factual sentence true. In traditional metaphysically or theologically oriented moral philosophies the attempt was made to validate the fundamental standards on the basis of revelation, a priori intuition, or logical proof. Absolute values were thus either concretely specified and dogmatically proclaimed or merely abstractly assumed and their specific content left open. From the logico-empirical point of view all of these approaches involve confusions of meaning or assumptions incapable of test. Absolute values as well as categorical imperatives can be expressed only in emotive language.

Critique of Theology*

It is now generally admitted, at any rate by philosophers, that the existence of a being having the attributes which define the god of any non-animistic religion cannot be demonstratively proved. To see that this is so, we have only to ask ourselves what are the premises from which the existence of such a god could be deduced. If the conclusion that a god exists is to be demonstratively certain, then these premises must be certain; for, as the conclusion of a deductive argument is already contained in the premises, any uncertainty there may be about the truth of the premises is necessarily shared by it. But we know that no empirical proposition can ever be anything more than probable. It is only a priori propositions that are logically certain. But the reason why we cannot deduce the existence of a god from a priori propositions which are certain is that they are tautologies. And from a set of tautologies nothing but a further tautology can be validly deduced. It follows that there is no possibility of demonstrating the existence of a god.

What is not so generally recognized is that there can be no way of proving that the existence of a god, such as the God of Christianity, is even probable. Yet this also is easily shown. For if the existence of such a god were probable, then the proposition that he existed would be an empirical hypothesis. And in that case it would be impossible to deduce from it, and other empirical hypotheses, certain experiential propositions which were not deducible from those other hypotheses alone. But in fact this is not possible. It is sometimes claimed, indeed, that the existence of a certain sort of regularity in nature constitutes sufficient evidence for the existence of a god. But if the sentence "God exists" entails no more than that certain types of phenomena occur in certain sequences, then to assert the existence of a god will be simply equivalent to asserting that there is the requisite regularity in nature; and no religious man would admit that this was all he intended to assert in asserting the existence of a god. He would

---

* Alfred J. Ayer, *Language, Truth and Logic* (New York, Dover Publications, Inc., 1946).

say that in talking about God, he was talking about a transcendent being who might be known through certain empirical manifestations, but certainly could not be defined in terms of those manifestations. But in that case the term "god" is a metaphysical term, then it cannot be even probable that a god exists. For to say that "God exists" is to make a metaphysical utterance which cannot be either true or false. And by the same criterion, no sentence which purports to describe the nature of a transcendent god can possess any literal significance. . . .

It is worth mentioning that, according to the account which we have given of religious assertions, there is no logical ground for antagonism between religion and natural science. As far as the question of truth or falsehood is concerned, there is no opposition between the natural scientist and the theist who believes in a transcendent god. For since the religious utterances of the theist are not genuine propositions at all, they cannot stand in any logical relation to the propositions of science. Such antagonism as there is between religion and science appears to consist in the fact that science takes away one of the motives which make men religious. For it is acknowledged that one of the ultimate sources of religious feeling lies in the inability of men to determine their own destiny; and science tends to destroy the feeling of awe with which men regard an alien world, by making them believe that they can understand and anticipate the course of natural phenomena, and even to some extent control it. The fact that it has recently become fashionable for physicists themselves to be sympathetic towards religion is a point in favour of this hypothesis. For this sympathy towards religion marks the physicists' own lack of confidence in the validity of their hypotheses, which is a reaction on their part from the anti-religious dogmatism of nineteenth-century scientists, and a natural outcome of the crisis through which physics has just passed.

It is not within the scope of this enquiry to enter more deeply into the causes of religious feeling, or to discuss the probability of the continuance of religious belief. We are concerned only to answer those questions which arise out of our discussion of the possibility of religious belief. The point which we wish to establish is that there cannot be any transcendent truths of religion.

For the sentences which the theist uses to express such "truths" are not literally significant. . . .

BIBLIOGRAPHY

Logical Positivism

Ayer, A. J., *Philosophical Essays*. New York, St. Martin's Press, Inc., 1954.

Bergman, Gustav, "Logical Positivism," in Vergilius Ferm, ed., *A History of Philosophical Systems*. New York, Philosophical Library, Inc., 1950.

Blau, J. L., *Men and Movements in American Philosophy*. Englewood Cliffs, N. J., Prentice-Hall, Inc., 1952.

Carnap, R., *Philosophy and Logical Syntax*. London, Kegan Paul, Trench, Truebner & Co., 1935.

Childs, J. L., *American Pragmatism and Education*. New York, Holt, Rinehart and Winston, Inc., 1956.

Copleston, F., S.J., *Contemporary Philosophy*. Westminster, Md., The Newman Press, 1956.

Joad, C. E. M., *A Critique of Logical Positivism*. Chicago, University of Chicago Press, 1950.

Perry, R. B., *Philosophy of the Recent Past*. New York, Charles Scribner's Sons, 1926.

Readings in Contemporary Philosophy, J. L. Jarrett and S. M. McMurrin, eds. New York, Holt, Rinehart and Winston, Inc., 1954.

Library of Living Philosophers, P. A. Schilpp, ed. Evanston, Ill., Northwestern University Press, 1939.

Werkmeister, W. H., *A History of Philosophical Ideas in America*. New York, The Ronald Press Company, 1949.

Works of John Dewey

Dewey, John, *Philosophy and Civilization*. New York, Minton, Balch & Company, 1931.

———, *The Quest for Certainty*. New York, Minton, Balch & Company, 1929.

———, *Essays in Experimental Logic*. Chicago, University of Chicago Press, 1916.

———, *A Common Faith*. New Haven, Conn., Yale University Press, 1934.

———, *How We Think*. Boston, D. C. Heath & Company, 1910.

———, *The Influence of Darwin on Philosophy*. New York, Holt, Rinehart and Winston, Inc., 1910.

———, *Psychology*, 3rd rev. ed. New York, American Book Company, 1891.

——, Logic: Theory of Inquiry. New York, Holt, Rinehart and Winston, Inc., 1938.

Works of Charles Sanders Peirce

Peirce, Charles Sanders, Chance, Love and Logic, ed. with intro. by Morris R. Cohen, and with suppl. essay by John Dewey. New York, George Braziller, Inc., 1956.
——, Collected Paper of Charles Sanders Peirce, Charles Hartshorne and Paul Weiss, eds. Cambridge, Mass., Harvard University Press, 1931.
——, Philosophical Writings of Peirce, J. Buchler, ed. New York, Dover Publications, Inc., 1955.

Works of William James

James, William, The Meaning of Truth. New York, Longmans, Green & Company, 1909.
——, A Pluralistic Universe. New York, Longmans, Green & Company, 1909.
——, Philosophy of William James, Drawn From His Own Works, intro. by Horace M. Kallen. New York, Modern Library, Inc., 1925.
——, Selected Papers on Philosophy. London, J. M. Dent & Sons, Ltd., 1929.
——, Some Problems of Philosophy. New York, Longmans, Green & Company, 1911.
——, The Will To Believe. New York, Longmans, Green & Company, 1903.

5

The Alienation
of Man:
Two Views

EXISTENTIALISM

DURING THE PERIOD after the first world war up until the present
a philosophical movement has arisen and flourished in Europe.
This movement has come to be known as Existentialism. It is an
extremely difficult movement to characterize. The reasons are
many. In the first place Existentialism, as the name implies, is a
philosophy of existence. Now existence can be contacted; it can
be experienced; it can be asserted; but it cannot be defined. The
reason for this is that our minds grasp essences, the intelligibilities
of things. But existence is not an essence. It is that by which an
essence exists. We certainly know the difference between the
merely intelligible and the real, but this reality which makes all
things real, precisely because it is not an intelligibility, cannot be
grasped conceptually as we grasp intelligibilities.

Secondly, a few of the philosophers most responsible for the
spread of the movement refuse to call themselves Existentialists.
One of the reasons for this is undoubtedly that these philosophers
differ from each other so radically at times that they are unwilling to be placed in the same group with their adversaries. For
there are certainly different brands of Existentialism. There is

one type which is professedly atheistic. Another professes a sort of biblical Protestantism. A third is associated to a greater or less extent with Catholicism. A fourth is politely agnostic and skeptical. There are, furthermore, Existentialists who have little or nothing to do with philosophy as such. They associate themselves with the movement, but they are content to restrict their Existentialist writings to the fields of literature, criticism, plays, and novels. Even within the area of philosophy another distinction is possible. There is one type of Existentialism which is openly irrational or anti-intellectual. There is another type which seems to incline more toward Rationalism and Kantianism. There is still a third type which limits itself to an analysis of psychological states, and which will have little or nothing to do with other areas of philosophy.

At the same time, however, there are marked similarities in Existentialist thinking. Certain general lines of agreement can be sketched. The movement has by no means reached its full potentiality, and, as a result, an indication of dominant themes rather than a complete analysis of the philosophy of each Existentialist may at present prove more profitable. The men who are in general responsible for Existentialism include three who may be regarded as initiators and four more who are at present writing and lecturing. Of the first group there is Soren Kierkegaard (1813-55), a Danish philosopher who is primarily a moralist. Kierkegaard was interested in recovering the individuality which he thought had been almost completely lost in modern society. He rebels constantly against the anonymity of the crowd and appeals for an individual decision on the part of the individual person. This saving decision he regards as a free commitment to Christianity. Secondly, there is the German philosopher, Friedrich Nietzsche (1844-1900), who wanted to substitute a new morality for the favored few—the Supermen. There is not a whole lot of similarity between Nietzsche and Kierkegaard, but they do have this much in common—both are interested in freeing men from the deadening influence of a traditional and crowd morality. Thirdly there is Edmund Husserl (1859-1938), the German Phenomenologist. Husserl is important for Existentialism in so far as he provides it with a systematic approach to its problems, an approach which attempts to reconcile essence with existence without returning to a previous Rationalism and without at the same time yielding to a meaningless philosophy of individual existence.

The four present day Existentialists with whose thinking we shall be primarily concerned in this chapter are Jean Paul Sartre (1905-   ), Martin Heidegger (1889-   ), Karl Jaspers (1883-   ), and Gabriel Marcel (1877-   ). The four exemplify pretty well the various types of Existentialistic philosophy now in vogue in Europe. Sartre is openly and frankly atheistic. Marcel, on the other hand, is a believing and convinced Catholic. Jaspers makes much of a philosophic faith in order to transcend the finite order of things. And Heidegger seems equally convinced that the finite modes of being can be transcended, only to encounter a Being which, while distinct from all its finite modes, is still itself finite. Yet despite their dissimilarities they are remarkably alike, and together they have raised Existentialism to the status of a system of philosophy to be reckoned with.

Basically Extentialism is a reaction against Hegel in particular and against all forms of Idealism and Abstractionism in general. If philosophy is supposed to explain reality, then according to the Existentialists it should deal with reality. And it should deal with reality as it is, as it exists, and not with an abstraction or a mere concept of it. Hence, unless one gets into contact with existence, one does not get into contact with the real. This contact with the real is, furthermore, much more than a mere intellectual understanding of it. When we face the real, we react to it in all sorts of ways: intellectually, volitionally, sensibly, and emotionally. These reactions, too, are real, and perhaps more so than the mere things which are there. And here we have an indication of another cardinal point in Existentialism. Previous philosophy has been content merely to investigate the object. It has treated objects abstractly, and such a treatment has pretended that knowing about objects was equivalent to knowing about reality. But the subject is real, too. The reactions of the subject are equally real. Neither can one understand this phase of reality by treating it as if it were just another object among objects.

Subjectivity

This brings us to another important point. The Existentialists insist that the subject must be investigated precisely as subject. This does not mean to imply that the existence of objects is denied or doubted. But subjectivity is the entrance to the object, and one can, perhaps, acquire a better understanding of reality by beginning with the subject than has been acquired by beginning with the object. Hence it is that man and the study of man become all important in Existentialism. For man alone is a subject. He not only exists, as do all other things, but he also ek-sists, as Heidegger says.[1] Man can rise above the mere things about him, know them, refer them to himself and other things, seek their meaning and value, their origin and their end. Man is, as Heidegger calls him, the Shepherd of Being,[2] who becomes aware of being himself and refers all things back to it. Yet it is also possible for man to be unaware of his high calling. He can refuse to ek-sist and can merely exist, as do all the other things about him. He can sink to the level of a thing, a mere object. He can lose himself in the crowd, alienate himself from himself, as the mass of men has succeeded in doing. In his *Works of Love*[3] Soren Kierkegaard paints a startling picture of man in present day society. Man had become a mere cipher, a fractional man who commands no respect, who has lost his individuality and his responsibility. He has succumbed almost completely to the herd instinct, is content with the safety of the crowd, is featureless and indistinct.

It takes only a little reflection on our own present situation to realize how correct Kierkegaard was. The propaganda to which the people of Germany were subjected under Hitler and that to which the peoples of other countries are still being submitted had for its purpose nothing else than to bring about this very

[1] Martin Heidegger, *Sein und Zeit* (Halle, Max Niemeyer Verlag, 1931).

[2] Martin Heidegger, *Über den Humanismus* (Frankfurt-am-Main, Klostermann, 1949).

[3] Soren Kierkegaard, *Works of Love*, trans. by David F. and Lillian M. Swenson (Princeton, N.J., Princeton University Press, 1946).

effect. Everyone knows how well it succeeded in most cases. One could well pause here for a moment to reflect on the soporific effects of mass advertising in this country, of the dictates laid down by fashion, different social groups, different age groups, etc. All this has tremendous effect on men in society, in industry, and in the professions, so that very few are willing or even capable of doing anything but capitulate to a blind following of the herd. It matters little that individuality and free decision are lost. It is unimportant that no one any longer is interested in rebelling against the arbitrary dictates that are laid down for the masses. The herd tramples blindly ahead, and there is simply a fear of being left behind or ostracized. It is this complete capitulation of the individual to the masses, this abdication of individual thought, action, and decision that the existentialist is fighting.

It is from this viewpoint that F. Heineman[4] describes Existentialism as a rebellion against alienation, and he pursues the theme through various philosophies which have succeeded in alienating man in one way or another. Hegel had alienated man from God by regarding him as an externalization of divinity. Marx and Engels had rebelled against man's alienation from economic security and the goods of the earth. The Existentialists feel that modern man has been alienated from himself. Hence they emphasize the need for man to recover his individuality, his selfhood, through subjectivity. All of them find the possibility for such recovery in a free decision made knowingly in a given situation. But they differ radically, of course, in what such a decision means and implies. For Kierkegaard it is a decision really to be a Christian as opposed to calling oneself a Christian. For Heidegger it is a commitment to being. For Sartre it involves the realization that being is an absurdity. From such a realization follows the decision to act responsibly, since the individual alone must bear the full responsibility for his actions. This commitment, of whatever sort it is, brings man into vital contact with existence and raises him up to his true stature above the things which are merely there. Thus it is through self determination, through free choice, that man literally creates his self. He forges

[4] Heineman, F., *Existentialism and the Modern Predicament* (New York, Harper & Brothers, 1953), chap. 1.

his essence, as it were, in the fire of situations which demand of him a commitment one way or another. It is in this sense that his existence is prior to his essence. For man is thrown into existence among the other existing things. Only if he is willing to choose, to decide, to commit himself irrevocably to action can he ever hope to give himself meaning, to realize his possibilities, to determine his individuality.

The Concept of Dread

Now it is precisely in these situations in which he must commit himself that man comes into most profound contact with the real. Such situations often arouse deep feelings and emotions, and these, too, affect man's self determination. In this area the Existentialists have contributed a good deal of real insight and clear analysis. One of the most real of these emotions is dread. It is carefully distinguished from fear. When we are afraid, we are always afraid of something definite. Fear is felt in the presence of a known danger. But dread is felt before the indefinite and the nameless. It is just because one does not know what he fears that he experiences dread. It is a fear of nothing, and simply because it is nothing it is all the more dreadful. This nothingness closes in on man from all sides. All around him things come to an end and are no more. There is a lack, an emptiness, an absence in being which continually shows itself. It is experienced in the non-arrival of an expected friend, in the failure of a hope. According to Sartre it is at the very heart of man himself. Not only can man lose himself, negate himself, but he is continually being reduced to a nonself by the others who know him and in knowing him reduce him to a mere object. The tragedy here is that man is not only a subject. He is also a thing. But he is forever incapable of bringing about a fusion between his selfhood and his objectivity in a world of things. Hence man is a frustration, a being incapable of overcoming the division within himself.

Death

The Existentialists push the concept still further. This nothingness which haunts being is something positive. For Heidegger it helps to bring being into bolder relief. For Sartre it is at the very essence of man and being, turning everything into absurdity. It is for this reason that death, too, is singled out for special consideration. For death is the negation of human existence, and each man marches irrevocably toward his dissolution. But it is not just of death in general that such philosophers speak. This has been precisely the difficulty. People have been unwilling to face death as a personal thing. They say, "One must die." Or, "People die." Or again, "All men are mortal." What the Existentialists insist on is the fact that *I* must die. It is I who must cease to be. There will be an end, not just for men, for people in general, but for me. In the face of such a realization the truth is borne in upon me that I am heading for nothingness, for non-being. Before this startling contact with my own non-being comes the further realization of all my as yet unfilled possibilities. This calls for decision, for commitment, before it is forever too late. I see the necessity of choosing, of determining myself, of fulfilling my latent capacities. No one can with complete awareness face this fact without making an end to detachment, to indifference, to drifting with the crowd. Thus there is opened up for the individual the opportunity for activity, made all the more real now in the presence of final inactivity.

Contingency

But death is not the only phenomenon which recalls to us our finitude and our precarious grasp on existence. There is also chance and fortune to which each man is subject. The most carefully laid plans can be shattered by pure accident. A life most carefully and reasonably lived can be ruined in a moment by a random happening. Nor can any one adequately protect himself against such happenings. We live in a world where chance plays a part, and there is always the possibility that it will play an important part in my life. Nor is this all. There is suffering, too, in all its many forms from which no man is ever free. It presses in upon us and makes us realize how short and uncertain our existence can be. There are threats from without as well as from within. We live in an age of conflict and distrust. The society in which we exist at present has its factors of decay growing within it. And it may be actually threatened from without by other societies which possess different ideologies and conflicting goals.

It is not difficult to see that Existentialism is not merely a rebellion against Idealism and Abstractionism. It is a philosophy which has arisen out of the insecurity and disillusionment of the time itself in which we live. Two world wars in twenty-five years with all the brutality and inhumanity they contained have left an indelible mark on the thought of the European philosopher. The bombings, the concentration camps, the uncertainty of day by day existence have all left men doubtful and distrustful of the very roots from which western civilization has sprung. What good has been accomplished by an analysis of being, by a speculative definition of man as a rational animal, by an abstract theory of morality? None of this has had any effect at all in preventing the horror and the catastrophe through which millions today have passed. Being is not as the Rationalists have defined it. Nor is the man who has lived on the brink of death for years the same as the one defined by the philosophers. A reappraisal is necessary, a new approach to being and man has to be undertaken, if we are ever to understand them as they are and not just as they are abstractly conceived. We live in a time of crisis and have done so for some time. This crisis has brought out new aspects of being and new insights into man. Man can, if he chooses, be an individual; being is not just a world of essences, but a shifting, uncertain, precarious thing which we have so far not really understood. But what, then, is being? What after all is man?

Being and Man

Here, too, the answers differ. Rather, it is, perhaps, more correct to say that the gropings after meaning differ from Existentialist to Existentialist. But there are as always similarities. Jaspers, Heidegger, Sartre, and Marcel all admit a difference between being and man. In the words of Heidegger there are things (*Seinde*), man (*Dasein*), and Being (*Sein*). For Heidegger Being is related to things through man and vice-versa. Heidegger, perhaps, more than anyone else is searching for the meaning of Being in a metaphysical sense. His complaint is that all previous metaphysics has identified Being with beings, and is, as a result, invalid. There is also a common agreement that Being is in some sense, at least, transcendent, although this is not meant to assert that Being is infinite or divine. Being transcends both things and man, but for Heidegger and Sartre it is still finite. Jaspers speaks of an ultimate All-Encompassing (*Umgreifende*), but it would seem that man's only entrée to it is through faith. For Sartre, Being is definitely finite and contingent. It is simply there without distinction or differences in itself. Hence in itself it is absurd. It needs man to interpret it, to put patterns upon it, to refer it to himself and others. Marcel alone identifies Being ultimately with God, who is truly transcendent and infinite.

There is substantial agreement, too, that Being is objective. We get more of it than its mere appearances. There is definitely a reality with which we can and do make contact. According to Jaspers, however, this is impossible through the old dichotomy between subject and object.[5] It is precisely this dichotomy that has rendered metaphysics a science of partial being rather than a science of Being as such. For Being is subjective as well as objective. But metaphysics in speaking about Being in the abstract has reduced the subjective pole to the objective. The problem is a basic and difficult one. A science is expressed in terms of concepts, which are necessarily abstract. These concepts objectify reality; they reduce it to essences; they stratify it and twist it out of the dynamism of the moment. Worse still, any concept of Being as subjective immediately destroys whatever subjectivity was present in the reality. Even when I talk about myself, I talk about myself not as a self, but as a thing. Yet the self is not a thing. It is different in its selfhood from all other things. This selfhood is real; it is being, and must be considered in any adequate treatment of Being. This subjective side of Being, this Being-as-subject, is what has been ignored by the Greeks and all other systems of metaphysics which followed. Being has been investigated only from the viewpoint of Being-as-object; and, how-

[5] Karl Jaspers, *The Way to Wisdom*, trans. by Manheim (New Haven, Conn., Yale University Press, 1951), chap. 3.

ever true such an investigation may have been, it is still partial and inadequate.

Yet even when the difficulty is realized, it still seems insurmountable. How can we possibly investigate the subject in its subjectivity? To speak about it at all is to speak of it in human terminology. This terminology is but an expression of our concepts. But to conceptualize something is to objectify it, to treat it as an essence, an abstraction. And once the subject is made abstract, it is no longer a subject. In an attempt to free himself from the dilemma, Jaspers finally settles for the subjective pole, and it is fairly easy to see how man is finally able to transcend his subjectivity only through faith. For Jaspers ontology is a science only of phenomenal, empirical being. The knowledge that we have of being reaches only to these phenomena. Such a knowledge is necessarily incomplete. For there is more to being than the phenomena. Hence our knowledge must remain open, because there is much more to being than this. There is existence at the root of everything, and this existence is got at from the side of the subject. Yet while we can become aware of existence in the very exercise of it, we cannot know it. For, as we have seen, to know anything is to conceptualize it, to make it into an abstraction. But even the awareness we have of existence is not sufficient. We are only aware of existence in the past, in retrospect. We never grasp it in its existential now. Hence the awareness we have of existence is awareness of possible, not actual, existence. From both sides, then, we are ultimately cut off from a knowledge of Being in itself. There is only one possible solution left. Our awareness of existence as possible points toward Being from the one side, as does the knowledge we possess of Being in its appearances from the other. These appearances of Being are so many signs pointing beyond themselves to Being in itself. The Transcendent is there beyond knowledge and beyond awareness. Everything leads us closer to it, everything assures us that it is just beyond the horizon of our endeavors. Yet there is no knowledgeable way to grasp it. It is here on the boundary of the appearances, on the rim of the phenomena, that man transcends his epistemological limitation in an act of faith in the reality of the All-Encompassing.

Heidegger, on the other hand, seems to lean in the other direction. Being is able to reveal itself to the person who remains open to it. The tendency here is to allow the subject to be absorbed by the object. Yet here, too, transcendence is possible only within the realm of the finite. The Being which reveals itself and with which man makes contact is larger and more inclusive than man, but still a finite Being whose horizon is the world.

Sartre

Yet always the distinction is maintained between Being, man, and beings. This is certainly true of Heidegger, Jaspers, and Marcel. Things are there, at hand, to be used. Somehow it would seem they participate in Being; yet none of them is Being. Each is merely a being, being-in-the-world as opposed to Being-in-itself. Sartre, on the other hand, is content to ignore the transcendence of Being as understood by the others. According to him, Being is divided into the thing-in-itself and the thing-for-itself. The thing-in-itself is completely contingent; it is without meaning; it is simply there. In itself it is, therefore, an absurdity with no reason for its existence or its obtruding presence. An insight into the chaos and meaninglessness of such being can only result in a complete nausea, a flight from the irrationality of things. This being of the thing-in-itself is not transcendent, but it is transmental. It is there, but at the same time we can have no knowledge of it. It presses itself upon us in all its underived contingency and absurdity. Individual existents stand alone, each one a completely unique being existing without cause and without meaning.[6]

Obviously there must be more to Being than just the thing-in-itself. We could not even speak about a universe composed only of absurdities. Hence Sartre introduces the being-for-itself. This is man who is conscious and who is responsible for whatever significance and rational structure the universe possesses. Consciousness is not the being of the In-itself. Hence consciousness is a negation of absurdity, an imposition of the reasonable on the absurd. Yet consciousness, in so far as it is a negation of being-in-itself is also a nothingness. But it is a positive kind of nothing-

[6] Jean Paul Sartre, *La Nausée* (Paris, Librairie Gallimard, 1938).

ness—if such a thing can be conceived—which opposes itself to
being and sets up an order of intelligibilities and rationalizations.
These very intelligibilities are opposed to the absurdity of being-
in-itself; they are a negation of being-in-itself. Man is other than
being-in-itself in so far as he is conscious. Now it is consciousness
which is the distinctive mark of man. Hence Sartre can assert
that man in his very humanity is a nothingness. This nothingness,
this otherness from being, is necessarily temporary. It is a lacuna
in being which being is constantly striving to overcome. And
being-in-itself will win. It will succeed finally in reducing the
otherness to itself, and consciousness will be no more. Man will
be snuffed out like a candle, and eventually absurdity will reign
unchallenged. It is not a very inspiring picture, to say the least.

Yet this march of absurdity does not go on unchallenged.
Man realizes the situation, for he is himself a being-in-itself as
well as a being-for-itself. Hence he is constantly striving to reconcile the two factors. Hegel had tried it and the result was a completely unreal Idealism. For Sartre, Hegel's attempt was nothing
more than the human projection of the will to be God. For
God is conceived by Sartre as nothing else but the possible fusion
of the In-itself and the For-itself. Such a fusion is, however,
impossible. There can be no fusion of that which is with that
which is totally other, of being with nothingness. Man is a useless passion, condemned ultimately to absurdity. It follows, therefore, that man achieves whatever stature he will ever possess by
recognizing the situation for what it is. This involves a necessary
rejection of God and a willingness to be completely responsible
for his own acts for as long as he exists as man. Man is responsible
only to himself, and he assumes this responsibility in his free
choices. Thus he becomes the sum of such choices, and in this
sense he makes his own essence out of the brute fact of his
existence.

Heidegger

For Heidegger the picture of man is not such a grim one.
Heidegger sees the uniqueness of man in his relation to Being. The
Rationalists had defined man as a thinker, while the Empiricists

had made him a maker, a technician, a *Fachmensch*. Man is none of these things. To be a man is to have the capacity to evaluate Being and to re-direct oneself toward it. Man is properly the Shepherd of Being. This is precisely what modern man has lost sight of. He is not at home in the universe because he is not at home with Being. He has allowed himself to become either the thinker or the technician, and he is by nature neither. It is no wonder that man is a wayfarer and a wanderer on the earth, for in losing his proper relationship to Being he has lost himself. Being is absent from man, because Being is not the simple totality of all that is. But man has looked no farther than at all that is. We live in a time marked by such an absence of Being. We are estranged from Being just as we have been estranged from God. Being and God have hid themselves, and we must wait for the time when they again make themselves known.

Yet we live not without hope. For man can expose himself to Being. He can freely let Being in its overtness manifest itself to him. The vision will remain a dim one, for Being is shrouded in mystery and one of its most important characteristics is that, when it does appear, it always appears veiled. Yet some realization and salvation is possible, and this possibility is seized by man's free choice to expose himself to Being. It is this freedom which is at the root of all truth, for it is only by such a choice that man comes to a knowledge of that which is.[7] It is understandable that Heidegger should come to think that eventually the poet could get a clearer glimpse of the face of Being than could the philosopher. For what the philosopher calls Being the poet calls the Holy. He seemed to find in Hölderlin, the German mystic poet, a more immediate contact wth Being than he could hope to express in philosophical language.

. . . Into all the veins of life,
    Rejoicing everything at once, let the heavenly share itself out!
Ennoble! Rejuvenate! So that no human good, no
Hour of the day may be fittingly hallowed
Without the Joyful Ones and without such joy, as now,
When lovers are reconciled, as it behooves them.

[7] Martin Heidegger, *Vom Wesen der Warheit* (Frankfurt-am-Main, Klostermann, 1949), chap. 5.

When we bless the meal, whom may I name and when we
Rest from life each day, say, how shall I give thanks?
Shall I name the High Ones then? No god loves what is unseemly;
To grasp him our joy is scarcely large enough.
Often we must keep silent; holy names are lacking,
Hearts beat and yet does speech still hold back?
That which thou seekest is near, and already coming to meet thee.[8]

Marcel

Like Heidegger, Gabriel Marcel is also seeking an insight into
Being. Like all the Existentialists he rebels against all forms of
Subjectivism. His tendency is toward description and the phenomenological approach. Yet he does not deny essences and
natures. Even granting natures and essences, however, Marcel
emphasizes the need of a philosophy always in touch with concrete experience, and he regards the employment of abstract,
scientific methods as an intrusion in philosophy. Being and existence are there to be experienced, and it is the task of philosophy
to penetrate into experience, to analyze it, and to discover the
factors which make it what it is. This requires a subjective as
well as an objective approach. It is here that Marcel makes the
distinction between problems and mysteries. A problem is always
objective. Problems can be taken in order and solutions arrived
at. But my own subjective existence is quite different. It is always
there, always changing, ever displaying new facets in new situations. It is impossible to objectify it, for it resists every attempt
to do so. I must live with it and I find that its reality, like the
reality of all concrete existence, is basically and ultimately a
mystery. Yet to recognize it as a mystery is already a step forward. And while one can never completely grasp the mysterious,
one can penetrate further and further into it. One can find
intelligibility, order, and structure there. In this point he differs
radically from Sartre, of course, as we have seen.

Marcel's greatest individual contribution has been, perhaps, his
analysis of the presence of Being in its various modes, and his
insight into the relationship of one's body to oneself. The basic

---

[8] Martin Heidegger, *Existence and Being*, trans. by Douglass Scott (Chicago, Henry Regnery Co., 1949).

distinction he makes is that between being and having. One has a horse or a car or a house. But one is one's body. The body belongs to one's subjective being; one exists in it and through it. There is an identification here which is not possible in relation to any other material object.

Like the others he, too, conceives man as living in a "broken world." The Materialism of the past has caught up with us. Not only do we think of man as just another of the things about us, but modern society has even begun to treat him as such. Human awareness has practically been lost, and human freedom has been reduced to the breaking point. The answer, as Marcel sees it, is to return to knowledge and awareness. And he means a knowledge and awareness of oneself as human and existent. Perhaps it is already too late, but one can stand on faith for the present. Thus faith becomes a rallying point around which those with philosophic insight can be gathered. Once they are gathered, then, perhaps, the philosophic enterprise can be begun anew.

The Contributions of Existentialism

In attempting to evaluate some of the insights provided by Existentialist philosophy it would be absurd to deny that this movement has provided much that is worth while. It has been realistic with a vengeance and has certainly succeeded in stressing the importance of the existing real in any system of thought. While Existentialism has found metaphysics seriously lacking, it has at the same time issued a clear call to return to metaphysics or give up any hope of explaining the universe and man. With its insistence on existence and existential situations it has drawn the line very clearly between possibilities, concepts, and constructs on the one hand and realities, things, and real relations on the other. It has faced the indubitable evidence that reality is more than mind, or subjective impressions, or even scientific formulae, and has pointed with a good deal of clarity to a realm of being distinct from man, into which man is thrown, and which he is challenged to understand and explain. It has re-emphasized the clear cut distinction between being and not-being, and in that emphasis of either/or has insisted again on the fundamental truth of the principle of contradiction. And if it has not succeeded, or even tried to make previous metaphysics respectable, it has shown clearly that metaphysics is much more than mere idle speculation or a consideration of questions that never should have been asked in the first place.

At the same time Existentialism has struck a decisive blow at all forms of Idealism by showing their complete inadequacy in being able to explain the existing individual in his situational reality. The Existentialists have brought a new clarity to the distinction between the possible and the real and have demonstrated the irreducibility of the one to the other. The suffering, the dread, the confusion, the anxiety of man as he exists are all palpably and experientially certain and in a completely different order from the rational animal of the Idealists and the Abstractionists. Nor have they dealt more kindly with the *scientific* philosophers, who in the name of evidence and concreteness have attempted to explain man and reality in terms of scientific formulae abstractly representing some sort of verifiability in experience. Existentialism has shown that the uniqueness of the individual escapes such Abstractionism; that existence itself cannot be submitted to it, yet is none the less real for all of that. Again the Existentialist thinking has proved that philosophy must of necessity include more than logic, and that a mere analysis of language is hardly sufficient to explain man, being, and knowledge.

Existentialism has, furthermore, cast new light upon the subjective side of being, and especially on the being that is man. It is particularly rich in insights here, and in its phenomenological approach to the subject has succeeded in laying bare hitherto unknown aspects of man's psychological make-up. It has, perhaps, even been correct in criticizing the complete objectivization of all knowledge and has rightfully insisted on an investigation of the subject as subject. Whether the subject necessarily escapes all attempts to be scientifically investigated and can only be approached through intuition or through the emotions remains to be seen, but certainly it would seem to require a different approach than that by which objects are grasped as objects. Here, too, in its study of the subject Existentialism has clearly made the old theories of Materialism and Behaviorism impossible. Whatever man is, he is evidently different from the things among which he moves. Whatever human reaction to situations may be, it is clearly different from mere response to stimulus, nor can it be explained in terms of the old theories of interactionism. The uniqueness of man, his transcendence of the world in which he finds himself, these put him in a class distinct and separate from the world of mere things.

In this area, also, Existentialism has emphasized the faculties and powers of man which clearly give him the possibility to assert and manifest his distinction from things. There is the reality of his freedom, his need for decision, his power of self determination. There is insistence on the fact that man can and must recognize his position, his innate potentiality for development. In accepting this fact and acting on it, man assumes the responsibility that is his, increases his uniqueness as an existing individual, and widens the already wide gap that separates him from things. It follows from this that good and evil are more than merely subjective interpretations of human activity. Good and evil are meanings restored to the objective, existential order of things; for the good man is the one who exists more fully and more completely, who projects his existence into activity which is in accord with what he is and what he is meant to become. This is the authentic person, the one who exists and acts according to the kind of being he is. Evil, on the other hand, is rightfully seen as a lack of proper being, a curtailment of reality, a refusal to exist and act as befits the being who is and should be different from all others.

It is all not just that simple, of course; but the Existentialists have dramatically forced philosophy back to a consideration of the real, of man, and of being. The various forms of Existentialism contain exaggerations, just as they lack many elements which are necessary for any complete philosophy. But Existentialism has in the main been a healthy influence and for all of its subjectivity has constantly pointed beyond mere Subjectivism.

DIALECTICAL MATERIALISM

Existentialism has been only partially successful as a philosophy attempting to show man how he might recover his lost inheritance. Its influence has been limited mostly to Europe and even there to a select group. There is another philosophical system which claims it can lead men to the recovery of their inheritance and so rescue them from the alienation which has been their lot. This system of thought has had a great deal of success in all areas of contemporary life, and by one means or another has established control over a great part of the earth. This is Dialectical Materialism, or, as it is more popularly known, Communism. It is not to our purpose here to enter upon an investigation of every phase of the Communistic system. It is a complex system involving not only philosophy, but economics, law, politics, morality, political science, etc. To consider the influence of Dialectical Materialism in each of these fields would lead us too far astray. We shall consider primarily the philosophy of Dialectical Materialism and merely point out some of the effects this philosophy has had in these areas.

The Historical Origin of Dialectical Materialism

Hegel, it will be remembered, had explained reality in terms of an Absolute Idea which was both all perfect and not all perfect at one and the same time. The existing order of finite being was nothing else except the attempt of this Absolute Idea to overcome the contradiction within itself. The finite order possessed the Idea as immanent to itself, had meaning only as a temporal expression of the Idea, and in comparison to the Idea, had to be considered as non-being rather than being. It was, furthermore, in this process of expressing itself that the Absolute overcame the contradiction within itself, and so achieved an even more perfect possession of itself. Again from the viewpoint of the finite this reconciliation of being with non-being resulted in becoming and thus explained the historical process of change and becoming. This notion of thesis merging with antithesis and resulting in a synthesis of the two is what Hegel meant by his dialectic. He conceived it as an eternal process and as the basic structure of all that was real. Since reality was considered as ultimately an Idea, Hegel's philosophy can be called a Dialectical Idealism.

As we have also seen, there were serious difficulties with this system of thought. One of the most basic was the inability to safeguard and maintain the reality of the finite. The whole realm of finite being, including man, tended more and more to be absorbed by the Absolute. Man and the material universe lost their hold on being and had to be regarded as mere appearances of what was truly real. It was against this dehumanization of man and against the dematerialization of all that was most evident that left-wing Hegelians like Ludwig Feuerbach reacted. In 1839 he severed his connection with Hegel, at least to the extent that he rejected the master's Idealism. He kept, however, the Hegelian dialectical method, applying it not to the idea but to matter.

Thus Feuerbach considered spirit or the Idea as a reflection of nature and not nature as a reflection of spirit. According to Feuerbach it was nature or matter which was real and spirit the pale reflection of this basic reality.[9] Thus spirit is regarded by Feuerbach as the negation of matter, the division of matter against itself. Hence the dialectical process is retained, but it is now applied to matter instead of spirit. The reality is nature and man. God, then, was conceived as an illusion formed by man in so far as he is able to form a concept of himself and purify this concept to infinity. God is man alienated from himself, and this alienation will continue, until man is restored to himself by reason and philosophy. Thus religion must be done away with, for it is the worship of an irrational illusion. Theology, in turn, must give way to the true science of man—anthropology. It was a rather crude materialism, but there were others who would see to the refining process.

KARL MARX (1818-1883). Marx's contribution to the process of materialization was chiefly in the field of political philosophy. He accepted Feuerbach's inversion of Hegel and applied it to the whole theory of the state. Instead of conceiving the state as prior to the family, as Hegel had done, Marx asserted it should be the other way around. The state arises according to the economic forces at work, which bind the individuals together according to a given ideology. The state is the socialization of the individual in relation to the mode of production which is in force.

This, however, is not the case with the present state. It is really

[9] G. Wetter, *Dialectical Materialism*, trans. by Peter Heath (New York, Frederick A. Praeger, Inc., 1958), p. 11.

a controlling factor, just as Hegel conceived it. It controls individual men because it controls the means of production upon which men depend for survival. At present, therefore, the Hegelian dialectic appears within the state as a struggle between the proletariat and private property, which has been alienated from the proletariat and taken over by the state. This private property really belongs to the proletariat, for man's labor is a projection of his individual nature. Yet the products of his labor have been taken from him by those who control the state. Man's labor, then, is divided from him. And since labor is the projection of his nature, it can be said that in the present state man's nature remains divided, alienated from him. Just as Feuerbach thought of God as an alienation of man, so Marx considered the present state as a further alienation of man. The proletariat, then, in abolishing private property will usher in a qualitatively better world.

FRIEDRICH ENGELS (1820-1895). Engels was closely associated with Marx and was instrumental in helping him compose the *Communist Manifesto*. Like Marx, of course, he accepted the inversion of Hegel from Feuerbach, but added to it a deeper insight and appreciation of the connection of thought with reality.

According to Hegel, dialectics is the self-development of the concept. The absolute concept does not only exist—unknown where—from eternity, it is also the actual living "soul" of the whole existing world. It develops into itself through all the preliminary stages which are treated at length in the *Logic* and which are all included in it. Then it "alienates" itself by changing into Nature, where, without consciousness of itself, disguised as the necessity of Nature, it goes through a new development and finally comes again to self-consciousness in man. This self-consciousness then elaborates itself again in history from the crude form until finally the absolute concept again comes to itself completely in the Hegelian philosophy. According to Hegel, therefore, the dialectical development apparent in Nature and History . . . is only a miserable copy of the self-movement of the concept going on from eternity, no one knows where, but at all events independently of any thinking human brain.[10]

By inverting the process, Engels put the dialectical development in matter, where he thought it primarily belonged. The whole thought process, therefore, is nothing else but the mental repro-

[10] Friedrich Engels, *Ludwig Feuerbach* (Moscow and London, 1950-51), p. 350. Quoted by G. Wetter, *op. cit.*, p. 45.

duction of the dialectical motion going on in the real world. Thus motion is threefold and provides the basis for the application of the dialectic in three areas: nature, history and human thought. Reality is, then, a process which never comes to an end and which repeats itself simultaneously on three different levels. Knowledge and truth, too, are never ending processes, constantly being renewed and perfected as history and time advance. Later Dialectical Materialists will attempt to overcome, at least to some extent, this complete Relativism.

VLADIMIR ILYICH LENIN (1870-1924). In regard to the philosophical basis of Dialectical Materialism, Lenin achieved two things. He helped clarify a theory of knowledge, and he distinguished the Materialism of communism from that of Mechanism. In his theory of knowledge Lenin espoused the "copy theory," which we shall look at more closely later. The problem of the nature of matter had arisen with progress made in the natural sciences. The atom was no longer considered the ultimate element in the material universe. Other sub-particles had been discovered and physicists were talking about the disappearance of matter, the dematerialization of matter, and, as a result were drifting into Idealism. Lenin insisted that a distinction had to be made between the scientific and the philosophical concepts of matter. The scientist is interested in discovering the ultimate physical constituents of matter. For the philosopher, however, matter is simply that which acts upon us and produces the reaction we call sensation. From this viewpoint there seems to be little difference for Lenin between Materialism and Realism.

There is a further distinction which Lenin also made. He was able to see that motion—by which matter is in process—included more than simply local motion. He recognized qualitative as well as quantitative change, and hence he was able to distinguish the Materialism of Communism from the crude Mechanism of earlier days. This, too, we shall consider more in detail later.

Dialectical Materialism as a Philosophy

The system known as Dialectical Materialism includes more than philosophy. It is a complete world outlook, dominated by its own proper methodology and joined with a militarism in the practical order. As a Materialism, of course, it makes much of the natural sciences. How, then, does it regard philosophy in relation to other sciences? Philosophy is considered different from the natural sciences in so far as it is a coordination and interpretation of these sciences. Lenin had been content to reduce philosophy to a theory of knowledge and a theory of matter, but later Soviet philosophers have taken a wider view about the subject matter of philosophy. G. F. Alexandrov writing in 1954 defines the subject matter of Dialectical Materialism as follows:

(The subject matter of Dialectical Materialism consists) in the most general laws of motion, change and development in nature, society and knowledge, investigation of which gives rise to a unitary, scientific world picture.[11]

Philosophy then, at least for the time being, has its own proper subject matter. Soviet philosophers look forward to the time when the natural sciences will have obviated most of the difficulities about which philosophers are at present concerned. Ultimately Lenin will be correct. The proper areas of philosophical investigation are logic and epistemology. But at present, at least, we may still speak of a philosophy of nature, society, etc.

PHILOSOPHY OF NATURE. Dialectical Materialists insist that reality is objectively given independently of our minds and that this reality is material. This is about as close as they come to a definition of matter in the philosophical sense. It is there. It opposes itself to us and causes what we call sensation. Matter is, furthermore, eternal and uncreated and it is in a state of progressive evolution. Motion is, therefore, one of the properties of matter, and it is through motion that the evolution of matter is explained.

Now motion can pose a difficulty for the Dialectical Materialist. It can lead him to conclusions which make it necessary to transcend the material order. Lenin saw the difficulty as motion was explained by the Mechanists. Where motion is held to be some sort of extrinsic force exerted on matter, which is purely passive, then the whole problem of a sufficient cause arises. This can lead,

11 *Ibid.*, p. 251.

if one is not extremely careful, to the necessary existence of a first cause. Hence Lenin rejected the idea of motion as merely local motion, extrinsic to the subject which is moved and conceived motion rather as an intrinsic property of matter. This intrinsic property of matter was then spoken of as the source of all change and development on the material level. Thus motion is just as eternal as matter, and he thought he had avoided the necessity of a regress to a cause distinct from matter.

What, then, is the nature of matter? Soviet philosophers point out that matter is evidently composed of opposites. In the atom, for example, some of the particles are positively charged; some are negatively charged. Matter is both stable and in transition. Motion itself is at one and the same time something and the denial of the something which it is. Hence, matter contains opposites, is divided against itself. It is because of this inner tension in matter and out of it that change and evolution take place. This change operates according to definite laws and these laws in operation produce the dialectical process which gives this form of Materialism its name.

Motion itself is a contradiction: even simple mechanical change of place can only come about through a body at one and the same moment of time being both in one place and in another place, being in one and the same place and also not in it. And the continuous assertion and simultaneous solution of this contradiction is precisely what motion is.[12]

THE DIALECTICAL PROCESS. Matter is a dynamic combination of opposites. It is out of this intrinsic tension that motion necessarily arises. The first stage in the process is a negation of one of the contradictories inherent in matter. Thus A gives way to Not-A. The negation of A, however, is not purely and simply a negation. Not-A has its positive aspect, which is more perfect by reason of its transcendency over A. Yet Not-A is itself also a combination of opposites, so that it too gives way to its negation. The resulting synthesis is the effect, the term of motion. This process is repeated eternally. The dialectic of matter goes on simply because this is the nature of matter.

[12] Friedrich Engels, *Herr Eugen Dühring's Revolution in Science (Anti-Dühring)* (New York, International Publishers Co., Inc., 1939), p. 135.

This law (the law of the negation of the negation) can only be understood, however, in the opinion of the Soviet philosophers, on the basis of Engels' first two laws: the law of the unity and struggle of opposites, the central principle of the materialist dialectic, is concerned with the nature and origin of development; the second expresses the form of development as a transition from quantitative to qualitative change; while the third, the law of the negation of the negation, relates to the tendency and direction of the development. The first tells us *why* development occurs, the second *how*, and third *whither* it is going.[13]

This dynamic process springing out of the very essence of matter is not restricted to mere mechanical change. There comes a point at which this intrinsic dynamism bridges the gap between quantity and quality. When it does so, the effect is a qualitatively different reality, a new type of being, emerging by a sudden "leap" from the former. Thus by raising the temperature of water one degree at a time there suddenly emerges the new and qualitatively different reality we call steam. These qualitative leaps are highly important for Dialectical Materialism, since they enable one to explain how the higher and more perfect levels of being arise from the lower in the dialectical process of evolution. Thus, one can admit, for example, that life and thought are qualitatively different manifestations of matter which are still explicable, however, in terms of a materialistic evolution.

APPLICATION OF THE DIALECTICAL PROCESS TO OTHER AREAS. The basic tension of opposites present in matter is used by Dialectical Materialism to explain the process of history and the development of the state. It is admitted that history as a process is shaped by the motives of men. But what is responsible for human motives? The answer is that human motives are themselves shaped by the ideologies of the age. Social consciousness thus determines individual consciousness. The fundamental driving force in all men is the struggle to exist. This struggle necessarily involves the production of and the exchange of the necessities of life. These necessities of life in turn involve the purposive activity of man, labor, and the instruments of labor. Now the exploiting class—the bourgeoisie—has always controlled labor because it has always controlled the means of production. Opposed to this is the exploited class—the proletariat. Thus society, like nature, is com-

13 G. Wetter, *op. cit.*, pp. 355-356.

posed of opposites. It is in the struggle of these opposites, the class struggle, that history can be best understood.

In the same manner the state is regarded as the basic element created by the mode of production. Private property, for instance, is seen as the result of a long evolutionary process. It was not so in the beginning. The acquiring of property, of course, creates classes. This results in a struggle between classes. The state, then, comes into being as an authority to maintain order and to keep the various classes from destroying one another. Since the exploiting class possesses the wealth and the power, the state is nothing else but a tool in the hands of this class.

LIFE AND KNOWLEDGE. Here, too, as in the realm of nature, Dialectical Materialism attempts to distinguish itself from the older Materialism. It recognizes real qualitative differences between the organic and the inorganic, between the living and the non-living. The living is achieved by another of those qualitative leaps, which characterized the transition from one level of inorganic matter to another. Here, of course, the transition is a more drastic one, and Lenin is willing to admit that it is more difficult to explain.

Life, the mode of existence of albuminous substance, therefore consists primarily in the fact that at each moment it is itself and at the same time something else; and this does not take place as the result of a process to which it is subjected from without, as is the way in which this can occur in the case of inanimate bodies. On the contrary life, the exchange of matter which takes place through nutrition and excretion, is a self completing process which is inherent in and native to its medium, albumen, without which it cannot exist. And hence it follows that if chemistry ever succeeds in producing albumen artificially, this albumen must show the phenomena of life, however weak these may be. It is certainly open to question whether chemistry will at the same time also discover the right food for this albumen.[14]

But how this takes place remains a problem. Further insight is required to explain

how matter, apparently devoid of sensation, is related to matter which, though composed of the same atoms (or electrons), is yet endowed with a well defined faculty of sensation. Materialism clearly formulates

[14] F. Engels, *Anti-Dühring*, p. 92.

the as yet unsolved problem and thereby stimulates the attempt to solve it, to undertake further experimental investigation.[15]

The problem, however, does not seem to disturb more recent Marxist writers.

As the natural sciences develop, ideas as to the ways and means whereby life has originated from inorganic nature are liable to change, and are in fact doing so. But the truth of the teaching of Marxist philosophical materialism remains beyond all doubt, that at some time or other in the remote past life must have arisen from non-living matter, from inanimate structures in nature, on the basis of the natural laws of their development, without the intervention of any forces of an immaterial, spiritual or 'divine' character.[16]

Once the gap has been bridged between the non-living and the living, the ascent from the non-thinking to the thinking is not any more difficult. Here again the fight is against the Mechanists, who deny any qualitative difference between mind and matter. Pavlov, the famous physiologist, was convinced that physiology could adequately explain mind and thought as mere functions of the brain. This position is no longer held by Dialectical Materialists. Mind is, of course, the highest evolution of matter to date, but it is recognized as having operations of its own which can no longer be immediately reduced to the laws governing the grosser areas of matter. Mental processes may be produced by the material, but they can no longer be explained simply in terms of the material, as we know it. The only adequate solution would seem to be to admit of a spiritual principle at the source of such operations. But this, of course, the Dialectical Materialist is unwilling to do.

The theory of knowledge in Dialectical Materialism admits the extramental existence of a materially real world. This reality in its process of evolution brings to perfection the latent seeds of life it contains. It is one reality which expresses itself in two different forms—the material and the ideal. Yet springing as it does from matter, thought is, nevertheless, sharply distinguished from sensation. Man as man has clearly transcended the level of the ani-

---

[15] V. Lenin, *Materialism and Empirio-Criticism* (New York, International Publishers Co., Inc., 1927), p. 34.
[16] M. Leonov, quoted by G. Wetter, *op. cit.*, p. 496.

mals. At the same time it is made quite clear that this in no way indicates the existence of anything like immaterial substance.

Even though thought and consciousness may exhibit an ideal, spiritual character, they are nevertheless phenomena of the one material world and have no existence as substances in their own right.[17]

Neither are there any unknowable Kantian things-in-themselves. The world and its laws are fully knowable, and the knowledge derived from this world is authentic knowledge having the objective validity of objective truth. There are, of course, things which, as a matter of fact, are not yet known. But there is every reason to think that through the efforts of science and practice these will become known. The theory of knowledge is opposed to all forms of Scepticism and Agnosticism on the the one hand, and to all forms of Rationalism and Idealism on the other.

THE PROCESS OF KNOWLEDGE. In explaining the process of knowledge there are again certain phases of the older Materialism which must be rejected. The first of these is a nominalism, which regards sensation and thought as mere symbols which substitute for an external reality. Dialectical Materialists insist they know the real, for sensation and thought are the real as it evolves in that area we call knowledge. There is only one reality here, which exhibits itself both as matter and as matter which is aware of itself. The second element to be rejected is the notion that the mind is purely passive in receiving impressions from without. Just as reality causes sensation and thought in its self-perfecting process; so, too, thought is itself an active evolutionary process reflecting that of the external world. Knowledge is a transition from a state of ignorance, and in this transition contradictions are continually being resolved.

The transition from ignorance to knowledge is effected as follows. The external object acts causally upon the senses and produces an image, or copy, of itself. Lenin explains the process as the transformation of the energy of external excitation into a state of consciousness. This image reflects the appearance of the object and presents these appearances to the mind in a unified complexity. There is, therefore, at least causal objectivity in sen-

[17] *Ibid.,* p. 494.

sation. Whether or not there is also formal objectivity in this sense image, it is rather difficult to say. The general tendency seems to be to say that there is, although to what extent and how such formal objectivity is achieved is not very clear.

The next step in the process is the mind's grasping the intelligibility contained in the sense image. This is not easy, but by analysis and synthesis, by insight into the complexity of the image, by abstracting various elements represented in the image, the mind arrives at some sort of knowledge of the essence of the object.

Conception, correctly as it expresses the general character of the picture of appearances as a whole, does not suffice to explain the details of which this picture is made up, and so long as we do not understand these, we have not a clear idea of the whole picture. In order to understand these details we must detach them from their natural or historical connections and examine each one separately, its nature, special causes, effects, etc.[18]

Thus it is that through thought the mind penetrates into the essences of things, seeking out the inner unity behind the outward appearances. Together, sense image and thought present a unified and objectively essential knowledge of an external object. Thus is mere sensism overcome on the one hand, and Kantian Subjectivism transcended on the other. The mind does not impose meaning on the object, but grasps meaning contained concretely in the singular.

Every mysterious, subtle, and insidious difference between the appearance and the thing-in-itself is an absolute philosophic fallacy. In fact each one of us has observed innumerable times the simple and palpable transformation of the 'thing-in-itself' into the 'thing-for-us.' This transformation is knowledge.[19]

All this, of course, takes place purely on the material level.

If one inquires further as to what thought and consciousness are and from whence they spring, then it is found that they are products of the human brain.[20]

KNOWLEDGE AND TRUTH. While Dialectical Materialism teaches that man can attain to an objective knowledge of material reality,

---

[18] F. Engels, *Socialism: Utopian and Scientific* (New York, International Publishers Co., Inc., 1935), p. 46.
[19] V. Lenin, *op. cit.*, p. 93.
[20] F. Engels, *Anti-Dühring*, p. 32.

it also admits that the senses can be defective, that observation can be uncritical, and that all experience is acquired against the background of class consciousness and class prejudice. Hence, it admits that knowledge can be erroneous. If this is the case, then how can true knowledge be distinguished from false? What is Dialectical Materialism's standard of truth? Both Marx and Engels agree on the answer. The norm of truth is practice. It is here on the level where knowledge can be made to work that we become aware of its truth.

From the moment we turn to our own use these objects, according to the qualities we perceive in them, we put to an infallible test the correctness or otherwise of our sense perceptions. If these perceptions have been wrong, then our estimate of the use to which an object can be turned must also be wrong, and our attempt must fail. But if we succeed in accomplishing our aim, if we find that the object does agree with our idea of it, and does answer the purpose we intended it for, then that is positive proof that our perceptions of it and of its qualities, so far, agree with reality outside ourselves.[21]

This reference to practice, says Engels, is a certain refutation of Agnosticism, as it is also a clear indication that we can and do know things in themselves.

It is also necessary to remember, however, that this criterion of practice can never be complete. It offers an adequate norm against Skepticism. But on the other hand practice does not prove that a given idea is absolutely true. It merely indicates that the knowledge we possess conforms to reality, at least to the extent that it can be practically applied to that reality. The same reservation must be made about truth itself. There is objective truth, and the human mind possesses truths at present which are absolute and unchangeable. Engels himself asked the question and answered it in the affirmative.

Are there any truths which are so securely based that any doubt of them seems to us to amount to insanity? That twice two makes four, that the three angles of a triangle are equal to two right angles, that Paris is in France, that a man who gets no food dies of hunger, and so forth? Are there then nevertheless eternal truths, final and ultimate truths? Certainly there are.[22]

[21] F. Engels, *Socialism: Utopian and Scientific*, p. 14.
[22] F. Engels, *Anti-Dühring*, pp. 101-102.

Most of the truth we attain, however, is not of such an absolute nature. There is room for constant progression in truth, for deeper understanding. The scientific knowledge of one age is always deepened and enriched by the knowledge acquired by a succeeding age. There are many things which we do not yet know, but which we shall come to know as a result of further study and experimentation. In most of the sciences, therefore, relative truth predominates.

It is interesting to note here the differences between Dialectical Materialism and the relativism we have studied in earlier chapters. Where other systems of thought, e.g., Pragmatism and Naturalism, settle for a complete relativity of all truth, Dialectical Materialism insists that the relativity of truth is due to the present condition of investigation and not necessarily to the incapacity of the human mind to attain truth. In this respect it is much more objective than either Pragmatism or Naturalism and has a much greater respect for the innate capacity of the human mind. We must distinguish, too, between the Pragmatism advocated by Dialectical Materialism and that of James and Dewey. The Pragmatism of James and Dewey is much more subjective and idealistic. There is little concern with the objective origin of knowledge or its objective validity in the American Pragmatists. With them it is more a question of utility. In this respect Dialectical Materialism is completely opposed to the Pragmatism we have studied in chapter three.

This relativity in most areas of knowledge and truth has its ramifications also in the field of morality. Dialectical Materialism regards most traditional morality as the product of the bourgeoisie's effort to protect itself and its holdings. Hence, it has nothing but contempt for most traditional morality. It admits there are some basically unchangeable moral standards, but what these are is quite difficult to determine with certainty. So it settles for a practical norm, and this norm is the interests of the class struggle. Whatever serves the success of the proletariat revolution, this is morally good. Whatever hinders this movement is morally bad. It is a morality of any means to an end.

Conclusion

In this section we have considered Dialectical Materialism only from the viewpoint of its basic philosophical teachings. It is from this viewpoint a realistic Materialism, which makes use of the Hegelian dialectic to explain motion and a materialistic evolution. Like Naturalism it recognizes nothing beyond nature and matter. It denies, consequently, any being or reality which is not material. Thus it is necessarily atheistic, and, while it tries to maintain a real difference between mind and matter, ultimately it is forced to agree that mind is the product of matter and just as mortal as the body. The morality of the system springs from this same conception of reality, and the norm of morality is the term toward which the whole evolutionary process is tending—the victory of world Communism.

Most people today are more aware of Dialectical Materialism as an economic, social, and political philosophy, which has been taken over by the communist party. From this viewpoint it is a philosophy of aggressive militarism which is striving not only theoretically but practically to dominate the world. Its theory of world domination, its ruthlessness in carrying out that theory, its complete antagonism to the way of life and traditions of the western world, its rejection of God and Christianity, all these aspects of Dialectical Materialism have made it a force to be resisted at all costs. All this we have touched upon only in passing or not at all, since our purpose has been to achieve some insight into the basic philosophy of the system. But there is one element in all this we might consider briefly before bringing this chapter to a close.

What is especially frightening about the whole situation is this. A great many of the people who are unalterably opposed to Communism are just as materialistic in their philosophy as is any Communist. It is this same group which is quite unwilling to admit the possibility of any certain knowledge about the universe, or the nature and destiny of man, or the capacity of man to achieve truth. They are, if anything, more relativistic and skeptical than any Dialectical Materialist against whom they shout their opposition. They insist that Communism destroys human rights, yet they deny that anyone can know with certainty whether there are such rights and what they are. They object to the evils of the Communist system, yet they are unwilling to admit any objective distinction between good and evil. They reject Communism as false, yet they can see no way in which the human mind can come to any knowledge of truth. One may well wonder on what grounds they base their opposition to Communism. And how long such opposition will last, if ever it is put to the test.

CRITICISM OF EXISTENTIALISM

Despite the many good effects which Existentialism has had on philosophy, it is not without serious weaknesses. The tendency to stress existence has resulted, especially in the philosophy of Jean Paul Sartre, in almost a complete loss of essence. Now essence is the intelligibility of a thing, and once essence is suppressed, then things necessarily lose all meaning. The universe becomes a chaos, without order, without reason, without any intelligibility. As we have seen, this is precisely the conclusion which Sartre draws. Heidegger and Marcel have sought to avoid such a drastic position, but Jaspers has not succeeded entirely in doing so. Existence transcends essence to such an extent in his thought, that reality becomes a ceaselessly moving and shifting object, which can never be adequately grasped by intellect. The most one can do is to remain open toward it, waiting for it to determine itself in this way or that, hoping to be able to grasp it partially in this or that stage of its constant becoming.

But activity and existence are never found independent of all structure. What exists, after all, always exists as some kind of thing. Wherever we make contact with existence, we make contact with something determined, something limited, something actuated and made real as this or that type of reality. Nor is a complete and exhaustive understanding of an object necessary to make us realize that things have meaning and intelligibility. However imperfect is our knowledge of the real at times, even such imperfect knowledge would be an impossibility were reality not basically determined and intelligibly structured. The same is true of activity. It is all very well to describe it as a projection of existence, but this projection will follow structured lines since it emanates from a structured source. Just as it is always a certain kind of being which exists, so, too, it is a certain kind of being which acts. To ignore essence and intelligible structure is to ignore experience and to fall back not just into subjectivity, but into Subjectivism.

This tendency, too, is present in Existentialist philosophy. Any intelligibility which Sartre finds in the objective realm of being has been put there by the mind which opposes itself to such a realm. The mind makes its intelligibility and imposes it upon that which is in itself a seething, twisted mass of absurdity. Jaspers has frankly accepted the Kantian theory of knowledge and understandably finds it impossible to know the order of existing things with anything like objective certainty. The result of such Subjectivism is a direct impediment to any sort of objective knowledge of the reality which Existentialists are so fond of emphasizing. This is undoubtedly why Existentialist thought has turned more and more to the subjective side of being, attempting to substitute inner intuition of psychic states and analysis of awareness for a less certain knowledge of distinct objects. Sartre has completely cut himself off from any understanding of the object in its objectivity; and Jaspers, while he has not removed intelligibility from the object, has admitted that any adequate knowledge of it is impossible. Hence many of the Existentialists are guilty of exactly the same thing for which they have criticized previous systems of metaphysics. They found the old metaphysics inadequate because it considered being only from the viewpoint of the object and lost sight of being in its subjectivity. Yet these same critics have tended more and more to philosophize only in terms of the subject and have to a greater or less extent lost sight of being in its objectivity.

It is for this reason, too, that phenomenology plays such an important part in Existentialist philosophy. When essence and nature is minimized, one can do little else but describe. This descriptive approach has certainly had its value, and it has been raised to a high level of perfection in Existentialism. It has succeeded, for example, in presenting exact data and evidence which up to this time had either been vaguely reported or grossly misrepresented. Yet it is not enough merely to clarify evidence and present it exactly. Evidence must also be interpreted; facts must be explained. Philosophy cannot be content with substituting description for reason and explanation. Nor do reason and explanation have to be absolutely complete and all-exhaustive, as Jaspers seems to demand that they be, before they can be accepted. Being can still be called intelligible, even if it is not completely so to man. To refuse to accept the intelligibility which is there before us and to impose upon the real a subjective interpretation drawn from an analysis of being as it affects the subject psychically comes very close to substituting a different but still inadequate theory for the older philosophcal systems which the Existentialists have rejected.

The restriction of the investigation of being to being-as-subject has led the Existentialists, too, toward an almost complete neglect of any philosophy of nature. Nature is too often regarded as simply there, as a tool which man must use or as a snare which can and does reduce man to its level. The interest has been so great in showing that man is a unique individual, different from all other individuals in the universe, that a corresponding lack of interest has been shown toward anything that is not man. But natural being is also an aspect of being; it, too, exists, and it cannot logically be ignored by a philosophy of being and existence. The same is true of natural theology. Here, however, the reasons are different. Sartre begins with a postulatory atheism, as J. Collins calls it,[23] and hence has no need or interest in developing a philosophy of God. Jaspers, as has been pointed out, is unable to transcend philosophically the finite modes of being's manifestations, while Heidegger has criticized previous philosophies for reducing God to just another being among beings. But he has offered no approach to God which will satisfactorily replace the theories he has criticized. Marcel has rejected the Thomistic proofs for the existence

[23] James Collins, The Existentialists (Chicago, Henry Regnery Co., 1952), chap. 2. Cf. also John Wild, The Challenge of Existentialism (Bloomington, Ind., Indiana University Press, 1955).

of God, claiming they are no more than logically expressed descriptions of an experience which is really beyond proof.

There is a serious lack also in the ethics described by the Existentialists. Despite their insistence on freedom and the necessity of choice, the objective value of good, and the existential emptiness of refusing to act and exist as a man, they have failed to provide a really sound distinction between good and bad choices. The emphasis has been placed rather on choice and decision at any cost and little, if anything, is said about the possible moral differences between types of choice. It seems at times that any choice is necessarily good, any decision is valuable, and any refusal to choose is bad. Here certainly they tend to confuse the metaphysical good or perfection of activity with the different moral good of an activity which is in accord with the rational source from which it proceeds and is further ordered to an end which is consonant with that source. Choice must be further clarified and analyzed. It cannot simply be called good because it is a choice. Experientially we make distinctions between good and bad choices, and we recognize practically that one act is better than another.

It is difficult to get away from F. Heineman's criticism of Existentialism as a philosophy which, for the most part, has developed out of a particular situation, a situation which was not a normal one, to say the least.[24] Speaking especially of Sartre, he states that this is a philosophy which best describes life in the prison camps of Europe, life in the Resistance, life in an abnormally precarious predicament. This sort of thinking was developed in a time of crisis, in the wreckage of Europe, and in the aftermath of a time of terror and disillusionment. It was a time when men saw the old traditions destroyed, the old ideals fail, the once proud gods crumble like so many idols. But life and society in general is not like that, nor is being always like that. If Existentialism has any value, and we have seen that it does, then it must cut itself free from the bizarre, the partial, the passing, and the particular situation—at least to the extent that it can give us a more complete and more adequate insight into being in all its aspects.

[24] F. Heineman, *op. cit.*, chap. 1.

Thomistic Existentialism

Finally, it must be pointed out that the criticism launched against previous systems of thought has not been completely just. However inadequate idealist and rationalist systems of metaphysics have been, it is hardly correct to regard all prior metaphysics as idealistic or rationalistic. Certainly St. Thomas Aquinas has neither ignored existence nor reduced it to a mere conceptualization. Neither has he been unaware that being-as-object is different from being-as-subject. In regard to the first point, Thomistic metaphysics has always insisted that only essences could be conceptualized, and at the same time it has recognized that there is more to being than essence. Ultimately it is existence which is responsible for reality, and it is precisely of the existing essence that Aquinas writes his philosophy. Whatever reality essence possesses, it does so only in relation to the act of existence which actuates it, fulfills it, transfers it from the order of the abstract and merely possible into the order of the concrete, individual, unique existent.

Nor does the fact that essence can be conceived only in the abstract and independently of existence reduce Thomistic metaphysics to an Essentialism or an Idealism. For there is more to knowledge than conceptualization. There is a judgment by which we assert that essences are, that they exist outside the mind. There is, furthermore, the whole order of sensible experience from which our knowledge begins and at which our knowledge terminates as knowledge of the here and now existing singular. Nor does the fact that existence cannot be conceptualized mean that it must remain once and for all beyond the realm of knowldge. For in the judgmental assertion of existence, existence is understood as the term to which the apprehended intelligibility is here and now related. It is understood as that without which there would be no intelligibility, that in which intelligibility is ultimately grounded, and that because of which intelligibilty is real and not merely possible. As Etienne Gilson writes:

. . . reality is neither a wholly inexpressible mystery, nor is it a mere collection of materialized concepts; it is a conceivable reality hanging on an act which itself escapes representation, yet does not escape intellectual knowledge, because it is included in every intelligible enunciation.[25]

It is because St. Thomas neglected neither essence nor existence that he wrote a metaphysics that stays in contact with reality as it is. The being about which he philosophized is intelligible, and it is intelligible primarily because it is real. Just as existence grounds being, so is existence made understandable by essence. And because essence makes being understandable, it is essence we primarily understand when our intellects reach out to being. Yet we do not stop there, but go beyond essence to assert that what we understand actually exists and is actual precisely because it exists. It is because St. Thomas recognized there is more to being than that which can be conceptualized that he remained a Realist and avoided a metaphysics that sank into Rationalism or Abstractionism. At the same time because being included essence and, therefore, intelligibility, Aquinas recognized the basic meaningfulness of being. Because, too, the finite manifestations of being are meaningful and intelligible, St. Thomas demanded an adequate reason for the existence of such limited manifestations of being. He was, therefore, able to transcend being in its finitude and to assert the necessary existence of the fulness of Being. There is a primacy of existence over essence in the Thomistic metaphysics, but it is the primacy of the actual over the potential, the real over the possible, and not the primacy of the unintelligible and the chaotic over the intelligible and the structured. Aquinas, too, would admit that in a sense man determines his essence, but there must be an essence actually existing which is there to be determined. Man does not determine his essence in the sense that he carves meaning out of absurdity, by negating a meaningless other-than-himself. It is because the other-than-himself is intelligible that man can become this other intellectually and at the same time assert its existential uniqueness and individuality. The knowing agent becomes the thing known without ceasing to be himself and without the other ceasing to be other. The other is left intact in its otherness because its otherness is coincident

[25] E. Gilson, *Being and Some Philosophers* (Toronto, Pontifical Institute of Medieval Studies, 1949), pp. 209 ff.

with its being, and its being is necessarily unique and incommunicable. Yet the other is grasped in its intelligibility because its intelligibility is communicable and distinct from its uniqueness and
individuality.

Knowledge of the Subject

Yet here the other problem presented by Existentialism, and
especially by Jaspers, presents itself. If uniqueness and individuality is connected with existence, then how can we ever arrive at any
sort of knowledge of the subject? For one is an individual in his
subjectivity, and if this is unique and incommunicable, how is
any knowledge of the subject as subject possible? Does Thomism,
as it is charged of all non-Existentialistic metaphysics, treat only
of being as object? There is a further difficulty here. For, while
the subject is connected with existence, and the object more
closely with essence, it is not enough to say that we can know the
subject as subject simply by coming to some knowledge of existence. For the subject considered in its subjective uniqueness is
more than existence. It is an individuated, incommunicable, existing essence. Can we get at essence in its individuated uniqueness? It would seem to be impossible. For in a Thomistic metaphysics of material being, form is the principle of intelligibility
and matter is the principle of limitation and individuation. Now
matter as such is unintelligible. Therefore, it would seem to follow
that the individuation which depends on matter escapes intelligibility. Nor does it help to say that the material principle is only
a negative principle of individuation. For whatever is positive in
the individuality of material beings succeeds in hiding behind
the material principle which is its source to such an extent that
we never come into intelligible contact with it.

But is the same thing necessarily true of the individual existent
which somehow transcends the limitations of matter? Is there no
way to arrive at a knowledge of human individuality, of the
human subject? Obviously the case is not quite the same here.
For the human subject is a spiritual subject and its individuality
is rooted in a form which is spiritual and which, in some of its
operations, at least, transcends the matter which individuates it.

In these operations which transcend matter the human subject
acts as an individuated subject. Hence it seems possible that there
would be some knowledge of individuality and subjectivity attainable in relation to these operations which are both spiritual
and subjective. For the individuality of such a subject is contained
in its operations, and the operations are necessarily like the source
from which they spring.

It is only in terms of these operations which are peculiar to
the self as spiritual—the acts of thinking and willing—that the
self is able to come to some awareness of itself precisely as self,
stated St. Thomas. In the *De Veritate* he wrote as follows:

The knowledge which is had of the soul in general is that by which
the nature of the soul is known; the knowledge, however, which one
has of his own soul is a knowledge of the soul as it exists in this individual. It is by this latter type of knowledge that one learns that the
soul exists, for it is in this way that one perceives that he has a soul.
By means of the former type of knowledge it is learned what the
nature of the soul is and what are its proper accidents.

In relation, then, to the actual knowledge by which one knows that
he actually possesses a soul, I say that the soul is known through its
proper activity. For one perceives that he has a soul, that he lives
and exists in so far as he perceives that he senses, that he understands, and that he exercises other vital operations. Hence the Philosopher states in the tenth book of the Ethics: *We are aware that we
sense; and we know that we understand; and that we sense and under
stand because we exist.* Now one perceives that he understands only
when he understands something, for one must know something before
he can know that he knows. The soul, then, comes to an actual perception of its own existence in its act of knowing or sensing.

The soul also has an habitual knowledge of itself; i.e., it can apprehend its own essence from the fact that its essence is present to it;
just as someone who has the habit of a science is able to apprehend
what is contained in that science from the very fact that the habit
is present in his intellect. For the soul, however, to perceive that it
exists and to be aware of what takes place within it, no habit is
required. The mere presence of the essence of the soul to the mind
is sufficient; for from the essence of the soul proceed certain operations by which it is actually able to perceive itself.[26]

[26] *De Veritate*, 10, 8. Cf. also the *Summa Theologica*, I, 87, 1; *Contra
Gentiles*, II, 75; III, 46; *De Veritate*, 8, 6; II *De Anima*, chap. 3, lecture 9.

According to the Thomistic theory of knowledge we know only what is in act, what is actually intelligible. Now the knowing subject is in potency to know until it actually knows. Hence only when the intellect is actually knowing, is it also actually intelligible, since only then is it fully an intellect. Only then is it fully present to itself as the kind of being it is. In this actual presence to itself it is actually aware of itself and of the kind of being it is. Yet this knowledge which the subject has of itself in its act of knowledge is not due to a direct apprehension of itself. It does not conceptualize itself. The self does not, in other words, formulate an abstract representation of itself. This would be to know itself not as a self, but as an other. Consequently the subject knows itself only indirectly, as the source from which proceeds its actual knowledge, as the necessary term which exists and which is related in its act of knowledge to that which is known directly.

St. Thomas is being very careful here to satisfy all the demands of his metaphysics. In the first place, only that which is in act is a proper object of knowledge. Secondly, that which is in potency cannot reduce itself to act. Thirdly, there is a knowledge which the subject has of itself as subject which must be differentiated from the knowledge which the subject has of objects. This knowledge of the subject by which it is aware of its own subjectivity is an awareness of itself as uniquely existing in and through its activity. Hence it cannot be the same as the conceptualized knowledge by which it knows objects. Now the intellect is in act when it knows. But it cannot know without knowing something. Hence the intellect is actually knowable only when it is actually knowing something distinct from itself. Since it cannot reduce itself from potency to act, it must be put into act by an object really distinct from itself. To be in act toward such an object is to know that object. The intellect is united to the object in such a way so that the act by which the intellect is actually knowing and the act by which the object is known are identical. The intellect becomes the object, is identified with it, in its act of knowledge. Therefore, in knowing the object the intellect cannot avoid knowing itself, for here and now it is intentionally identical with the object. The knowing subject has become the other, yet at the same time it remains existentially distinct from the other. It is aware of itself as a self, as not the other on one level, yet it is identified with the other on another level. The self in knowing what a tree is is also aware that it itself is not a tree, that it exists differently than a tree, even though intellectually it has achieved a likeness to what it means to be a tree. What is conceptualized here is tree. But the subject is also aware that it is itself which has conceptualized tree, that it is the sort of being which can do this, that it is an *I* and remains an *I*, even while it knows an *other*. The Thomistic theory of knowledge has by no means ruled out a knowledge of the subject as such. At the same time it has managed to avoid the subjectivism which has plagued the attempts of Existentialism to establish a knowledge of subjectivity.

CRITICISM OF DIALECTICAL MATERIALISM

If Existentialism cannot hope ultimately to restore man to his lost inheritance, can Dialectical Materialism expect to fare any better? At first glance it might seem so. The system recognizes the objective validity of thought and the capacity of the mind to know truth. It faces a real world and acknowledges man's special position in that world. It provides man with a goal and instructs him in the use of the means to achieve that goal. To this extent, at least, Dialectical Materialism is a refreshing contrast to the skepticism and relativism characteristic of so much modern philosophizing. On the other hand, Dialectical Materialism has a fundamental and insuperable difficulty. It attempts to be a realistic philosophy, and at the same time is committed to ignoring one of the basic elements in reality. There must be more than matter constituting reality. If there were not, there would be nothing to think about. Pure matter is unthinkable, because pure matter is not even possible. It is always a material thing which exists, never just matter. And as soon as we begin to talk about things, we enter the realm of the intelligible; and the intelligible can never be identified with matter as such.

Materialism Confused with Realism

One gets the impression from reading Marx, and especially Engels, that their whole opposition to other forms of philosophy is based on the notion that to be a Realist one must be a Materialist. The whole struggle against Hegel is a struggle conceived in terms of the inadequacy of Idealism and the need to return to the real order in which man exists. Now there is nothing wrong with this. The difficulty arises, when one conceives such a return as necessarily involving a commitment to Materialism. None of the doctrines of Dialectical Materialism mentioned above would be rejected by a Realist. But just as there is more to reality than matter, so there is more to a realistic philosophy than a Materialism is able to concede. Refusing to make this concession Materialism condemns itself to an a priori position about the nature of reality and must ignore the evidence presented to it, or simply insist that such evidence is of no importance and will one day be able to be explained in terms of its own system. No one denies that it is right and good to save man. But, perhaps, this can be done without destroying God and eventually man, too, in the process. Materialism, of course, cannot do it. But a fully developed Realism can.

The Evidence of Thought

What is the evidence that there is more to reality than matter? As we have already seen in the criticism of Naturalism, the evidence which presents itself is thought. There is no need to repeat here what has been said previously, but let us note again that the only chance we have to find out what a thing is really like is by observing the way it operates. To understand what is involved in thinking is to understand that thought cannot be an activity of matter. The insistence that only matter is real is particularly surprising, when Dialectical Materialism is willing to admit that the thinking process cannot be explained in terms of matter. The reasonable conclusion would be that there must exist another principle, not material, which is the source of such activity. But Dialectical Materialists are willing to settle for the weak assertion that thinking springs ultimately from a material source, even though at present they cannot explain how this happens. In place of explanation there is substituted a blind act of faith in the natural sciences and their ability to one day explain this activity so different from the other activities arising from matter.

Inasmuch as the materialist dialectic assigns consciousness to the general category of reflection, it confronts natural science *eo ipso* with the still unsolved problem as to how the highest form of motion and reflection in matter, that of consciousness, has emerged concretely from the motion and reflection of its lower forms.[27]

The Structure of Matter and Motion

Dialectical Materialism conceives matter as composed of contradictions. But here, too, there are difficulties. Often what are called contradictions are only contraries, as, for example, the positive and negative qualities in mathematics. At other times the contradictions do not apply to the same subject, as is the case with the positive and negative charges within the atom. The positive charges belong to protons, the negative charges to electrons. Even if contradiction is understood in the broader sense of contrary, where is the common subject for these contraries? And where contraries are united in a common subject, it is not sufficient simply to state that such is the case. Such a composite of mutually exclusive elements requires a cause to explain it. For those things which by nature mutually repel each other cannot possibly be conceived as bringing about their own union in the same subject.

Motion, too, as the first intrinsic property of matter is spoken of as a contradiction in terms.

Motion is itself a contradiction: even simple mechanical change of place can only come about through a body at one and the same moment of time being both in one place and in another place, being in one and the same place and also not in it. And the continuous assertion and simultaneous solution of this contradiction is precisely what motion is.[28]

This is simply not true. There is always *something* which moves, changes, or becomes. But this becoming involves no contradiction.

[27] V. Ral'tsevich. Quoted in G. Wetter, *op. cit.*, p. 196.
[28] F. Engels, *Anti-Dühring*, p. 137.

The something which exists does not become in the same way that it exists. In other words it does not become what it already is. What becomes already has being in one respect and it lacks being in another respect. It may acquire the being which it lacks at present, but it cannot and does not acquire the being which it already possesses.

Neither does it help to explain motion simply by making it intrinsic to matter; nor by including in motion qualitative as well as quantitative change. Wherever there is any change from A to B, even if this change is intrinsic to the being which changes, there is necessarily required an extrinsic cause of the change. Otherwise one has to say that a being which lacked a certain perfection, and which it acquired by moving or changing, caused this perfection within itself. But if it caused this perfection in itself, then it must have already possessed this perfection, or it could not have caused it. But if it already possessed the perfection, there never was any reason for it to change in order to acquire it. And once an extrinsic cause of change is admitted as necessary, then a First Cause must also be admitted, or one is involved in the nonsense of an infinite series of causes, all being caused to cause by nothing.

The same objection may be made to the famous law of the negation of the negation. To explain the evolutionary process by the negation of one of two opposites is not sufficient. Negation never explained anything. If anything positive is achieved, this owes its reality, not to the negation of its opposite, but to a positive cause responsible for the perfection which is attained. Once again we are back to causes, and causes have a way of leading necessarily to a First Cause. The law of the negation of the negation may be a description of change. It is not an explanation.

In the light of what has already been said, it is clear how weak an explanation of qualitative change the "leap" is in Dialectical Materialism. This is used to explain how the inorganic becomes the organic, how non-conscious organisms become conscious, etc. We are told that due to long and consistent quantitative change there suddenly occurs a qualitative change, and a qualitatively different being emerges by a "leap." It is hardly necessary to point out that this is not an explanation. It is again a dogmatic assertion that the higher and more perfect can arise of itself out of the lower and less perfect. It is true that a long series of quantitative changes often precedes a qualitative change. They prepare the way for such a qualitative change. They may even be a necessary condition of such qualitative changes. But to be a condition is not the same thing as to be a cause, and it is a cause that is needed here to explain the qualitative change. Qualitative changes are facts of experience. It is the business of philosophy to explain why and how such facts take place. It is not an explanation to state that they happen because a being on a lower level suddenly "leaped" to a higher level. Neither does it help much to say that this is due to the intrinsic dynamism of matter. Even intrinsic dynamism has to be explained with reference to an extrinsic cause. Intrinsic dynamism is another phrase for matter already in motion. In such a case motion is presupposed and still has to be accounted for.

Further Contradictions in Dialectical Materialism

Marx and Engels had prided themselves on their inversion of the Hegelian dialectic and the application of the dialectic to matter. But as G. Wetter points out, this inversion is impossible.

In all this, Leninist dialectical materialism is blindly reiterating the Hegelian principle of the coincidence of dialectic, logic and epistemology without asking itself whether such an equation is still feasible, now that Hegel has been subjected to the materialist 'inversion' and 'matter' has replaced the Idea. And in fact this possibility is no longer open to it. In the first place, so far as the assimilation of logic and dialectic is concerned, the impossibility of reconciling this with the dialectical materialist position emerges all too clearly from the very disputes about the relation of formal logic to dialectic which are currently going on among the Soviet philosophers. . . . As for the other equivalence, that of dialectic and epistemology, this was possible for Hegel inasmuch as he regarded being—all being, that is—as consisting in its inmost essence of 'Idea'; the self-unfolding of the Idea in its being is therefore at the same time the process whereby it comes to self-knowledge, a knowledge which, thanks to the identity of thought and being, must necessarily remain true to reality. But if 'matter' is now substituted in place of the Idea, the argument is no longer applicable. For either consciousness is regarded thereafter as a property of only a part of matter, namely 'highly-organized' matter—in which case being and consciousness are no longer identical, the developmental process in matter in respect of its being is thus no longer immediately coincident with its development in respect of its consciousness, the accordance of consciousness with reality is no longer given *eo ipso* by its very occurrence, and the problem of the bridge between knowledge and reality is raised once more in its most acute form. Alternatively, despite the 'inversion' of Hegel, being and thought are again equated, the only difference being that it is now called 'matter' instead of 'Idea'; and in fact an identification of this sort is not infrequently met with in the epistemological disquisitions of Soviet dialectical materialism, especially where it is said that the 'brain' is a part of 'Nature,' and hence that in this its organ Nature comes to consciousness of itself, just as the Hegelian 'Idea' does in the case of 'Spirit.' But this would presuppose that 'matter' so conceived is already by origin in some way *essentially* 'consciousness,' and does not merely become so in the case of its highest product; in that case, however, we should again have fetched up in Hegel's idealism, and the whole difference between Hegel and dialectical materialism would be simply a matter of terminology, in that 'matter' or 'Nature' is used instead of the word 'Idea.'[29]

A similar difficulty is noted by N. Berdyaev, who points out that "dialectical" properly refers to complexity, to mind, to opposing intelligibilities. "Materialism" on the other hand refers to a peculiarly one-sided view of reality, completely simple and narrow minded in its approach. Nor does the criterion of truth escape the charge of inconsistency. If experience and practice are norms by which truth can be determined, then we are faced with this situation. Knowledge depends for its validity on its reference to experience. But this reference to experience is itself knowledge and can only be grasped experientially. Hence a vicious circle is set up. The experience which verifies knowledge must itself be validly known before it can do so.

The same difficulties are inherent in other areas as well. We have already seen with what difficulty thought is identified—at least at its source—with matter. To apply "matter" to thought is eventually to lose the ordinary meaning of the term "Matter." The same is true of the word "liberty." To insist, as Dialectical Materialism does, that all being is subject to necessary causal

[29] G. Wetter, *op. cit.*, p. 521.

laws, and then to define liberty as the awareness of the causes by which one is determined, is certainly to give a meaning to liberty which is not the ordinary one. However dialectical this Materialism may become, it still remains the old Materialism and inherits all the difficulties and basic inconsistencies which cling to Materialism.

The Philosophy of History

Here, too, an attempt is made by Dialectical Materialism to apply the philosophy of nature and matter. As we have seen, the form taken by the state is determined by the mode of economic production. If this is true, then it should follow; 1. that where there are different modes of production, there will be different types of states; 2. where the modes of production are similar, the states should be of the same type. But this simply is not what has happened. There have been similar states all having different modes of economic production; e.g., Greece and Rome had modes of production based on slavery, yet the governments of Greece and Rome ranged all the way from monarchy through democracy to imperialism. In the United States, on the other hand, which has maintained a fairly consistent type of government, the modes of production have varied greatly.

These modes of production, furthermore, are supposed to have determined the ideology of society. Where the mode of production changes, so too does the ideology of the society change. But what causes the mode of production to change? This question has to be answered also. It would seem that discoveries and inventions have been mostly responsible for changes in the modes of production. Will Dialectical Materialists claim, then, that these inventions and discoveries are due to the opposition of contraries in matter? They would rather seem, as Christopher Dawson points out, to be part of the intellectual and spiritual history of man. The invention of a tool or a machine marks the triumph of mind over matter, and not just the blind evolutionary process of unconscious forces. In a purely material universe a mechanical invention would be an impossibility.[30]

[30] C. Dawson, *Essays in Order* (New York, The Macmillan Company, 1931-32), p. 238.

The same objection may be made to their theory of morality. If morality is a mere product of the economic situation in which men find themselves, then different economic situations should logically produce different standards of morality. But again it is a matter of historical fact that Christian morality with its un-changing norms has been accepted by different societies differing widely in their economic situations and modes of production. We might ask here, also, just how it is possible to prove that the economic system or the mode of production is the basic motive behind men's actions. Just how is it possible to reduce all other motivation to this one?

THE CLASS STRUGGLE. Here again we find history forced into a preconceived mould. There have, of course, been frequent exam-ples of classes exploiting other classes. No one would dream of denying this. But Marx went much further than simply noting this as an historical fact. From the experience he had of two such aspects of the social and economic situation he proceeded to generalize, until he stated that these were the only two classes in the world. The exploiting class he then identified with the property holders and the owners of the means of production. The exploited class he identified with the workers. Again this is ridiculous. There are certainly property owners who do not ex-ploit their workers. And there are just as certainly working classes who are not only making a good living, but who have a more than ordinary amount of this world's goods and its conveniences.

Secondly, to assert as Marx does, that this struggle between the classes has been responsible for all the great social changes which have taken place in history is another great oversimplifica-tion. C. E. M. Joad in his *Guide to Philosophy* has put the matter as well as anyone.

In general it may be said that the rigorous application of logic to life is apt to result in an interpretation of events which is too final, too sharply cut, and too clearly defined. What actually happens in history is determined not only by the working out of fundamental principles and discernible underlying trends, but by a thousand and one irrelevant and disturbing factors whose genesis escapes detection and whose operations evade analysis. A thousand cross-currents deflect the stream, a thousand side-winds blow athwart the course of history; personal intrigues, sexual jealousy and desire, love of power, thwarted ambition, slighted vanities and injured prides, religious enthusisam, re-forming zeal, party strife, even the disinterested desire for the public good, all these on occasion play a part in determining events. Nor is the influence of the exceptionally gifted individual to be ignored: great men may be the mouthpieces of movements, but the movements are such as only *they* have made inevitable. To seek to confine all these factors, as various as human nature is various, within the Procrustean bed of a single formula, to derive them all from the working out of a dialectical process conceived in terms of material forces brought into operation by different techniques of production, is to do violence to the complexity of fact in the interest of theory. Human affairs are not cut and dried, as logic is cut and dried; they are not painted in colors of black and white, but deepen and fade through innumerable shades of intermediate grey, and, as a result, their outcome is not predictable in the sense in which, if the application of the Dialectic were valid, they should be predictable. Human history hangs upon the threads of a thousand chances; let but one of these be different, and the tale of history would have to be retold.[31]

Lastly, it should also be pointed out that according to its own theory of economic and political development the communist state is itself due to progress continually, until it is in turn replaced by another. The communists deny this, of course, since the communist state is by definition a classless society. Once this stage has been reached, they say, there will still be progress, but there will no longer be any "leaps" of the qualitative kind to usher in a new society. One can, of course, be skeptical about the possibility of a classless society. One can also see the necessity in present day communistic theory for distinguishing between progress and qualitative leaps. But such present day theory is hardly consistent with the more basic theory of Dialectical Materialism on the inevitability of evolutionary progression.

Private Property

The struggle of opposites manifests itself again within present day society as a struggle between the proletariat and the property which has been alienated from it. Man's labor is a projection of his individual nature; and, therefore, in his labor he places ir-

[31] C. E. M. Joad, *Guide to Philosophy* (New York, Random House, 1939), p. 489.

revocably the stamp of his individual nature upon the products of such labor. In so far as private ownership of these products has been taken over by capital, man's nature has been alienated from him. The key to the recovery of man's humanity lies in the overthrow of private property. This in brief is the principle behind the war waged by Dialectical Materialism against private ownership of property.

To what extent is private ownership of property a right of man? St. Thomas makes a distinction on the nature of natural rights. In the first place a natural right may be spoken of absolutely without any qualification. Thus, for example, there is a natural order of man to woman for the purposes of procreation, and parents have the unqualified right to bring up their children. Secondly, a natural right may refer to that which follows upon or flows from what is an unqualified natural right. It is here that St. Thomas locates the right of private ownership. If one considers a certain piece of land in itself, for example, there is nothing in the land which makes it belong to one man rather than to another. But this same piece of land considered from the viewpoint of cultivation or peaceful use can then have a relationship to one man rather than to another. This is to consider something in relation to reason, and in this sense natural right belongs only to human beings, for only they are reasonable. St. Thomas calls such rights the *Jus Gentium*. The first type of natural right is present prior to reason, and is, therefore, common to both rational and irrational animals. Hence the *Jus Gentium* marks a certain restricted area of natural rights.[32]

This right to possess things is always ordered to their use. In a later article Aquinas states that only God has an absolute right of possession, since He created these things and gave them their proper natures. Yet man, too, has been made by God and has been given a corporeal nature which demands the use of such things as food, clothing, shelter, etc. Since he needs these things for his survival, and since the beings of a lower order are for the good of beings of a higher order, St. Thomas sees in this need of man and in his superiority over the lower orders of nature a right

[32] *Summa Theologica*, II-II, 57, 3.

to possess things so that he might use them for his own well-being and perfection.[33]

In the following article St. Thomas pushes the question further and inquires whether men have the right to personal possessions. Again he answers affirmatively for three reasons. In the first place personal possessions are necessary, when one considers how much more solicitous men are about their own belongings than they are about those which are common property. One need only think of the condition of some of the city parks to be convinced of the truth of this. Most men are anxious to avoid work and to leave to others the work involved in keeping up common property.

Secondly, he points out that human affairs ordinarily proceed much better, if individuals have the care of individual things. Otherwise there is always the possibility of confusion. As V. Bourke suggests, it is much better for ten men each to have possession of one cow than for these same ten to possess one-tenth of each of the ten cows.[34] Lastly, it is much better for men to have their own possessions for the peace and order of the community. There is always a much greater chance for quarrels where many men possess something in common.[35]

This does not mean that communal possession is necessarily immoral, or that private ownership of goods is not subject to difficulty and abuse. Private ownership of property can be and has been abused. But to argue from such abuse of private ownership to its abolition, as does Dialectical Materialism, is to miss the point. One might just as well argue that fire should be abolished because it does damage here or there, or that water should be done away with because now and then someone drowns in it.

Conclusion

In concluding this criticism of Dialectical Materialism we can point out that it is a system of thought which claims to be realistic, but which certainly takes an inadequate view of reality.

[33] *Ibid.*, 66, 1.
[34] V. Bourke, *Ethics* (New York, The Macmillan Company, 1955), p. 374.
[35] *Summa Theologica*, II-II, 66, 2.

Its Realism is identified with Materialism and as a result is forced to ignore the evidence in reality which indicates that reality must be more than just matter. These inadequacies continually appear in its interpretation of history, the origin of the state, the influence of economics, morality, nature, and man. Joined as it is with the communist purpose of world domination and kept strictly in accord with this purpose by the leaders of the Communist Party, Dialectical Materialism is a limited and dogmatic system of thought. It asserts much, but proves very little. As a result, much of what is termed philosophy is little more than propaganda.

If man is to be saved from alienation and restored to his inheritance, this restoration cannot be a partial one. Man must be understood for what he is: something greater than the nature of which he is a part and a little less than the angels. Always it is his intellect which identifies him as the special sort of being he is. And it is this intellect which points to the spirit he possesses. His importance lies here, for it is only spirit which can evaluate matter and being and understand the destiny of both man and the universe.

Dialectical Materialism has injected itself into the crisis of modern philosophy. This philosophy, in spite of its boast of elevating man to the summits of rational power, has run its course within the framework of a steady debasement of human personality and intelligence.

Such debasement has, in its turn, rather complex origins. It is due in part to the misunderstanding and the rejection of a metaphysical concept, to the pretense of its ability to dispense with metaphysics or transcendent truth in order to concentrate exclusively on the empirical world. It is due in part, also, to the will to restore in another guise, in the guise of the Idol, the object toward which the cult of man is directed.

Man rushes breathlessly from Rationalism, which limits the intellect, in so far as it would make pure and abstract reason the preponderant part of intelligence, to Individualism, to Naturalism (the logical consequence of this negation of intuitive intelligence), to Relativism (consequence of Naturalism), to Positivism, and to Irrationalism. But it is only a part of man, and not the whole man, that finds contentment in such doctrines. With Positivism, a new form of Materialism has breached the walls of thought—a Materialism tougher than the old one, more radical and intransigent, but rich with all the contributions of modern thought. Is it the idea that matters, or is it the fact? Is it spirit that is of importance, or is it matter?[36]

SUMMARY

Existentialism

1. Existentialism is a philosophy which attempts to explain reality by beginning with man as the focal point. It attempts to restore man to his humanity and individuality, which he has lost to Rationalism and Idealism and the forces at work in modern society.

2. It attempts to accomplish this through free decision, through commitment, to what it means to exist as human.

3. Hence the object is approached through the subject and subjectivity itself is studied, since only man is properly a subject. Thus Existentialism concerns itself with the basic and stark human emotions as a way of getting at the subject.

4. Heidegger sees man's return to himself as a return to Being. Sartre sees it as a decision to stand alone in the face of nonsense and nothingness.

Jaspers sees it as a commitment to the transcendent through faith.

Marcell sees it as a decision to embrace Being as revealed and thus for the present make Faith substitute for philosophy.

5. Thus Existentialism marks a return to Realism and has used a method which has produced many fine insights into man's psychological make-up.

6. It has clearly distinguished man from mere things. It has stressed his capacity to choose and the need to exercise this capacity.

Dialectical Materialism

1. In its historical origins Dialectical Materialism goes back to Hegel. But instead of following Hegel's Idealism, men like Feuer-

[36] C. J. McFadden, OSA, *The Philosophy of Communism* (New York, Benziger Brothers, Inc., 1939), Conclusion.

bach, Engels, Marx, and Lenin applied the dialectic of Hegel to the material order.

2. The subject matter of philosophy consists in the most general laws of motion, change, and development in nature, society, and knowledge.

3. Reality is matter whose chief property is motion. This motion results in the dynamic development of matter and explains the evolutionary process.

4. It is this process which produces not just local motion and quantitative change, but qualitative change as well. There are "qualitative leaps" which explain the transition from one level of being to another, from inorganic to organic, from the living to the sensing and the thinking.

5. This basic process is also applied to history and the state. Thus history is seen as a conflict of classes and the state as an imposition by authority to keep the classes from destroying one another.

6. Mind is considered as the product of matter, but different from matter, at least in so far as matter ordinarily manifests itself. Knowledge is the conscious grasp of a reality distinct from mind, yet this consciousness is the same reality now become aware of itself as mind. Knowledge, then, is a reflection, a copy, of reality.

7. The criterion of true knowledge is practice. Dialectical Materialism admits both absolute and relative truth.

8. The norm of reality is whatever aids the proletariat to achieve its goal—a classless society in which the products remain the common property of the workers.

Criticism

1. EXISTENTIALISM
   a. The exaggerated emphasis on existence and activity results in a loss of essence and, therefore, of intelligibility.
   b. All intelligibility becomes completely subjective, a substitute by the subject for the absurdity of the real.
   c. The over-emphasis on being-as-subject has resulted in a neglect of natural philosophy and ethics.

   d. Existentialism has not yet freed itself from the bizarre and a particularized situation.

   e. A Thomistic existentialism recognizes the primacy of existence over essence without destroying that which makes existence intelligible. Neither does it lose being-as-subject in its study of being-as-object.

2. DIALECTICAL MATERIALISM

   a. Dialectical Materialism identifies Materialism with Realism. In turn it regards any Realism which does not identify itself with Materialism as Idealism.

   b. The activity of thought remains a difficulty for any materialistic philosophy.

   c. If matter itself is a combination of opposites, this composition requires an explanation.

   d. Motion is not a contradiction in terms. Something does not become in that respect in which it already is.

   Even intrinsic motion requires a cause, and this cause must be something positive, not just a negation of a prior perfection.

   e. Dialectical Materialism involves a series of contradictions.

      1. No Materialism can be dialectical.

      2. Practice as a criterion of truth presupposes the truthfulness of the mind, which must judge on the conformity of its idea to practice.

      3. "Matter" loses its meaning when applied to thought.

      4. "Liberty" is made to mean awareness of determinism.

   f. Economic production as the moving force explaining history, the nature of the state, and morality cannot be historically justified.

   g. It is an oversimplification to explain historical change simply in terms of class struggle.

   h. Dialectical Materialism's attack on private property is based on the abuse of such ownership rather than on the nature of private ownership as such.

SELECTED READINGS

Existentialism and Subjectivity*

Atheistic existentialism, which I represent, is more coherent. It states that if God does not exist, there is at least one being in whom existence precedes essence, a being who exists before he can be defined by any concept, and that this being is man, or, as Heidegger says, human reality. What is meant here by saying that existence precedes essence? It means that, first of all, man exists, turns up, appears on the scene, and, only afterwards, defines himself. If man, as the existentialist conceives him, is indefinable, it is because at first he is nothing. Only afterward will he be something, and he himself will have made what he will be. Thus, there is no human nature, since there is no God to conceive it. Not only is man what he conceives himself to be, but he is also only what he wills himself to be after this thrust toward existence.

Man is nothing else but what he makes of himself. Such is the first principle of existentialism. It is also what is called subjectivity, the name we are labeled with when charges are brought against us. But what do we mean by this, if not that man has a greater dignity than a stone or table? For we mean that man first exists, that is, that man first of all is the being who hurls himself toward a future and who is conscious of imagining himself as being in the future. Man is at the start a plan which is aware of itself, rather than a patch of moss, a piece of garbage, or a cauliflower; nothing exists prior to this plan; there is nothing in heaven; man will be what he will have planned to be. Not what he will want to be. Because by the word "will" we generally mean a conscious decision, which is subsequent to what we have already made of ourselves. I may want to belong to a political party, write a book, get married; but all that is only a manifestation of an earlier, more spontaneous choice that is called "will." But if existence really does precede essence, man is responsible for what he is. Thus, existentialism's first move is to make every man aware of what he is and to make the full responsibility of his existence rest on him. And when we

* Jean Paul Sartre, *Existentialism*, trans. by Bernard Frechtman (New York, Philosophical Library Inc., 1947).

say that a man is responsible for himself, we do not only mean that he is responsible for his own individuality, but that he is responsible for all men.

The word subjectivism has two meanings, and our opponents play on the two. Subjectivism means, on the one hand, that an individual chooses and makes himself; and, on the other, that it is impossible for man to transcend human subjectivity. The second of these is the essential meaning of existentialism. When we say that man chooses his own self, we mean that every one of us does likewise; but we also mean by that that in making this choice he also chooses all men. In fact, in creating the man that we want to be, there is not a single one of our acts which does not at the same time create an image of man as we think he ought to be. To choose to be this or that is to affirm at the same time the value of what we choose, because we can never choose evil. We always choose the good, and nothing can be good for us without being good for all.

If, on the other hand, existence precedes essence, and if we grant that we exist and fashion our image at one and the same time, the image is valid for everybody and for our whole age. Thus, our responsibility is much greater than we might have supposed, because it involves all mankind. If I am a workingman and choose to join a Christian trade-union rather than be a communist, and if by being a member I want to show that the best thing for man is resignation, that the kingdom of man is not of this world, I am not only involving my own case—I want to be resigned for everyone. As a result, my action has involved all humanity. To take a more individual matter, if I want to marry, to have children, even if this marriage depends solely on my own circumstances or passion or wish, I am involving all humanity in monogamy and not merely myself. Therefore, I am responsible for myself and for everyone else. I am creating a certain image of man of my own choosing. In choosing myself, I choose man. . . .

Existentialism and Humanism*

But there is another meaning of humanism. Fundamentally it is this: man is constantly outside of himself; in projecting himself,

* Jean Paul Sartre, *op. cit.*

in losing himself outside of himself, he makes for man's existing:
and, on the other hand, it is by pursuing transcendent goals that
he is able to exist; man, being this state of passing-beyond, and
seizing upon things only as they bear upon this passing-beyond, is
at the heart, at the center of this passing-beyond. There is no universe other than a human universe, the universe of human subjectivity. This connection between transcendency, as a constituent
element of man—not in the sense that God is transcendent, but
in the sense of passing beyond—and subjectivity, in the sense that
man is not closed in on himself but is always present in a human
universe, is what we call existentialist humanism. Humanism, because we remind man that there is no law-maker other than himself, and that in his forlornness he will decide by himself; because
we point out that man will fulfill himself as man, not in turning
toward himself, but in seeking outside of himself a goal which is
just this liberation, just this particular fulfillment.

' From these reflections it is evident that nothing is more unjust
than the objections that have been raised against us. Existentialism
is nothing else than an attempt to draw all the consequences of a
coherent atheistic position. It isn't trying to plunge man into
despair at all. But if one calls every attitude of unbelief despair,
like the Christians, then the word is not being used in its original
sense. Existentialism isn't so atheistic that it wears itself out showing that God doesn't exist. Rather, it declares that even if God did
exist, that would change nothing. There you've got our point of
view. Not that we believe that God exists, but we think that the
problem of His existence is not the issue. In this sense existentialism is optimistic, a doctrine of action, and it is plain dishonesty
for Christians to make no distinction between their own despair
and ours and then to call us despairing. . . .

The Framework of Philosophy*

THE QUESTION OF THE ENCOMPASSING. In order to see most
clearly into what is true and real, into what is no longer fastened
to any particular thing or colored by any particular atmosphere,

* Karl Jaspers, *Reason and Existenz*, trans. by William Earle (New York,
The Noonday Press, 1955).

we must push into the widest range of the possible. And then we experience the following: everything that is an object for us, even though it be the greatest, is still always within another, is not yet all. Wherever we arrive, the horizon which includes the attained itself goes further and forces us to give up any final rest. We can secure no standpoint from which a closed whole of Being would be surveyable, nor any sequence of standpoints through whose totality Being would be given even indirectly.

We always live and think within a horizon. But the very fact that is a horizon indicates something further which again surrounds the given horizon. From this situation arises the question about the Encompassing. The Encompassing is not a horizon within which every determinate mode of Being and truth emerges for us, but rather that within which every particular horizon is enclosed as in something absolutely comprehensive which is no longer visible as a horizon at all.

THE TWO MODES OF THE ENCOMPASSING. The Encompassing appears and disappears for us in two opposed perspectives: either as Being itself, in and through which we are—or else as the Encompassing which we ourselves are, and in which every mode of Being appears to us. The latter would be as the medium or condition under which all Being appears as Being for us. In neither case is the Encompassing the sum of some provisional kinds of being, a part of whose contents we know, but rather it is the whole as the most extreme, self-supporting ground of Being, whether it is Being in itself, or Being as it is for us.

All of our natural knowledge and dealings with things lie between these final and no longer conditioned bases of encompassing Being. The Encompassing never appears as an object in experience, nor as an explicit theme of thinking, and therefore might seem to be empty. But precisely here is where the possibility for our deepest insight into Being arises, whereas all other knowledge about Being is merely knowledge of particular, individual being.

Knowledge of the many always leads to distraction. One runs into the infinite unless one arbitrarily sets a limit by some unquestioned purpose or contingent interest. And in that case, precisely at these limits, one always runs into bewildering difficulties.

Knowledge about the Encompassing would put all the knowable as a whole under such conditions. . . .

The Limited and the Transcendent*

That which is logically graspable, consistent, univocally present to consciousness as such is rational in the narrowest sense, the understandable. What is a-logical to the understanding, the Other at the limits of understanding, must itself be felt as rational.

We only grasp the a-logical in transcending. We are natures which not only inquire into the things in the world, but also into ourselves and into the Whole. Thus, to be sure, we are real only as empirical existents, as consciousness as such, and as spirit; but therein we are also beyond ourselves and beyond every determinate mode of our empirical existence, beyond every determinate content of thought, and in this "beyond" we first come to ourselves and to Transcendence.

Already in the merely logical explication of the Encompassing which we have tried, we have transcended in thought toward that which cannot be objectified, toward that which passes beyond every determinate objectivity. For the clarification of the modes of the Encompassing, we have used words and concepts which had their original meaning for definite things in the world; now, however, they are used to go beyond the limits and are not to be understood in their original sense, but rather as objectifying aids in bringing the non-objective, the Encompassing to expression.

The question is what this transcending thought means. It should have an influence upon inner life; it aims at making communicable the non-objective, that which does not appear like things in the world. It is only for consciousness as such that the object of thought is directly intelligible simply as the presence of the object or concept, as identical for every understanding, and whose concrete content is given through what can be perceived and through the trivialities of what can be identically and universally felt by everybody. In transcending thought, on the one hand, comprehension is only possible through an encounter in real experience of that Encompassing about which one is talking. . . .

* Karl Jaspers, *op. cit.*

Meaning of Transcendence*

Transcendence is firstly the relationship between being and Being starting from the former and going toward the latter. Transcendence is, however, at the same time the relationship leading from the changeable being to a *being in repose.* Transcendence, finally, corresponding to the use of the title "Excellency," is that *highest being itself* which can then also be called "Being," from which results a strange mixture with the first mentioned meaning.

Being and Nothingness†

The conception of the sciences is everywhere aimed at being and, indeed, at separated areas of being. It was necessary to start from this conception of being, and, following it, to conform to an opinion close to the heart of the sciences. They believe that with the conception of being the entire field of what is explorable and subject to questioning has been exhausted, that except for being there is "nothing else." This opinion of the sciences is tentatively taken up with the question about the essence of metaphysics and apparently shared with them. However, every thoughtful person must already know that a questioning about the essence of metaphysics can only have in view what distinguishes metaphysics, and that is the transcendence: *the Being of being.* Within the horizon of scientific conception, which only knows being, that which is not being (namely Being) in any way at all can, on the other hand, present itself only as nothingness. Therefore, the lecture asks about "this nothingness." It does not ask haphazardly and vaguely about "the" nothingness. It asks: how about this totally different other to each being, that which is not being? In this it is shown that man's existence is "held onto" "*this*" nothingness, into this completely other of being. Put differently, this means and could only mean, "Man is the seatholder for nothingness." This sentence means that man is holding the place open

* Martin Heidegger, *The Question of Being,* trans. by William Kluback and Jean T. Wilde (London, Vision Press, Ltd., 1956).
† Martin Heidegger, *op. cit.*

for the complete other of being, so that in its openness there can be such a thing as being present (Being). This nothingness which is not being but *is* just the same, is nothing negative. It belongs to being present. Being and nothingness are not side by side. One intercedes on behalf of the other in a relationship, the amplitude of whose essence we have scarcely considered yet. Nor do we consider it as long as we refrain from asking which "it" is meant that "is" (giving) here. In what kind of giving does it give? In what respect does there belong to this "there is Being and nothingness" such a thing which submits to this gift of existence while preserving it? Lightly we say: there is. Being "is" just as little as nothingness, but both *are*.

Man as Ex-sistent*

In this *Da-sein* there is preserved for mankind that long unfathomed and essential basis on which man is able to ex-sist. "Existence" in this case does not signify *existentia* in the sense of the "occurrence" (*Vorkommen*) and "being" (*Dasein*), *i.e.* "presence" (*Vorhandensein*) of an "existent" (*eines Seinden*). Nor does "existence" mean, "existentially" speaking, man's moral preoccupation with himself—a preoccupation arising out of his psychophysical constitution. Ex-sistence, grounded in truth as freedom, is nothing less than exposition into the revealed nature of what-is-as-such. Still unfathomed and not even conscious of the need for any deeper fathoming of its essence, the ex-sistence of historical man begins at that moment when the first thinker to ask himself about the revealed nature of what-is, poses the question: What is what-is? With this question unconcealment and revealment are experienced for the first time. What-is-in-totality (*das Seinde im Ganzen*) reveals itself as ... "Nature," which does not as yet mean a particular field of what-is, but what-is-as-such-in-totality (*das Seinde als solches im Ganzen*) and, moreover, in the sense of an unfolding presence (*aufgehenden Anwesens*). Only where what-is is expressly raised to the power of its own revelation and preserved there, only where this preservation is conceived as the quest for

* Martin Heidegger, "On the Essence of Truth," in *Existence and Being*, trans. by R. F. C. Hull and Alan Crick (London, Vision Press, Ltd., 1949).

what-is-as-such, only there does history begin. The initial revelation of what-is-in-totality, the quest for What-is-as-such, and the beginning of the history of the West, are one and the same thing and are contemporaneous in a "time" which, itself immeasurable, alone opens the Manifest to every kind of measurement.

But if ex-sistent *Da-sein*, understood as the letting-be of what-is, sets man free for his "freedom" which confronts him, then and only then, with a choice between actual possibilities and which imposes actual necessities upon him, then freedom is not governed by human inclination. Man does not "possess" freedom as a property, it is the contrary that is true: freedom, or ex-sistent, revelatory *Da-sein* possesses man and moreover in so original a manner that it alone confers upon him that relationship with what-is-in-totality which is the basis and distinctive characteristic of his history. Only ex-sistent man is historical. "Nature" has no history.

Man's Unawareness of Being*

But the forgotten mystery of *Da-sein* is not obviated by being forgotten; on the contrary, forgetting gives the apparent disappearance of the forgotten a presence of its own. Inasmuch as the mystery denies itself in and for the sake of forgetfulness, it leaves historical man to rely on his own resources in the realm of the practicable. Abandoned thus, humanity builds up its "world" out of whatever intentions and needs happen to be the most immediate, filling it out with projects and plans. From these in their turn man, having forgotten what-is-in-totality, adopts his measures. He insists (*beharrt*) on them and continually provides himself with new ones, without giving a thought to the reasons for taking measures or the nature of measurement. Despite his advance towards new measures and goals he mistakes their essential genuineness. He is the more mistaken the more exclusively he takes himself as the measure of all things.

With that measureless and presumptuous (*vermessen*) forgetfulness of his he clings to the certainties of self-hood, to whatever happens to be immediately accessible. This insistence (*Beharren*) is—unknown to him—supported by the circumstance that his

* Martin Heidegger, *op. cit.*

Da-sein not only *ex-sists* but *in-sists* at the same time, i.e. obstinately holds fast to (*besteht auf*) that which actuality (*das Seinde*), as though open of and in itself, offers him.

As *ex-sistent, Da-sein is in-sistent.* But the mystery dwells also in insistent existence, though here the mystery is the forgotten essence of truth, now become "inessential."

Problem and Mystery*

. . . Metaphysical thought-reflection trained on mystery. But it is an essential part of a mystery that it should be acknowledged; metaphysical reflection presupposes this acknowledgement, which is outside its own sphere. Distinguish between the Mysterious and the Problematic. A problem is something met with which bars my passage. It is before me in its entirety. A mystery, on the other hand, is something in which I find myself caught up, and whose essence is therefore not to be before me in its entirety. It is as though in this province the distinction between *in me* and *before me* loses its meaning.

The Natural. The province of the Natural is the same as the province of the Problematic. We are tempted to turn mystery into problem.

The Mysterious and the Ontological are identical. There is a mystery of knowledge which belongs to the ontological order (as Maritain saw) but the epistemologist does not know this, makes a point of ignoring it, and turns it into a problem.

A typical problem: the 'problem of evil.' I treat evil as an accident befalling a certain mechanism which is the universe itself, but before which I suppose myself placed. Thereby I treat myself, not only as immune to the disease or weakness, but also as someone standing outside the universe and claiming to put it together (at least in thought) in its entirety.

But what access can I have to ontology as such? The very notion of access here is obviously inapplicable. It only has meaning in a problematic enquiry. If a certain place has already been plotted

* From Gabriel Marcel, *Being and Having*, trans. by K. Farrer (London, A. & C. Black, Ltd., 1949).

out, the question is then how can I gain access to it. Impossible to treat being in this way.

Proofs for God's Existence*

From this point of view, what becomes of the notion of proving the existence of God? We must obviously subject it to a careful revision. In my view, all proof refers to a certain datum, which is here the belief in God, whether in myself or in another. The proof can only consist in a secondary reflection of the type which I have defined; a reconstructive reflection; a reflection which is a recovery, but only in so far as it remains the tributary of what I have called a blindfold intuition. It is clear that the apprehension of the ontological mystery as metaproblematic is the motive force of this recovery through reflection. But we must not fail to notice that it is a reflexive motion of the mind that is here in question, and not a heuristic process. The proof can only confirm for us what has really been given to us in another way.

Faith and Proof†

It may perhaps be objected that if faith is understood in this sense, it does not seem to agree very closely with what is commonly meant by the word. The objector might ask me whether I have not systematically tried to shirk the fundamental question; that question will always be the existence of God. I am faced by two alternatives. Either I am in danger of reducing faith in God to an incommunicable psychic event, which implies the end of any sort of theology, and that means of all universality; or else I must try to find a way of framing something resembling a proof of the existence of God. The answer must be that everything we have said in the course of these lectures tends to show that this dilemma must be rejected—I should rather say transcended. It might well be that the idea of a proof, in the traditional sense of the word, of the existence of God, implied a paralogism or a vicious circle.

* Gabriel Marcel, *op. cit.*
† Gabriel Marcel, *The Mystery of Being,* Vol. II, *Faith and Reality,* trans. by René Hague (London, The Harvill Press, Ltd., 1951).

To assess this correctly, it would be necessary to proceed to an analysis of the phenomenological conditions of the act of proving. Proving always implies a 'I undertake to. . . .' But this claim seems itself to be guaranteed not by the personal consciousness of a power, but by an essential unity which cannot but be apparent to a thought which has acquired for itself a certain degree of inner concentration.

One fact, however, remains: the proofs that have been given of the existence of God have not always seemed convincing—far from it—even to the historians of philosophy who expounded them the most minutely. We might say briefly that when they spoke of 'proofs' they put the word in inverted commas. We certainly cannot maintain that these historians failed to understand what they were saying. Should we then say that they had exposed a sophism which had escaped the notice of those who took the thought behind those proofs at its face value? That would be just as difficult to assert.

If the cosmological proof or the ontological proof 'mean nothing' to a man—which implies that so far as he can see they do not get their teeth into reality, they skate on its surface—it may be that he is no further advanced on the high road of thought than those who are satisfied by them (I have in mind, briefly, the fact that the Kantian argument set up in the Transcendental Dialectic does not seem to have finally exploded the proofs.) From another angle, however, I am no more inclined to think that those who wish to uphold the proofs can legitimately counter-attack by claiming that their opponents are guilty of a kind of fundamental ill-will which is basically pride. That is, indeed, too easy a method of discrediting one's opponent.

What is lacking here is the necessary minimum of agreement about ends, about the supreme value. But every proof presupposes, if it is to be given, at least this minimum of agreement. When that is lacking, the conditions in which proof is even possible are no longer present. The history of modern philosophy, as I said before, seems to supply abundant illustrations of the progressive replacement of *atheism*, in the grammatically privative sense of the word, by an *anti-theism* whose mainspring is the will that God should not be. If, then, we consider the ineffectual character of the proofs of the existence of God, we cannot but notice again that deep split in the world of men to which I called your attention at the beginning of last year's lectures. So we stumble on this paradox: the proofs are ineffectual precisely when they would be most necessary, when, that is, it is a question of convincing an unbeliever; conversely, when belief is already present and when, accordingly, there is the minimum of agreement, then they seem to serve no useful purpose. If a man has experienced the presence of God, not only has he no need of proofs, he may even go so far as to consider the idea of a demonstration as a slur on what for him is a sacred evidence. Now from the point of view of a philosophy of existence, it is this sort of testimony which is the central and irreducible datum. When, on the other hand, the presence of God is no longer—I shall not say felt, but recognized, then there is nothing which is not questionable, and when man models himself on Lucifer, that questioning degenerates into the negative will which I have already described.

A Broken World*

'Don't you feel sometimes that we are living . . . if you can call it living . . . in a broken world? Yes, broken like a broken watch. The mainspring has stopped working. Just to look at it, nothing has changed. Everything is in place. But put the watch to your ear, and you don't hear any ticking. You know what I'm talking about, the world, what we call the world, the world of human creatures . . . it seems to me it must have had a heart at one time, but today you would say the heart has stopped beating.'

These general remarks may help us to see in what sense the world we live in today really is a broken world. Yet they are not enough to enable us to recognize and acknowledge how deep and how wide the break really goes. The truth of the matter is that, by a strange paradox . . . in the more and more collectivized world that we are now living in, the idea of any real community becomes more and more inconceivable. Gustave Thibon . . . had very good grounds indeed for saying that the two processes of

* Gabriel Marcel, *The Mystery of Being*, Vol. I, *Reflection and Mystery*, trans. by G. S. Fraser (London, The Harvill Press, Ltd., 1950).

atomization and collectivization, far from excluding each other, as a superficial logic might be led to suppose, go hand in hand, and are two essentially inseparable aspects of the same process of devitalization. To put it in general terms, and in simpler language than Thibon's, I would say that we are living in a world in which the preposition 'with'—and I might also mention Whitehead's noun, 'togetherness'—seems more and more to be losing its meaning; . . . . It is, or so it seems to me, by starting from the fact of the growingly complex and unified social organization of human life today, that one can see most clearly what lies behind the loss, for individuals, of life's old intimate quality. In what does this growingly complex organization—this socialization of life, as we may call it—really consist? Primarily in the fact that each one of us is being treated today more and more as an agent, whose behavior ought to contribute towards the progress of a certain social whole, a something rather distant, rather oppressive, let us even say frankly rather tyrannical. This presupposes a registration, an enrolment, not once and for all, like that of a new born child in the registrar's office, but again and again, repeatedly, while life lasts.

The Dialectic of Materialism*

The analysis of Nature into its individual parts, the grouping of the different natural processes and natural objects in definite classes, the study of the internal anatomy of organic bodies in their manifold forms—these were the fundamental conditions of the gigantic strides in our knowledge of Nature which have been made during the last four hundred years. But this method of investigation has also left us as a legacy the habit of observing natural objects and natural processes in their isolation, detached from the whole vast interconnection of things; and therefore not in their motion, but in their repose; not as essentially changing, but as fixed constants; not in their life, but in their death. And when, as was the case with Bacon and Locke, this way of looking

* Friedrich Engels, *Herr Eugen Dühring's Revolution in Science* (Anti-Dühring), trans. by Emile Burns (New York, International Publisher's Co., Inc., 1939), pp. 27-31.

at things was transferred from natural science to philosophy, it
produced the specific narrow-mindedness of the last centuries, the
metaphysical mode of thought.

To the metaphysician, things and their mental images, ideas,
are isolated, to be considered one after the other apart from each
other, rigid, fixed objects of investigation given once for all. He
thinks in absolutely discontinuous antitheses. His communication
is: "Yea, yea, Nay, nay, for whatsoever is more than these cometh
of evil." For him a thing either exists, or it does not exist; it is
equally impossible for a thing to be itself and at the same time
something else. Positive and negative absolutely exclude one another; cause and effect stand in an equally rigid antithesis one to
the other. At first sight this mode of thought seems to us extremely plausible, because it is the mode of thought of so-called
sound common sense. But sound common sense, respectable
fellow as he is within the homely precincts of his own four walls,
has most wonderful adventures as soon as he ventures out into
the wide world of scientific research. Here the metaphysical mode
of outlook, justifiable and even necessary as it is in domains whose
extent varies according to the nature of the object under investigation, nevertheless sooner or later always reaches a limit beyond
which it becomes one-sided, limited, abstract, and loses its way in
insoluble contradictions. And this is so because in considering individual things it loses sight of their connections; in contemplating
their existence it forgets their coming into being and passing away;
in looking at them at rest it leaves their motion out of account;
because it cannot see the wood for the trees. For everyday purposes we know, for example, and can say with certainty whether
an animal is alive or not; but when we look more closely we find
that this is often an extremely complex question, as jurists know
very well. They have cudgeled their brains in vain to discover
some rational limit beyond which the killing of a child in its
mother's womb is murder; and it is equally impossible to determine the moment of death, as physiology has established that
death is not a sudden, instantaneous event, but a very protracted
process. In the same way every organic being is at each moment
the same and not the same; at each moment it is assimilating
matter drawn from without, and excreting other matter; at each

moment the cells of its body are dying and new ones are being formed; in fact, within a longer or shorter period the matter of its body is completely renewed and is replaced by other atoms of matter, so that every organic being is at all times itself and yet something other than itself. Closer investigation also shows us that the two poles of an antithesis, like positive and negative, are just as inseparable from each other as they are opposed, and that despite all their opposition they mutually penetrate each other. It is just the same with cause and effect; these are conceptions which only have validity in their application to a particular case as such, but when we consider the particular case in its general connection with the world as a whole they merge and dissolve in the conception of universal action and interaction, in which causes and effects are constantly changing places, and what is now or here an effect becomes there or then a cause, and vice versa.

None of these processes and methods of thought fit into the frame of metaphysical thinking. But for dialectics, which grasps things and their images, ideas, essentially in their interconnection, in their sequence, their movement, their birth and death, such processes as those mentioned above are so many corroborations of its own method of treatment. Nature is the test of dialectics, and it must be said for modern natural science that it has furnished extremely rich and daily increasing materials for this test, and has thus proved that in the last analysis Nature's process is dialectical and not metaphysical. But the scientists who have learnt to think dialectically are still few and far between, and hence the conflict between the discoveries made and the old traditional mode of thought is the explanation of the boundless confusion which now reigns in theoretical natural science and reduces both teachers and students, writers and readers to despair.

An exact representation of the universe, of its evolution and that of mankind, as well as of the reflection of this evolution in the human mind, can therefore only be built up in a dialectical way, taking constantly into account the general actions and reactions of becoming and ceasing to be, of progressive or retrogressive changes. And the more recent German philosophy worked with this standpoint from the first. Kant began his career by resolving the stable solar system of Newton and its eternal permanence—

after the famous initial impulse had once been given—into a historical process: the formation of the sun and of all the planets out of a rotating nebulous mass. Together with this he already drew the conclusion that given this origin of the solar system, its ultimate dissolution was also inevitable. Half a century later his views were given a mathematical basis by Laplace, and another fifty years later the spectroscope proved the existence in space of such incandescent masses of gas in various stages of condensation.

This newer German philosophy culminated in the Hegelian system, in which for the first time—and this is its great merit—the whole natural, historical, and spiritual world was presented as a process, that is, as in constant motion, change, transformation and development; and the attempt was made to show the internal interconnections in this motion and development. From this standpoint the history of mankind no longer appeared as a confused whirl of senseless deeds of violence, all equally condemnable before the judgment seat of the now matured philosophic reason, and best forgotten as quickly as possible, but as the process of development of humanity itself. It now became the task of thought to follow the gradual stages of this process through all its devious ways, and to trace out the inner regularities running through all its apparently fortuitous phenomena.

That Hegel did not succeed in this task is here immaterial. His epoch-making service was that he propounded it. It is indeed a task which no individual will ever be able to solve. Although Hegel—with Saint Simon—was the most encyclopaedic mind of his age, yet he was limited, in the first place, by the necessarily restricted compass of his own knowledge, and, secondly, by the similarly restricted scope and depth of the knowledge and ideas of his age. But there was also a third factor. Hegel was an idealist, that is to say, the thoughts within his mind were to him not the more or less abstract images of real things and processes, but, on the contrary, things and their development were to him only the images made real of the "Idea" existing somewhere or other already before the world existed. This mode of thought placed everything on its head, and completely reversed the real connections of things in the world. And although Hegel grasped correctly and with insight many individual interconnections, yet, for the reasons just given, there is also much that in point of detail also is botched, artificial, laboured, in a word, wrong. Hegelian system as such was a colossal miscarriage—but it was also the last of its kind. It suffered, in fact, from an internal and insoluble contradiction. On the one hand, its basic assumption was the historical outlook, that human history is a process of evolution, which by its very nature cannot find intellectual finality in the discovery of any so-called absolute truth; but on the other hand, it laid claim to being the very sum-total of precisely this absolute truth. A system of natural and historical knowledge which is all-embracing and final for all time is in contradiction to the fundamental laws of dialectical thinking; which however, far from excluding, on the contrary includes, the idea that the systematic knowledge of the external universe can make giant strides from generation to generation.

The realisation of the entire incorrectness of previous German idealism led necessarily to materialism, but, it must be noted, not to the simple metaphysical and exclusively mechanical materialism of the eighteenth century. Instead of the simple and naively revolutionary rejection of all previous history, modern materialism sees history as the process of the evolution of humanity, and its own problem as the discovery of laws of motion of this process. The conception was prevalent among the French of the eighteenth century, as well as with Hegel, of Nature as a whole, moving in narrow circles and remaining immutable, with its eternal celestial bodies, as Newton taught, and unalterable species of organic beings, as Linnaeus taught. In opposition to this conception, modern materialism embraces the more recent advances of natural science, according to which Nature also has its history in time, the celestial bodies, like the organic species which under favourable circumstances people them, coming into being and passing away, and the recurrent circles, in so far as they are in any way admissible, assuming infinitely vaster dimensions. In both cases modern materialism is essentially dialectical, and no longer needs any philosophy standing above the other sciences. As soon as each separate science is required to get clarity as to its position in the great totality of things and of our knowledge of things, a special science dealing with this totality is superfluous. What still independently survives of all former philosophy is the science of thought and its laws—formal logic and dialectics. Everything else is merged in the positive science of Nature and history.

Production and Society*

The materialist conception of history starts from the principle that production, and with production the exchange of its products, is the basis of every social order; that in every society which has appeared in history the distribution of the products, and with it the division of society into classes or estates, is determined by what is produced and how it is produced, and how the product is exchanged. According to this conception, the ultimate causes of all social changes and political revolutions are to be sought, not in the minds of men, in their increasing insight into eternal truth and justice, but in changes in the mode of production and exchange; they are to be sought not in the *philosophy* but in the *economics* of the epoch concerned. The growing realisation that existing social institutions are irrational and unjust, that reason has become nonsense and good deeds a scourge is only a sign that changes have been taking place quietly in the methods of production and forms of exchange with which the social order, adapted to previous economic conditions, is no longer in accord. This also involves that the means through which the abuses that have been revealed can be got rid of must likewise be present, in more or less developed form, in the altered conditions of productions. These means are not to be *invented* by the mind, but *discovered* by means of the mind in the existing material facts of production.

Economics and Morality†

We therefore reject every attempt to impose on us any moral dogma whatsoever as an eternal, ultimate and forever immutable moral law on the pretext that the moral world too has its permanent principles which transcend history and the differences be-

* Friedrich Engels, *op. cit.*
† Friedrich Engels, *op. cit.*

tween nations. We maintain on the contrary that all former moral theories are the product, in the last analysis, of the economic stage which society had reached at that particular epoch. And as society has hitherto moved in class antagonisms, morality was always a class morality; it has either justified the domination and the interests of the ruling class, or, as soon as the oppressed class has become powerful enough, it has represented the revolt against this domination and the future interests of the oppressed. That in this process there has on the whole been progress in morality, as in all other branches of human knowledge, cannot be doubted. But we have not yet passed beyond class morality. A really human morality which transcends class antagonisms and their legacies in thought becomes possible only at a stage of society which has not only overcome class contradictions but has even forgotten them in practical life.

Mind and Nature*

Such a result comes of accepting in quite a naturalistic way "consciousness," "thought," as something given, something from the outset in contrast to being, to Nature. If this were so, it must seem extremely remarkable that consciousness and Nature, thinking being, the laws of thought and the laws of Nature, should be so closely in correspondence. But if the further question is raised: what then are thought and consciousness, and whence they come, it becomes apparent that they are products of the human brain and that man himself is a product of Nature, which has been developed in and along with its environment; whence it is self-evident that the products of the human brain, being in the last analysis also products of Nature, do not contradict the rest of Nature but are in correspondence with it.

BIBLIOGRAPHY

Berdyaev, N., *The Origin of Russian Communism*. New York, Charles Scribner's Sons, 1937.
Cochrane, Arthur C., *The Existentialists and God*. Philadelphia, The Westminster Press, 1956.
    * Friedrich Engels, *op. cit.*

Collins, James, *The Existentialists*. Chicago, Henry Regnery Co., 1952.

Copleston, F., S.J., *Contemporary Philosophy*. Westminster, Md., The Newman Press, 1956.

Dempsey, Peter, OFM. Cap., *The Psychology of Sartre*. Cork, Cork University Press, 1950.

Desan, Wilfred, *The Tragic Finale*. Cambridge, Mass., Harvard University Press, 1954.

Engels, Friedrich, *Herr Eugen Dühring's Revolution in Science (Anti-Dühring)*. New York, International Publishers Co., Inc., 1935.

——, *Ludwig Feuerbach*. New York, International Publishers Co., Inc., 1934.

——, *Socialism; Utopian and Scientific*. New York, International Publishers Co., Inc., 1935.

——, *The Origin of the Family, Private Property and the State*. Chicago, Charles H. Kerr Co., 1902.

Gilson, E., *Being and Some Philosophers*. Toronto, Pontifical Institute of Medieval Studies, 1949.

Hawkins, D. J. B., *Critical Problems of Modern Philosophy*. London and New York, Sheed and Ward, Ltd., 1957.

Heidegger, Martin, "On The Essence of Truth," and "What is Metaphysics?" in *Existence and Being*, trans. by R. F. C. Hull and Alan Crick (London, Vision Press, Ltd., 1949).

Heineman, F. H., *Existentialism and the Modern Predicament*. New York, Harper & Brothers, 1953.

Hook, S., *Marx and the Marxists*. Princeton, N. J., D. Van Nostrand Co., Inc., 1955.

Jaspers, Karl, *Reason and Existenz*, trans. by W. Earle. New York, The Noonday Press, 1955.

——, *The Way to Wisdom*, trans. by R. Manheim. New Haven, Conn., Yale University Press, 1951.

Joad, C. E. M., *Guide to Philosophy*. New York, Random House, 1938.

Kierkegaard, Soren, *Either/Or*, Vol. I trans. by David F. and Lillian M. Swenson, Vol. II trans. by Walter Lowrie. Princeton, N. J. Princeton University Press, 1944.

——, *Fear and Trembling*, trans. by Walter Lowrie. Princeton, N. J., Princeton University Press, 1941.

——, *The Sickness Unto Death*. Princeton, N. J., Princeton University Press, 1946.

Lenin, V., *Marx, Engels, Marxism*. New York, International Publishers Co., Inc., 1935.

——, *Materialism and Empirio-Criticism*. New York, International Publishers Co., Inc., 1927.

Marcel, Gabriel, *Man Against Mass Society*. Chicago, Henry Regnery Co., 1952.
———, *The Philosophy of Existence*. New York, Philosophical Library, Inc., 1949.
Maritain, Jacques, *Existence and the Existent*, trans. by Lewis Galantière, and Gerald B. Phelan. Garden City, N. Y., Doubleday & Co., Inc., 1957.
Marx, Karl, *Capital*, trans. by Eden and Cedar Paul, Everyman's Library Series. New York, E. P. Dutton & Co., Inc., 1934. 2 Vols.
———, *The Communist Manifesto*. Chicago, Henry Regnery Co., 1954.
McFadden, C. J., O.S.A., *The Philosophy of Communism*. New York, Benziger Brothers, Inc., 1939.
Murdoch, Iris, *Sartre*. New Haven, Conn., Yale University Press, 1953.
Sartre, Jean-Paul, *Existentialism*, trans. by B. Frechtman. New York, Philosophical Library, Inc., 1947.
———, *La Nausée*. Paris, Librairie Gallimard, 1938.
———, *L'Être et le Néant*. Paris, Librairie Gallimard, 1938.
Sheed, F., *Communsim and Man*. London, Sheed & Ward, Ltd., 1938.
Sheen, F., *The Cross and the Crisis*. Milwaukee, Wisc., The Bruce Publishing Co., 1938.
The Philosophy of Communism, C. Boyer, S.J., ed. New York, Fordham University Press, 1952.
Wetter, G., S.J., *Dialectical Materialism*, trans. by Peter Heath. New York, Frederick A. Praeger, Inc., 1958.
White, Morton, *The Age of Analysis*. Boston, Houghton Mifflin Co., 1955.
Wild, John, *The Challenge of Existentialism*. Bloomington, Ind., Indiana University Press, 1955.

6

The Problem
of
Knowledge

THE VARIOUS SYSTEMS of modern thought that have been considered in this book are varied enough. At the same time these different philosophies possess a certain similarity. There is a dominant theme running through most of them. At times this theme is explicitly stated, at other times it is there only implicitly, but it is there nevertheless. This theme is the problem of knowledge. In all systems of modern thinking human knowledge has been seriously restricted. In all but a few of these systems the search for certain knowledge still goes on, but the area in which it is sought has become a definitely circumscribed one. Outside of that area most modern philosophers are unanimously agreed that the search is bound to be a vain and useless one. A brief resumé of the philosophies we have studied from the viewpoint of what can be known will make this obvious.

KANTIANISM

In his philosophic synthesis Immanuel Kant reduced the object of human knowledge to a combination of experience and intellectual interpretation. This experience he spoke of was itself a unified series of sense impressions. Upon these sense impressions were imposed the subjective laws according to which the intellect functioned and because of which experience became meaningful and intelligible. Each element of the combination was absolutely essential for any sort of real knowledge. Without the subjective impressions in the sense order there would be nothing with which the intellect could work. Without the application of the intellectual forms there would be nothing intelligible in our experience. The result was, of course, a Subjectivism in which all meaning was contributed from the side of the knowing subject. This was bad enough, but Kant's contribution went further than that. Not only was meaning imposed by the mind of the knower, but it was imposed upon sense experience and only upon sense experience. In other words, the only possible area which the mind could make understandable was the limited area of experience. Where there was no experience, there was necessarily no knowledge. Such a theory of knowledge led immediately to two necessary consequences.

In the first place it made all true and certain knowledge the exclusive property of the natural sciences, for only these sciences are concerned entirely with sense experience and with formulating the laws according to which the things we encounter in experience operate. More than that, Kant made every scientific law a mental construct, which represented more the way the mind functions in dealing with experience than it did the actual operations of a material universe. A scientific law told us how we had to think of things, not necessarily how things were. Secondly, as we have seen, the Kantian theory of knowledge exiled from the realm of knowledge any object not contained in the realm of experience. There was no other choice but to state that metaphysics was an impossibility. There could no longer be any knowledge of God and the soul. And if man had a destiny beyond matter, there was now little use in speculating about it. Man had become the measure of all things and faith was nothing more than an assent to pure possibility. Kant had found his synthesis. The object of the intellect was not being but sensible being. Human intelligence had been cut off from being and left to consider only things. No wonder Heidegger would later complain about the absence of being in the world of men. If man was no longer at home with being, it was because being could no longer be allowed to enter into the universe of man.

IDEALISM

The Idealists, too, restricted the field of the knowable. That which can be known is obviously that which is intelligible. Now the intelligible just as obviously requires a mind in which and for which it is intelligible. Furthermore, if that which is intelligible is real, and if that which is real is also intelligible; then, just as being is intelligible, so is that which is intelligible being. Hence being becomes synonymous with mind, and from this point there are two paths one can travel. The first one leads to the position that the mind with which the real is identified is my mind. This is by far the more drastic position, for it immediately creates the problem of the existence of other minds. Since it is very difficult to prove the existence of such other minds, Solipsism becomes not just a philosophical theory, but a very real danger. Not only may I be alone in the universe, but I may very well be the universe.

There is, however, another road which can be taken. One may speak of mind as something absolute, something thinking on a cosmic level, something projecting its thoughts so as better to understand itself. Hence we have the existence of finite and even contradictory intelligibilities. In such a system a pluralistic universe is much more easily explained. But it, too, has its difficulties. The finite may be a manifold, yet it is hard to see how there can really be a finite. If mind penetrates the cosmos to such an extent that the cosmos is merely an intelligibility, which has existence only because it is being thought, whose very existence is to be thought, then how can such a universe be really distinct from the mind thinking it? What is the future of finite personality and individuality in such a universe? Again it is not being which we know, but being in so far as it is intelligible. The intellect has been restricted to the idea. The fact that the idea has become synonymous with the real makes little difference. Whether one admits a reality beyond the idea, as Kant did, or whether one rejects such a reality is of no consequence. The Idealist necessarily moves in a restricted world of concepts and ideas, and human knowledge remains a knowledge of meanings and possibilities. This is a universe of logic and mathematics and universals. There is such a universe, of course; but it is a poor substitute for the real one.

NATURALISM

Just as Idealism centered upon the source of intelligibility and its expression in the idea, so Naturalism turns toward the object, toward that which is made intelligible. Now that which is made intelligible is sense experience, and the Naturalist finds in sense experience and its object the complete object of human knowledge. There is less insistence here on the subjective side of the knowing process than there is in Kant. Yet the area open to knowledge is the same as that defined by the German philosopher. For the Naturalist the universe of sensible experience is an unquestioned fact. It is there. And man is a part of it. From it he comes and to it he returns. In between those two points he can know something about that universe to the extent that it affects him. To attempt to transcend it in his knowledge is futile, since there is nothing beyond it. What the Naturalist knows is sensible being as experienced, for that is all there is to know. There is no need for metaphysics, simply because there is nothing beyond physics.

Now in a purely physical universe the highest and most exact knowledge that can be obtained is that made possible by the physical sciences. Again, therefore, there is great stress laid upon scientific knowledge. Just as metaphysics is supplanted by biology, chemistry, and physics, so, too, is ethics replaced by humanism, anthropology, and sociology. These are the sciences proper to a universe of sensible experience, for these are the lines along which the functioning of such a universe is reasonably predictable. So the ethics of Naturalism is a theory of what is most useful and naturally good for man. There is much talk of the development of human capacity, always in an harmonious way, of course. There is much that smacks of Epicureanism, Stoicism, and Humanism. Some of it sounds a bit too much like Cicero's De Senectute to ring completely true, but what else can one talk about in a universe whose only stability is a constant evolutionary process, which has no destiny or goal beyond itself? Once again it is a case of the limitation of knowledge to a restricted area of being. Then suddenly we are told that this is all there is or can be of being.

PRAGMATISM

Pragmatists have long since given up the hope of any knowledge of essences or of any certainty about realities that transcend sensible experience. The Pragmatist considers any attempt to acquire such knowledge an unrewarding labor at best and a wearisome and endless quest at the worst. He does not deny, as does the Naturalist, that there is anything beyond nature; but he regards all such questions as insoluble. It matters not so much whether there is a God or not, whether the soul is immortal or not, but how these questions and their possible answers affect the business of everyday living. Hence knowledge is restricted to what we can know about results here and now. Metaphysics is relegated to the category of wearisome dispute and idle speculation, and meaning is reduced to what something means in a practical, progressive, material universe. Meaning becomes synonymous with practicality, and, hence, the only meaningfulness any theory can have is one which is discovered in and restricted to the empirical order.

Nor does truth fare any better at the hands of the Pragmatist. Something must be meaningful before it can be true. Now if meaning is restricted to experience, truth will rise no higher. We can know what is practically good for us, and to the extent that something is good for us it will also be true for us. Of course, there are many things in and about experience which can never be known. Hence meaning and truth remain open areas, always able to be further modified, further enriched, further qualified. The most one can hope for in such a situation is for some sort of relative consistency, according to which his present knowledge will be harmoniously organized and kept from being self contradictory. Since any new experience may invalidate all previous experiences, human knowledge can provide at its best only a high degree of probability which may serve as a basis for action, but which can never provide any degree of certainty. We have already seen the difficulties involved in such a theory of knowledge. It is sufficient here to point out the increasing skepticism which accompanies the increasing restriction placed on human knowing.

LOGICAL POSITIVISM

In Logical Positivism, from one viewpoint at least, we find the whole process pushed one step further. Not only do we find the rejection of the possibility of any knowledge beyond the realm of sense experience, but we find the question itself of the possibility of such knowledge an inane one. A Pragmatist would admit that God might possibly exist. He simply states that we can never discover if this possibility is a reality. So one does the next best thing. A Logical Positivist, however, refuses even to discuss the question. From the beginning it is evident to him that such a question should never have been asked. It is a completely vain and useless question, as is its contradictory: It is possible that God does not exist? There is only one possible knowledge for man, and that is a knowledge of the material, empirical universe. There is, furthermore, only one way to achieve such a knowledge, and that is by using the method of experimentation and verification which has proved so successful in the area of the natural sciences. Metaphysics is ruled off the court before the game begins. In fact, the rules of the game have been pre-established, and the main one—the principle of verifiability—is dogmatically asserted as the one to be observed at all costs. There is even a way to take care of any suspicions that might arise about the possible limitations of the verifiability principle. Linguistic analysis is sure to prove to the skeptic that so called metaphysical statements are nothing more than emotive expressions or confusions of language. The fact that these questions and statements keep popping up from time to time only indicates that man is an emotional and lyrical animal as well as a logician.

EXISTENTIALISM

As has been pointed out, Existentialism was basically a healthy reaction. In many ways it marked a return to the real, and it recognized this real as a proper object of knowledge. The approach to reality, however, was bound to cause difficulties. Espousing subjectivity, as it did, and using the subject as its point of departure, it is not surprising that in many cases it failed either to transcend the subject or to get beyond the realm of phenomenal being to which long ago Kant had restricted the human intellect. The German Existentialists, and Jaspers in particular, have not been able to overcome their Kantian presuppositions. In France intellect has been too distorted and kept too much on the subjective level to constitute really a valid opposition to the older Rationalism. Starting with the subject in most cases it was unable to transcend the subject. And it is just as inadequate ultimately in its subjectivity as was historic Rationalism in its objectivity.

This problem of knowledge has been without doubt one of the most important in modern thought. What can man know and to what extent can he know it are ever recurring questions. The answer has, for the most part, been a foregone conclusion. In very few instances has intellect been considered a faculty of being. The Kantian position of the limitation of intellect to sense experience has in most cases been accepted. In other instances the starting point of the investigation has been the idea or the concept, and this has entailed an attempt to prove that the concept adequately represents the external object. Such a proof is, of course, impossible, and modern philosophical systems are evidence of the impossibility of such a venture. As long as the concept has been the point of departure, the concept has remained that at which intellect has finally terminated. Modern Subjectivism, the substitution of probability and predictability for certainty, is only a logical outcome and inevitable conclusion of a theory of knowledge which long ago ignored evidence and started from preconceived assumptions of what science is or should be. This is always a dangerous procedure. Reality is, after all, what it is and as it is. It is the task of intellect to search it out.

DIALECTICAL MATERIALISM

In its theory of knowledge, Dialectical Materialism attempts to steer a middle path between the older Mechanism and Idealism.

This could result in a realistic theory of knowledge, were it not for the fact that Dialectical Materialism is committed to the rejection of any immaterial principle in reality. Hence, although it attempts to differentiate mind from matter, it must at the same time hold that matter is the ultimate source of mind. Knowledge is matter that has become conscious of itself, and the knowing process is a copy of the evolutionary process taking place on a lower level. Knowledge is, then, objective and based on the causality of external objects. It depends on experiential contact with an external world and is due to progress in accord with scientific investigation of experience. There is, of course, no hope here that knowledge will transcend the experienceable world, since this world and reality completely coincide.

KNOWLEDGE AND EXPERIENCE

Let us attempt to dispense with all preconceived notions of what knowledge is or should be and examine it as we find it in experience. For knowledge is a fact. We know, and we know that we know. It is, at the very least, an individual experience of which we are conscious, and which we can attempt to understand and analyze. No one will deny that he knows. If we begin with this fundamental fact of our human experience, perhaps we can arrive at some notion of what to know means. It is just possible that from an inspection of this basic experience we shall find knowledge to be more objective than we have previously suspected.

For a good many years now modern theories of knowledge have assumed that knowledge begins in the senses and must then be interpreted and given meaning by the intellect. Kant, as we have seen, succeeded in driving a deep wedge between sense experience and intellectual knowledge. But it is not only the non-scholastic philosophers who have been guilty of such a separation. The way the knowing process is described at times can very easily lead the reader to the idea that sensation takes place prior to and independently of any functioning of the intellect. The object of sense knowledge must first affect the external senses, pass through the internal senses, and finally be represented in the phantasm. Only then does the intellect begin its work of abstracting the intelligible species from the phantasm so that it can finally represent this intelligibility in a concept. The operation of the senses is distinct, of course, from that of the intellect, and the two functions can be separately described. But distinction does not mean separation, and in reality we do not first sense and then know. Rather we know that we sense. I see a table, and at one and the same time I know that I see a table. There is one unified source of a two-fold function here. It is man who knows and he knows by means of a principle which is in matter and which functions in matter. The intellective soul is the radical source of man's knowledge, and it is through it ultimately that he both senses and understands.

Knowledge a First Principle

Hence there is never any need to "prove" that the intellectual knowledge we have is really a knowledge of a real object. Our senses bring us into immediate contact with things, not just with their qualitative or quantitative modifications. The whole thing acts on us, for only a fully constituted being can act. And we respond fully, as a whole being, to that which affects us in one way or another. We do not just see red or feel heat. We see *something* red and feel *something* hot. And at one and the same time we know that we see it and feel it. In this respect man's sensitive powers and operations are completely different from those of an animal. Our sensation is completely human, which means that from the very beginning it is penetrated by intellect. Our seeing is a meaningful seeing, and our feeling is a meaningful feeling. In the same way our basic understanding is interwoven with sense and directed to a sense object and brought into immediate contact with such an object.

Nor does the knowing process stop here. There is more to human knowledge than mere meaningful seeing or hearing. We spontaneously assert that what we know in a sensible and meaningful way exists and is affecting us here and now. Through the senses we come into direct and meaningful contact with a sensible and external reality. The senses make contact with existence without realizing either what exists or that it exists. But the intellect, operating in immediate relation with the senses, knows what is sensed and that it is being sensed and asserts that knowledge in its judgments. "This red thing is;" "that cold thing is." All this is a fact of immediate experience. It is something which happens to all of us. It is basic in the knowing process. It cannot be proved simply because proof always begins from something more known and proceeds to something less known. But there is nothing more known than this sensible-intellectual knowledge of external, material objects. It cannot be proved precisely because it is a first principle. There is nothing prior to it. It is completely and clearly evident that such is the case. To doubt it is to call into question the unquestionable. It is to pretend that things are not as we must recognize them. And it results, consequently, in setting up a false problem, which, as a matter of fact, becomes an insoluble problem simply because from the very beginning it proceeds from a false and impossible starting point.

The Knowing Process

Let us attempt to follow the knowing process, as it takes place in a concrete situation. In the statement, "This apple is red," I am asserting something of a concrete, individual, existing thing. I am not speaking simply about a meaning. What I am speaking about has meaning, but there is more to it than that. It is *this* meaningful thing which I have encountered and of which I am aware. It is something to which I can point, something which I see, feel, taste, etc. It is here and now affecting me sensibly, and I am aware that this is the case. Hence, it is not just a term or an idea that I am speaking about. It is a real, concrete object with which I am in immediate sensible and intellectual contact. The "is" in the statement expresses this concrete act of existence which is being exercised here and now by the object confronting me. In the predicate I state further under what manner the existing thing is affecting me. In this case it is in the manner we call red, and the reason why it can so affect me is precisely because it exists as red. What the statement means is this: Here and now I see something which I recognize as an apple, and this apple exists in itself as red; hence it affects me and causes me to see it as red and recognize it as an apple. It is only because the apple exists that I express a statement of its existence. It is only because it exists as red that I see it as red. Whatever I say, I say about a real object. And I can make such statements because my knowledge comes from experiential contact with a real being and is referred back to that being.

That there are both sensible and intelligible elements in the object is equally evident. There is meaning here, for I recognize an apple, not an orange or a pear. Yet this meaning, which can refer to any apple and all apples, is in this case concretized and individuated. It is *this* apple about which I make the statement. If there were two apples, each the same color and size, there would be no way to distinguish them on the intellectual level. Each one is completely and perfectly an apple. Each one contains the meaning of apple. The only possible way I can distinguish between two such objects, each of which contains the same intelligible content, is to refer them to some area in which the distinction can be made. I do this by seeing them, by pointing to them. The distinction, then, is made in the only area in which it can be made—in the area of sense knowledge. *This* I see is not *that*. In such a case, when the intelligible content of two objects is the same, intellectual knowledge must be joined with sense knowledge, if one object is to be adequately distinguished from the other. And again this is exactly what happens. No one ever had any difficulty in knowing that one red apple was different from another red apple and in saying so. It is through the sensible experience we have that our intellectual knowledge is referred to its proper object.

Knowledge a Function of Man

As long as one realizes that it is man who knows and not just an intellect, it is easy to avoid the charges of rationalism and abstractionism which are brought against Aristotle's and St. Thomas' theory of knowledge. Both of them state that the *intellect* cannot know the singular in its singularity. But neither of them said that *man* cannot know the singular. St. Thomas, for example, writes that the mind primarily knows the formal intelligibilities of material things and secondarily the material element which is related to the formal intelligibility. Now every form is of itself universal and, consequently, a relationship to form will result only in a universal knowledge of the matter which is associated with it. Considered from this viewpoint, matter is not a principle of individuation. It is only when matter is considered as existing under determinate dimensions that it can be called an individuating principle. That is why man can be adequately defined as a composite of matter and rational form. In this case the form is known directly and matter only in general, as a term to which the form is related. But if we consider this man, Socrates, we can no longer form a definition of him because Socrates is composed of *this* form and *this* matter. *This* matter is matter as it exists under determinate dimensions. We can get no direct knowledge of such matter by way of intellect.

Yet St. Thomas is far from denying that we can get a direct knowledge of the singular. In the very next sentence he explains how:

It is clear that our mind cannot know the singular directly; but we can know the singular through our sense powers, for they receive the forms of things in a corporeal organ: thus they receive them under determinate dimensions and so are led to a knowledge of the material singular.[1]

It is because the senses themselves are associated with matter that material things can affect them in a material way. The sense power is immersed in a material organ. Whatever affects it must do so through the material organ. Hence a material object will act on the senses not just formally but materially as well. The impression which is received by the sense will be received under the dimensions of matter. These dimensions are determinate, concrete. The sense will respond, therefore, determinately and concretely to the determinate and concrete object here and now acting upon it. But to respond in this way is to know a singular object in its singularity. Nor will the mind be absent from such knowledge. As St. Thomas says, the mind will mingle itself with singulars so far as it is connected with the sense powers, which

[1] *De Veritate*, 10, 5.

are directed toward singular objects.[2] Aquinas further explains how this connection with the sense powers operates.

This connection takes place in two ways. In the first place in so far as the motion of the sensitive part terminates at the mind, as happens in the motion which arises from sensible things and proceeds to the mind. Thus the mind knows a singular by means of a certain reflection. Thus the mind in knowing its object, which is some universal nature, knows also its own act, it knows further the species which is the principle of the act, and it knows, too, the sense image from which this species has been abstracted. And thus it acquires some knowledge of the singular.[3]

The process can work from the other direction also. The operation can begin in the mind and proceed toward the sense faculties. In this way the mind immerses itself in singulars by means of the cogitative sense. This cogitative sense is a sense power with a corporeal organ which acts as an intermediary between the universal knowledge of the intellect and the particular objects to which such knowledge can be applied. As a matter of fact we can and do apply such knowledge to singular objects. We recognize, for example, that it is good for man to have some relaxation and entertainment. But we can obtain such needed relaxation by attending this play at this theater. And so we choose to go to the theater that evening. There must be some medium through which and by which our universal knowledge is applied to singular objects. If this were not so, we would never make judgments about singular objects. The cogitative sense is precisely this medium between the mind's universal knowledge on the one hand and the sensible concrete object on the other. Thus a sort of syllogism is found in which the major premise is universal. And this expresses the universal knowledge possessed by the intellect. The minor premise will be an application made by the cogitative sense. This will be a singular proposition. And the conclusion will be the choice of this or that way of acting.[4]

There is no problem in such a theory of knowledge about man's contact with reality. He perceives it sensibly and intellectually as the composite of sense and intellect which he is. And the

[2] *Ibid.*
[3] *Ibid.*
[4] *Ibid.*

balance in such a knowledge of the real is always maintained. There is meaning in the real which one experiences, and the human intellect gets at that meaning directly. There is more than this, however. There is meaning concretized and sensibly existing. It is this concretized, existing reality which the human sense powers attain. But in each case, what one knowing process gets directly, the other gets indirectly. The intellect is mingled with sense, and sense in turn is united with intellect. The radical source of both functions is the same—a substantial form existing in matter. It is always man who knows, and he knows the existing, sensible, intelligible real in an intellectualized sensation. And immediately he asserts that it is as he knows it. Aquinas does not write a rationalism, a philosophy of the abstract concept. Neither does he sink into a mere sensism. He writes a metaphysics of reality as it is known and grasped by a human being who confronts that reality and who knows it as only a man composed of spirit and matter can know it.

Knowledge and Being

The knowledge we have been speaking of is the kind of knowledge had by everyone in an immediate contact with what is real. And everyone responds spontaneously to such contact and asserts in one way or another that things are, that they exist in this way or that way. In other words, the human intellect makes contact with being and is aware that it does so, because this is what intellect is made for. All of our thinking is ordered to being, and we think the way we do because being is that way. To some extent, at least, every man is a metaphysician. For every man, whether he recognizes it or not, is constantly striving to understand that which is. And it is only because things are that they can become objects of intellect. What else is there to know, if not being? Outside of being there is nothing, and nothing cannot possibly become an object of knowledge. Only that which is real can be a real term of the intellect's function; and the real is that which exists. For it is existence which makes being be and makes each being be in this way or that way. There is no difference, in fact, between existing and existing in a certain way. Existence actuates whatever perfection a being contains within itself; or better, perhaps, it is responsible for whatever real perfection is found in being. The act of existence is the ultimate determining factor, nor is there anything that need be added to the act of existence to further explain it. The basic intelligibility of a being, the various accidental modifications of a being, all these are knowable only because they are real; and they achieve their reality from their existential acts. We know the possible only from the real, and, when we conceive the possible, we conceive it as that which is capable of existing. Here, too, there is a necessary reference to existence and being. We assert being in every judgment we make, and it is being itself which makes such judgments possible. St. Thomas expresses it as follows:

That which I call 'to be' is among all things the most perfect: this is clearly seen from this that act is always the perfection of a potency. No determined form is ever actually understood unless it is actuated by a 'to be.' For humanity or the nature of fire can be considered as existing in the potency of matter, or in the power of an agent, or even in an intellect: but that which possesses 'to be' is made actually existing. Hence it is clear that what I call 'to be' is the actuality of all acts and because of this the perfection of all perfections. Nor should it be understood that anything more formal than 'to be' can be added to what I mean by 'to be,' determining it as act determines a potency: for a 'to be' of this sort is entirely different from that to which it is added as a determining factor. Nothing can be added to 'to be' which is extrinsic to it, since there is nothing extrinsic to existence except non-being, which can be neither matter nor form. Hence 'to be' is not determined by something else as potency is by act but rather as act is determined by potency. For in the definition of forms the proper matter takes the place of a difference, as, for instance, when the soul is defined as the act of a physically organized body. In this way this 'to be' is distinguished from that in so far as it is the 'to be' of this or that kind of thing. Hence it is that Dionysius says that, although living things are more noble than things which merely exist, nevertheless 'to be' is more noble than to live: for living things do not only have life, but at one and the same time they possess existence.[5]

[5] *De Potentia*, 7, 2 and 9, trans. by the English Dominican Fathers (Westminster, Md., Newman Press, 1952).

Knowledge of Transcendent Being

This being which the human intellect knows in conjunction with the sense powers is, as we have seen, a concrete, individuated being. It is a kind of being directly proportioned to the kind of being man himself is. Hence he responds to it immediately and is aware that he does so. This being which we know directly and immediately is not, of course, the being of metaphysics. But it provides us with the necessary starting point, so that we can see there is more to being than the sensible and the material. Once we recognize the real as that which exists, then we understand that, wherever we find existence, we find being. We understand also that 'to be' is not the same as 'to be sensible.' Hence, while our direct knowledge is of the sensible, there remains the possibility of an indirect knowledge of being which is not sensible. For such being will be being because it exists, and we have some notion of what it means to exist. We assert existence constantly. We distinguish it from the material and the merely intelligible. We understand it as that which grounds the material and the intelligible, giving them whatever reality they possess.

From here philosophy can seek for a more penetrating insight into the reality which is confronted in concrete experience. An analysis of such experience will lead us to a knowledge of the composition and limitation involved in all material being. And from a knowledge of such composition and limitation we are led necessarily to assert the existence of the Simple and the Unlimited. And while it is true to say that we can never grasp this Unlimited Being, as we do the limited beings of our experience, yet it is equally true to say that we are able to arrive at some sort of knowledge of such a Being. We may know only *that it is* and not *what it is,* but in that assertion is contained the ultimate reason for the being of the limited things that are. So it is that from beings we are led to Being, from existents to Existence Itself, from the realm of the finite to that of the Infinite. Gilson expresses the necessity of such a transition in the following words:

. . . Once more, it is the being in things which is the ultimate reason of all the natural processes we have been stating. It is being as such which communicates its form as efficient cause, which produces change as a moving cause, and assigns to it a reason for being produced as a final cause. We are dealing, then, with beings which are ceaselessly moved by a fundamental need to preserve and complete themselves.

Now we cannot reflect upon an experience like this without noticing that it does not contain the adequate explanation of the facts it places before us. This world of becoming which is in motion in order to find itself, these heavenly spheres continually seeking themselves in the successive points of their orbits, these human souls which capture and assimilate being by their intellect, these substantial forms forever searching out new matter in which to realize themselves, do not contain in themselves the explanation of what they are. If such beings were self-explaining, they would be lacking nothing. Or, inversely, they would have to be lacking nothing before they could be self explaining. But then they would no longer move in search of themselves; they would repose in the integrity of their own essence at length realized; they would cease to be what they now are.

It is, therefore, outside the world of potency and act, above becoming, and in a being which is totally what it is, that we must look for the sufficient reason of the universe. But this being reached by thought is obviously of a different nature than the being we observe, for if it were not different from the being which experience gives, there would be no advantage in positing it. Thus the world of becoming postulates a principle removed from becoming and placed entirely outside it.[6]

Thomistic Realism

It is in this sense, then, that the philosophy of St. Thomas can be called a realistic philosophy. It is grounded in being, since it takes as its starting point the being which faces us at every turn and in every experience. It asks what it means to be, and it finds in the answer a richness and a perfection which leads beyond the experience with which it began. Such a metaphysics may transcend experience, but it will never leave being behind and settle for mere abstractions and conceptualizations. For it never loses sight of the fact that it is reality which is under investigation and that reality is irrevocably united to existence. It becomes necessary, therefore, for such a metaphysics to transcend matter and sense;

[6] Etienne Gilson, "The Spirit of Thomism," in *A Gilson Reader*, Anton C. Pegis, ed. (Garden City, N. Y., Doubleday & Co., Inc., 1957), pp. 249-250.

for there is no necessary connection between matter and sense and existence. Whatever reality such things have they have by privilege not by right. Reality on this level is a shared and limited reality, for the existence which is possessed is a limited existence. To be real can never be the same as to be material; to exist means more than to exist sensibly. And always it is the real in its very reality which this metaphysics is striving to understand, not just the real as modified, or qualified, or limited to this mode or that. One does not seek the source of light in a room by groping amid the dimly lit corners. Nor should one hope to find being by restricting the search to its limited and partial manifestations. Matter and sense are left behind only because a richer reality is being sought, and it is evident that it cannot be found in such an area.

Nor is this true just of the sensibly real. The whole of the contingent is like this. For what is contingent can either be or not be. And if it is, then it is by sufferance not by necessity. There can be no necessary connection between the contingent and being, but only a factual one. Being in its perfection cannot possibly be found in an area which could just as easily be void of being. Hence all that is imperfect and limited, all that changes and in changing manifests its limitation and lack of reality necessarily points beyond itself. It is only when existence itself is reached that reality itself is achieved. And in the light of that truly Real all that is partially and limitedly real falls into place and achieves significance on its own level.

LIMITATIONS OF SUCH A REALISM. It is obvious, of course, that such a knowledge of being which transcends the being of sensible things is less clear and direct than is our knowledge of what we experience through the senses. It is had by analogy, by discursive reasoning, and by judgments of separation. As a result, it is a difficult knowledge to obtain, and it requires training and reflection before it can be obtained. It is further a knowledge expressed in propositions and constructs. And while it results in a certain kind of intellectual insight, this insight is not the immediate insight which one has of sensible reality. Yet it must be remembered that such knowledge is no less certain for all of that. To understand *that* it must be so is one thing. To understand completely and exhaustively *how* it must be so is clearly another. The limitations under which such a knowledge labors come not from the system of metaphysics according to which we philosophize, but from the very nature of the being who knows. Reality is extremely rich and complex. As human beings we exist on a given level of it. Just as there are any number of gradations of being below us, so, too, are there gradations of being above us. We are properly at home in the material section in which we exist. We know that area of the real properly and immediately. Yet our human intellects reach out to all being precisely because we understand that there must be more to being than what we experience on our own level. It is not surprising that, when we contact such being, we should understand it only improperly, indirectly, and in relation to that which we know directly.

Those who would reduce all certain knowledge to that which is obtainable in the area of the natural sciences complain that metaphysical knowledge is not verifiable. If by this is meant that one cannot have sensible experience of the conclusions drawn on the metaphysical level, then, of course, such knowledge is unverifiable. But there is another sort of verifiability than the sensible. There is a verification on the intellectual plane, where one sees clearly that certain propositions and conclusions lead to impossibilities and irreconcilable contradictions. That limited being, for example, is necessarily composite; that every effect demands an adequate cause; that change requires a subject in which to take place; all these statements are verifiable in the sense that they are essential to any reasonable explanation of the experience which is common to everyone. Philosophy attempts to explain the real in terms of its ultimate causes. If the real is more extensive and more complex than we would like it to be, we do not become philosophers by limiting the real to this or that area of it, so that we can discuss it more simply and more clearly. We can do nothing except face the complexity and the richness of reality and seek an understanding of it in terms of a knowledge which is proper to us as humans and not angels. Such a knowledge will necessarily lead us beyond ourselves and beyond the level of being on which we exist. When it does that, we may be less at home than we are in the realm of sensible experience, but we are not lost. For we, too, have a share in being, and our intellects are made for being. Hence we shall achieve some knowledge of being, even if it be an indirect and analogous knowledge.

The same is true of our knowledge of God. We can know that He is, says St. Thomas, and not what He is. But to know that He is, is itself a positive and certain knowledge. To understand that a First Cause explains all other causes, a Necessary Being is demanded by the contingent beings of our experience, an Unlimited Being is required to make intelligible the limitation we find all about us, this is not nothing. We may never be able to grasp comprehensively the nature of God; we may never be able to express the meaning of God in a concept or a definition. But to know that there is and must be at the heart of reality a pure and perfect Being is of tremendous importance. It means that reality has a source and a goal; that it is meaningful and purposeful; that human action carries responsibility with it; that the universe in which we live is an intelligible one.

It is because of this richness and complexity of reality that the science of metaphysics can never be completely written by one man or by one age. Being ultimately is infinite and the human mind is constantly able to discover new facets of it, achieve new insights into it, draw new conclusions from it. The work of metaphysics is the work of many lifetimes, and it will necessarily continue for as long as there are human minds which are confronted with being. This is not to deny the validity of past knowledge. It is simply to recognize the fact that the human mind is finite; that whatever truth it has been able to find in the past is also finite; that this truth can also become more deeply appreciated, more clearly seen, more completely related to other facets of truth in other areas of knowing. The certainty which has been achieved is no less certain because it is understood more completely or its relationships more adequately apprehended.

This is the reason also that, while metaphysics is a true natural wisdom and leads to certain knowledge of ultimate causes, there is more than metaphysics required for a complete human knowledge of the real. There are depths of being which the human mind itself could not dream of. There are complexities in reality which the human intellect alone could not suspect. If being is ultimately divine and infinite, then only the divine and the infinite can adequately know it. And if, as a matter of fact the divine has revealed some of the truths of being, then it is to these sources of truth that man must go for a more complete grasp of the reality in which he finds himself. Philosophy itself needs the guiding hand of theology. Reason finds its completion in faith.

SUMMARY

1. Sensation and intellection are a unified operation of one human being. We have an intellectualized sensation of a real being, and we judge that such is the case.

2. It is only in terms of both senses and intellect that our statements about the reality we contact have any meaning. It is always *a* man who knows *this* or *that* thing. Thus Aquinas avoids both pure Rationalism and mere Sensism.

3. The basic reason for the intelligibility of any thing is existence; for only that is knowable which exists and only in so far as it exists. Non-being is not an object of knowledge.

4. Existence can be distinguished from its *de facto* connection with matter and essence. Hence, from contact with limited existence, as we find it in experience, we can rise to the necessity of an Existence, which we cannot experience.

5. This philosophy of existence begins with experienced existence and concludes to a necessary Existence without which the existence we experience is unintelligible. Hence, it is truly a philosophy of being, grounded in being and rising to Being in its plenitude.

6. Our knowledge of this ultimate and necessary Being is, of course, limited; but it is certain and absolute, as far as it goes. Thus knowledge can and does transcend the merely sensible order, and metaphysics is really a science of being and not just of concepts.

SELECTED READINGS

Man as Knower*

An examination of certain formulas of spontaneous language is enough to indicate the general bearing of the problem posed by the judgment of existence. When I say, "I see a man," or "I perceive the existence of this table," even the most cursory reflection makes it clear how improper expressions of this kind are. I can neither perceive nor see *man* nor *existence,* which are concepts of the understanding. What I want to say is that I know by my intellect that what I perceive by my senses is a man, or an existent. Still, expressions like these, however confused they may be, mirror perfectly the complex unity of psychological experience, since it is of that above all that there is question here. Posing the problem of the apprehension of a sensible being by a human composite, one is in experience from start to finish. It is enough then to note that we express our perceptions spontaneously just as they present themselves to us, that is, perceived by an intelligent subject, and that we formulate our judgments just as we conceive their terms, that is, concepts weighted with sensible images and often bound up with sensations. In short, man knows what he feels and feels what he knows.

The direct observation of these facts of internal experience is sufficient in itself. If, in addition, we quote St. Thomas, it will only be to assure those who wish to make classical realism over in their own manner that their predecessors did not wait for the twentieth century to take notice of such evidences as these. It matters little about the technical language St. Thomas uses, provided one sees beneath the words he uses the reality which they signify. Psychologies remain free to fashion for themselves another language in order to express more detailed experimental findings: to St. Thomas goes the merit of having insistently drawn the attention of the investigator to the important fact that the intellection of man is the act of a human intellect, and that the

* E. Gilson, *Réalisme Thomiste et Critique de la Connaissance* (Paris, J. Vrin, 1947).

sensation of man is the operation of a human sensibility. The sensibility of the animal is itself already more than the passive registering of impressions presented to it. The behavior of animals proves that they are capable of acquiring an experience which is purely sensible, and up to a certain point, of adapting themselves to the different situations in which they find themselves. This adaptation can attain to such a flexibility that their reactions often closely resemble the operations of a reasoning being. The aptitude of images to combine and organize into series which lead the animal to acts adapted to the circumstances is what the Middle Ages called the *aestimativa*. Inasmuch as he himself is an animal, man has one also; to it he readily leaves the task of directing many actions which, under normal circumstances and unless something unforeseen happens, his body performs the better the less his reason concerns itself with them. And yet, the medieval philosophers often gave man's *aestimativa* a distinct name; they called it *cogitativa*, or even *ratio particularis*—not at all meaning that it is a function of reason in man, but because it operates in man as the sensibility of an intelligent being. The expression *ratio particularis*, whence arises the apparent confusion, expresses the communication of distinct functions in the unity of the same subject, meaning then that as the memory of man is able to perform operations which that of the animal is not able to do, the sensory faculties of man are capable of operations still more like than are those of the animal to the operations of reason. And why? Because, says St. Thomas, our sensibility possesses *aliquam affinitatem et propinquitatem ad rationem universalem, secundum quandam refluentiam*. The expressions are purposely vague; it is the business of psychology today to give them a precise meaning. What concerns us is the fact itself; the osmosis which is produced between the understanding and the sensibility in the unity of the human knowing subject.

As one could have foreseen, the phenomenon is produced equally in the opposite direction: to the intellectualization of the sensibility by the understanding corresponds a sensibilization of the understanding by sensation. That is what is meant by certain scholastics tags, which are often repeated but not always meant in the full sense that belongs to them. Indeed, it is not enough to say that "one does not think without images." It is important to realize that even that which we conceive by the intellect is presented us by and in the given of sensation. Just as the thing perceived is a knowable without knowing itself, so the sensible species is possessed of an intelligible which the senses do not know. Now, it is not only there, but it is no place else at the moment when we know it by the intellect. We are not separated Intelligences thinking Platonic Ideas. Sensible things exist independent and separate one from the other, but there are no intelligibles for us separate from the sensible as one thing can be separated from another. This is why, says St. Thomas, the intelligibles of our human intellect are in the sensible species *secundum esse*. We think of them there because it is there that they exist. Is there question of apprehending some thing? We first must have a sensation. Is there question of thinking and of reflecting on that which we already know? We must have recourse, in order to conceive, to sensible images, themselves deposited in us by sensations.

Existentialism and Existence*

Just as essentialism is a metaphysics of being minus existence, existentialism is a philosophy of existence minus being. Hence the peculiar characters of the experience of existence upon which it rests. It can be described as a bare sensation of existence experienced by a sensibility which, for a few moments, is cut off from its intellect. It is, so to speak, a downward *extasis*, wherein finite acts of existing are merely felt in themselves, wholly unrelated to their essences and therefore deprived of all intelligibility. No concept there, nor even judgment, but the bare experiencing of an *is* which is not yet a *being*. No wonder, then, that, for contemporary existentialism to experience existence is to experience anguish, nausea and the utter absurdity of everything. But, where there is no thing, there can be no all. Such an experience is but too real, yet it merely proves that essence and purpose are part and parcel of actual being. Should they be removed, be it for a

* E. Gilson, *Being and Some Philosophers* (Toronto, Pontifical Institute of Medieval Studies, 1949), pp. 208-209.

split second, what is left no longer makes sense: it is that whose only essence and meaning is to have neither essence nor meaning. He who allows himself thus to sink into his own sensibility cannot but experience a metaphysical giddiness, a sort of existence-sickness, whence he will later conclude that existence itself is but a sickness of being.

How could it be otherwise? There is only one way to reach pure existence, and the mystics have always known it. Not the way that leads, through the denial of essences, to the maddening experience of some existing nothingness, but the one that once lead Augustine, Bonaventura and John of the Cross, through overcoming all essences without ever losing them, to reach their common source, itself beyond essences yet containing them all. Not despair, but perfect joy, is the reward of such an experience, and it is true that philosophy alone cannot achieve it; but this is not the only case in which philosophy points out a goal which it itself is unable to reach. Contemporary existentialism is right in asking questions about existence, but one may well wonder if its fundamental mistake is not to ask existences to account for themselves, instead of looking at being for their cause. Distinct as they are from being by that only which in them is not, nothingness necessarily becomes their specific difference. We are thus left face to face with Platonic becoming, without the world of Ideas to grant it what it may have of intelligibility; or with universal motion without the self-thinking Thought of Aristotle to sway it from on high; or with a world created out of nothing, which, having lost its Creator, must needs be created by nothing. Existentialism has not discovered existence; its only metaphysical discovery is to ask how existence can still make sense, if nothingness remains the sole principle of its intelligibility.

The Proposition: God Is*

We must understand that it is not God Who is here to be defined and made intelligible: it is the world. The problem of God is only the ultimate basis of the problem of the world and of

---

* A. D. Sertillanges, O.P., *Foundations of Thomistic Philosophy*, trans. by Godfrey Anstruther, O.P. (London, Sands & Co., Ltd., 1931).

life. Take away God, and life and the world are left unfinished, are not defined, but offer only something relative and insufficient, without ultimate reason for existence: what may be called a *system of nothings*. But, to manifest them, and make them thinkable for us, it is sufficient to be able to think of, and define God, and make Him apparent to us, precisely as exercising a function. The problem of God leads us to this: to comprehend the necessity of the Incomprehensible, to know that there is an Unknowable, to define the need of the Indefinable. So true is this, that if we were able to understand and define God, we would then be unable to account for the world. I mean that if God were to enter into the categories of thought, under any guise whatever, He could no longer be that first thing which the world requires in order to remain in what Renouvier calls "the limits of the possible intelligence." It is quite obvious, therefore, that there is no contradiction of any sort. The defined and the non-defined do not belong to the same object or the same subject, and the objection falls to the ground. On the question of the identity of essence and existence, of being, and that which is, in God, we are in entire agreement. We admit the consequences: we can no more attain to the being of God than we can to His nature. But it is by no means necessary to attain to God's being in this way in order to form a judgment of His existence. To affirm that God is, is not to be in contact with God's essence. *Being* may be taken in two ways. First as signifying the very entity of a thing, in which sense *being* is substance, quantity, quality and the rest, because "that only can be called being which enters, in some way, into the general categories of being." Secondly, as expressing the truth of a proposition, by means of the connecting-word *is*. In the first sense, the word *being* signifies God in His reality, and therefore stands for something unknowable. In the second sense it signifies nothing; it is only a predicate which can be applied equally well to a thing without real existence, as when we say: Thisness *is*, or nothing *is* inferior to being. When we say: God *is*, we simply affirm the reality, under whatever form it be, of the sufficient and necessary principle of all things. We predicate reality of the unknowable and unnamable principle, without which nothing can be known or named.

It will now be apparent that the very being of God, identical with His essence, has absolutely no need to be attained by the mind, in order that the proposition, *God is*, may be true and rigorously demonstrated. We do not put God among existing things in the sense that we attribute being to Him as a quality which He posseses in common with His creatures. In that sense God *is not*. If He were, He could no longer be called the source of being. That which causes being is above and outside the being which it causes. Since all causality implies an ultimate principle, we postulate one, and call it *God*. When we say *God is*, we consecrate this postulate to Him alone, but we do not, properly speaking, qualify its possessor. Our God is not *such* a one; were He *such*, He would be limited, and could no longer answer our requirements. The phrase, *God is*, is positive only as an expression of the insufficiency of the world and the correlative necessity of an ultimate principle: as a value of definition, in the proper sense of the word, it is entirely negative.

After that it is useless to dwell on the last argument; it is already answered. Our principles are derived from experience, and, it is objected, they cannot take us out of the realm of experience. Hence we cannot pass beyond that realm. I answer that we pass beyond experience only in the sense that we follow up our experiences to the source which explains them. If we cannot close the circle, if series of causes cannot give a reason for their efficacy save by means of a first cause, at once immanent and transcendent, then we must admit a first cause. This first cause is immanent by its action and life-giving presence, and, under this aspect, it is knowable, as a necessity of experience itself. As transcendent we declare it inaccessible and unknowable; we do not put it in any ideological framework or category. The relations we attribute to it are only conveniences of thought; in no sense are they realities. There are no real relations of God to the creature: there are only real relations of the creature to God, which we, by an instinctive need of *correlation*, make reciprocal. Whatever there is in the creature comes from God, subsists by God, and tends towards God, but without any change, or real qualification, or attachment, or real relation on God's side.

BIBLIOGRAPHY

Gilson, E., *Réalisme Thomiste et Critique de la Connaissance*. Paris, J. Vrin, 1947.
——, Being and Some Philosophers. Toronto, Pontifical Institute of Medieval Studies, 1949. Cf. especially the last chapter, pp. 208-209.
Henle, R. J., S.J., *Method in Metaphysics*. The Aquinas lecture of the Aristotelian Society of Marquette University. Milwaukee, Wisc., Marquette University Press, 1951.
Maritain, J., *A Preface to Metaphysics*, trans. by E. I. Watkin. New York, Charles Scribner's Sons, 1940.
——, *Existence and the Existent*, trans. by L. Galantière and G. B. Phelan. New York, Pantheon Books, Inc., 1949.
Phelan, G. B. "'The Existentialism of St. Thomas," proceedings of the American Catholic Philosophic Association, Vol. 21. Washington, Catholic University of America Press, 1946. Pp. 25-40.
Regis, L. M., O.P., *St. Thomas and Epistemology*. The Aquinas Lecture of the Aristotelian Society of Marquette University. Milwaukee, Wisc., Marquette University Press, 1946.
Sertillanges, A. D., O.P., *The Foundations of Thomistic Philosophy*, trans. by G. Anstruther. St. Louis, B. Herder Book Company, 1931.
Smith, G., S.J., "A Date in the History of Epistemology," *The Thomist*, Vol. 5, the Maritain volume. New York, Sheed & Ward, Ltd., 1943.
Wilhelmsen, F., *Man's Knowledge of Reality*. Englewood Cliffs, N. J., Prentice-Hall, Inc., 1956.

7

Reason
and the
Destiny of Man

Philosophy as a science is meant to lead to a certain knowledge of ultimates. The perfection of such knowledge will include also a grasp of the inter-relationship of things, an understanding of how one thing is ordered to another and to the supreme principle which rules and directs them. Such a knowledge will recognize that the goal to which a thing is directed is also the proper good of that thing, and that such a thing is best disposed, when it is properly ordered to this goal. Now just as the particular thing in the real order acquires a perfection through being directed to its proper goal, so an habitual knowledge of things with relation to their goals produces in the intellect a perfection of its own. This perfection is called wisdom.

In the real order, one area of being is naturally and properly subordinate to other areas. The art of medicine, for example, is superior to the art of the pharmacist; for health, with which medicine is concerned, is the goal of all the medications prepared by the pharmacist for the use of the physician. So, too, is the art of making weapons subordinate to the art of war. For someone to recognize such particular goals and know how to reach them is for him to be wise in a particular way. If, then, someone were able to know the absolute end or goal of all things and to see how all things are related to such a goal, he would be wise in the absolute sense. Hence, philosophy is called a natural wisdom because it comes to a knowledge at least of the existence of an absolute principle to which everything is directed and on which everything depends. A complete natural wisdom—if such a thing were possible—would, of course, demand more than this. It would have to include the knowledge of the nature of this ultimate principle and the way the beings which depend on it are meant to achieve this principle. It would include, that is, a knowledge of the goal of the whole universe and of each thing in it, as well as the complex inter-relationships between these things.

To what extent can philosophy lead us to such a knowledge? It can tell us certainly what is the goal of the universe, but it can do that only in a general way. Properly speaking, the goal of anything is that which is intended for it by its author. As we have seen, the author of the universe is a Supreme Intelligence. The goal, then, to which the universe is directed must be a goal which is perfectly in accord with such an Intelligence. Since every goal is a good, the goal of the universe must also be the good of this Supreme Intelligence. The good of any intelligence is truth, for this is what perfects an intellect. So, too, must the good of the Supreme Intelligence be truth. This Truth will be a Supreme and Most Perfect Truth, the foundation and principle of all truth. This is the Truth at the very heart of the being of all things. It is to a knowledge of such Truth that philosophical wisdom aspires.

It has already been pointed out to what extent philosophy can lead us to a knowledge of this Most Perfect Truth, Who is also Most Perfect Being. From limited and composite effects we can know with certainty that such a Being exists, and we can further come to a knowledge of some of the characteristics possessed by such a Being. On the other hand, since this knowledge is derived from limited, sensible things, we know much more clearly *that* He is than we know *what* He is. But knowledge is not adequate, unless it tells us what a thing is. It is in this intelligible grasp of the whatness, or essence, of a thing that knowledge reaches its perfection. The human intellect, however, is directed in its present state to an adequate knowledge only of those things which fall directly under the senses. Such things can never lead us to a knowledge of the very essence of God, for such sensible effects fall far short of representing the complete perfection of their cause.

Furthermore, even this direct knowledge which we have of sensible things is itself in many instances inadequate. There are all sorts of properties of sensible things which remain hidden from us. In many areas the human intellect can arrive at only a general grasp of the nature of such things. For we know natures and essences insofar as they manifest themselves through activities and operations which are proper to them. Only from such proper activity can we come to a metaphysical definition of the source of such activity. We can define a man, for example, as a rational animal, because we experience the activity we call thought. But, if one should ask whether a tiger is specifically different—in the philosophical sense—from an elephant, what can one say? The Only proper activity we experience is the same in the case of both. This activity represents their animal natures, but it is doubtful, to say the least, if there is any particular activity which will suffice to distinguish tigerness from elephantness. In such cases our knowledge must remain generic without ever becoming specific. Now, if our knowledge of sensible things must remain to a great extent inadequate and incomplete, it is obvious that we can come to no adequate or complete knowledge of that which in no way comes under our sense faculties. Furthermore, even if we had a complete grasp of the natures of sensible things, we would still not know how they are related to one another and how each fulfills its place in the universe. In other words, we would not know the plan of the Creator. Not knowing this, how could we possibly hope to achieve a perfect knowledge of the source of these relationships?

NEED OF REVELATION

Since, then, the end of a created intelligent being is to know God, and since such a being achieves only an inadequate knowledge of God, it is fitting that God should reveal himself to man, lest man despair of ever achieving his goal. That such a revelation has, as a matter of fact, been made St. Thomas considers clearly evident from the signs and wonders which have accompanied it.

There are the prophecies and their fulfillment, the raising of the dead, the cures, the inspiration given to human minds. There is, further, the wonderful spread of Christianity itself in the face of persecution and death. There is the acceptance of a doctrine which curbs sense pleasure, which rejects false worldly standards, which leads men to high moral lives. All this has happened not by chance, but evidently by a disposition of God.[1]

These effects which testify to the fact of a revelation are there. Christianity confronts us. Men must react to it one way or another. And historically they have done so. There is, for example, the Rationalist response, which regards revelation as a poetic and imaginative way of proposing truth to those who do not have the capacity to reach it by reason and philosophy. Such an attitude recognizes nothing in revelation which is beyond the capacity of human reason—at least beyond the capacity of human reason at its finest. Almost diametrically opposed to this is the attitude which might be termed pietistic. Such an attitude regards all attempts to bring reason to bear on revelation as scandalous and futile. God has spoken; what need is there of any further questioning? There is not nor can there be any connection between human science and the revealed word of Heaven. Athens cannot possibly have anything in common with Jerusalem. There is another attitude, of course, which simply rejects the possibility of the validity of any so-called revelation. Should persons with such an attitude turn philosophers, they restrict themselves necessarily to reason working simply as reason. We shall return to this point later.

The Thomistic attitude to revelation is not like any of these described above. St. Thomas certainly recognized human reason and the part that it must play in man's intellectual development. As we have seen, he grants to it a proper function, and he insists that in its own area it can achieve scientific and certain knowledge. At the same time he recognizes its limits, and he is far from ascribing to it the possibility of a complete and adequate knowledge of all being, both real and possible. He is not content simply to believe, nor does he think that human knowledge and

[1] The material for this part of the chapter has been taken in general from St. Thomas Aquinas, *Summa Contra Gentiles*, Vol. I, trans. by Anton C. Pegis (Garden City, N. Y., Doubleday & Co., Inc., 1957), Chap. 1-8.

investigation is necessarily a snare and a delusion. Neither would he insist, as the Rationalist does, that revelation is merely a crutch held out to those incapable of walking on more philosophical ground. There is no doubt that God could have revealed truth inaccessible to human understanding, since the divine intellect surpasses all created intellects infinitely more than the finest human intelligence surpasses the lowest. Where such truth is inaccessible to human understanding, the intellect can assent to it only because of other motives than those which move it to accept truths which it does clearly understand. This brings up the necessary distinction between knowledge and faith.

KNOWLEDGE AND FAITH

Knowledge is an actuation of a potency. In the knowing process the intellect is moved from the capacity to know to actually knowing. The moving causes are many, but always there is an object, which presents itself to the intellect. This object is intelligible, and its very intelligibility is the reason why the intellect assents and affirms that the object is as it appears to the mind. Not only does the intellect affirm that such is the case, but in knowledge taken strictly the intellect understands that it cannot be otherwise. The intellect is actuated and comes to rest in possession of the understood reality with which it is in contact. Hence, when we really know something, we assent to it because we must. There is no other alternative. We understand clearly, for example, that two plus two equals four, will always equal four, and can never equal five.

In faith, too, there is an intellectual assent. But in the case of faith there is no intrinsic evidence forcing the intellect to its conclusion. A proposition is proposed to the intellect, but the intellect does not understand that this proposition must be so, that it cannot be otherwise. When we affirm, for example, the truth of the proposition: God is triune, we do not understand why it must necessarily be so and cannot be otherwise. Hence, where faith is concerned, the motive for assent is not the intrinsic intelligibility of the object shining forth and moving the intellect necessarily to a conclusion. If left to itself in such a case, the

intellect would neither assent nor dissent. Another motivating
factor is necessary. This other factor is the will which, under the
influence of grace, leads the intellect to assent to a proposition
which, of itself, does not determine that intellect. Hence the
will plays a part in every assent to a revealed proposition which is
not clearly and adequately understood. The act of faith, then, remains a free act.

It is clear then, why St. Thomas states that no one can know
and believe the same thing in the same way and under the same
aspect. In the one case there is a clear understanding that this
is true and must be true. In the other there is no such clear understanding. Hence, once one knows something, he can no longer
believe it, and when one believes something, he does so because
he does not fully understand why it must necessarily be so. One
cannot believe that two plus two equals four. He knows that.
But one can believe that God is triune, because he cannot know
it.

Content of Revelation

Now while one cannot both know and believe the same thing
at the same time and under the same aspect, it is possible that
what for one person is an act of faith may very well be an act of
knowledge for another. For St. Thomas states that revelation
includes truths which may be known by the natural use of reason
and also truths which could never be known in this way. Revelation is given to men so that they might save their souls. God,
furthermore, wills that all men achieve the salvation for which
they were created. But there are many truths, all of which are
necessary for salvation, which can be acquired naturally only with
great difficulty and much labor. If God had not revealed such
truths, few men would come to any knowledge of God. Many,
for example, do not have the physical disposition necessary for
the work involved. They simply are not capable of refined and
exacting intellectual processes. There are others who may have
the ability, but who are almost constantly involved in temporal
matters, or the daily struggle of earning a living, caring for a
family, etc. Such persons do not have the adequate time and

leisure to devote to a study of the truths concerning God, man, and the universe. Lastly, there are persons who are simply too indolent to submit themselves to the energy and discipline which a study of God necessarily involves. There are few, says Aquinas, who are willing to pursue learning for its own sake.

Furthermore, the very difficulty and profundity of such truths, which are naturally able to be arrived at by human reason, involves a long and slow process. Not only must one go slowly in achieving such understanding, but technical training in method and approach is also required. Were the only way open to us for the knowledge of God that of reason, most men would remain all their lives in complete ignorance of God. The few who were able to acquire such knowledge might also doubt its validity. For the human intellect does not always see the power of demonstration, nor does it always manage to escape the influence of the imagination, and so falls into error. Others would be led astray by the spectacle of wise men, all differing in their views on certain questions. Hence, St. Thomas concludes that it is fitting for God to have revealed truths which reason left to itself can and does achieve. For where men are unable to use their intellects to full advantage, or where they might very easily doubt the conclusions reached by the intellect, they now have the unshakeable certainty of a truth revealed by a God who can neither deceive nor be deceived. In this case revelation complements and supports reason, leading it to a certainty which is naturally achievable— and which in some cases is actually achieved—so that men can go more freely and easily about the more important task of saving their souls.

It is one thing, however, for one man to believe what another may know rationally, and it is another for men to believe that which no created intellect can ever know. As we have seen, St. Thomas has no difficulty in stating that the revelation of such truth is entirely possible. An infinite mind quite possibly would be aware of some truth which created intellects could never fully understand. Since, then, God has actually chosen to reveal such truth to men, there is no difficulty in seeing that such a revelation is also fitting and meaningful. In the first place, no one strives eagerly toward a goal which is not known to him. Now men are

ordered to a good which surpasses every created good. Hence it
was right and proper that God should reveal this goal to men
so that they might more readily seek it. Such revelation also
makes it possible for men to have a true and more perfect knowledge of God. Only then can we say we truly know God, when
we understand that He is far above everything that it is possible
for man to think about Him. This is accomplished when God
reveals something about Himself which surpasses all human understanding. Such a revelation also has the further advantage of
reminding man that his intellect is finite and created and, consequently, preserves him in a humble seeking of the truth. Such
humble search for truth also has its rewards. For while man can
never fully understand what has been revealed, the very assent
to it is a perfection of his intellect; for it leads him beyond his
own limitations to an assertion of the unlimited truth of God.

Revelation, then, comprises two types of truth. There is that
which could be naturally achieved, but which involves a great
deal of time and difficulty. But there is also that which completely
surpasses all effort at human understanding and which is acquired
only through faith. It is the function of theology to apply human
reason to both types of truth and attempt to show their relationships, to inquire into their meanings in so far as human reason
can, to refute opposed errors, and to clarify their sources and their
importance. This revelation which surpasses human reason to a
greater or less extent demands, then, an assent of faith. Such an
assent is, however, always a reasonable one; for the human intellect, while it cannot understand the truth proposed to it, can
and does understand that it is good and worthwhile to believe
such truth. There are, as we have seen, the signs and wonders
which accompany such a revelation and indicate that it is from
God. There is the inner harmony and coherence of one revealed
truth with all the others. There is the dignity and beauty of the
revelation which leads men to a life of moral worth and a complete and final fulfillment.

Revelation Not Opposed to Reason

Just as the truth revealed by God is to the benefit and perfection
of human reason, so, too, is it impossible for human reason to

think anything which would be in contradiction to what is revealed. The very principles of reason are given us by God, for He has created us as the rational beings we are. These principles of reason within us are, then, contained in the Divine Wisdom. Hence, whatever is opposed to them is also opposed to Divine Wisdom. To say, therefore, that reason could possibly be opposed to what is revealed is to say that Divine Wisdom is capable of contradicting Itself. Where the source is the same, that which proceeds from the source must also be in harmony. From the beginning, then, one knows that an argument which claims to disprove a truth revealed by God is either only probable or sophistical and so cannot have the force of a valid demonstration. Not only is there no discord between the truth revealed by God and the truth which human reason is capable of attaining, but the higher truth presents to human reason the best opportunity for intelligent exercise. What we know of God from reason is based on a knowledge of the effects, which bear a certain likeness to their creator. This likeness is, however, very imperfect and cannot possibly become an illustration of revealed truth. Yet such illustrations are worthwhile considering, provided one does not presume that in such weak resemblances there is contained anything like a demonstrative proof or adequate comprehension of what we accept by faith.

St. Thomas has succeeded in drawing a clear-cut distinction between philosophy, revelation, faith, and theology. Human reason has its value and its proper function. It is meant to investigate rationally an intelligible universe and come to a knowledge of the first cause of that universe. Yet this human reason achieves a knowledge which at best remains inadequate. Revelation is fittingly presented to man as a means of overcoming this inadequacy. This revelation must of necessity be true, since it proceeds from a God who is Perfect Truth as well as Perfect Being. Hence, human reason understands this much, that it is good and reasonable to assent to a truth which it cannot fully comprehend. But reason remains reason, and having accepted such a truth on faith, it then proceeds under the light of faith to reach a fuller and more perfect understanding of the truth which has been revealed. Hence philosophy, revelation, faith, and theology remain always distinct from one another. The method, object, and purpose of

philosophy, for example, is different from that employed by
theology. Yet, although they are distinct, there is no reason why
they should be separated. Reality is very complex. The very complexity demands different approaches. Hence, just as it is not
enough to be a biologist or a chemist, so, too, is it not enough
to be a metaphysician. Man is made for a vision of being and
truth. On this earth he approaches that vision through the various
avenues of natural knowledge. He may approach it most perfectly as a metaphysician, but "most perfectly" by no means
signifies adequately. When human knowledge reaches its limit,
as it were, there is given to man a higher truth surpassing the
abilities of his human intellect. It is only by submitting that intellect through an act of faith that he assures himself eventually
of a knowledge that will go directly and adequately to the source
of all being and truth. In other words, when he can no longer
know, man believes in order that one day he may know perfectly
the truth he has always sought. St. Thomas expresses it as follows:

There is, then, in man a threefold knowledge of things divine. Of
these, the first is that in which man, by the natural light of reason,
ascends to a knowledge of God through creatures. The second is that
by which the divine truth—exceeding the human intellect—descends
on us in the manner of revelation, not, however, as something made
clear to be seen, but as something spoken in words to be believed. The
third is that by which the human mind will be elevated to gaze perfectly upon the things revealed.[2]

Modern Attitudes Toward Philosophy and Revelation

This understanding of the harmony which exists between metaphysics, faith, and theology is quite different from the attitude
which is more or less prevalent today on the part of those who
philosophize independently of a revelation. For such philosophers
regard revelation as an extrinsic, restrictive influence imposed arbitrarily upon the human intellect. It is a throttling of intelligence,
a dogmatic and unphilosophical curtailing of the mind's right
to investigate truth and the necessity that the mind has of following truth down whatever paths it leads. The philosopher cannot

[2] *Summa Contra Gentiles*, Vol. IV, chap. 1, trans. by Anton C. Pegis (Garden City, N. Y., Doubleday & Co., Inc., 1957).

possibly have anything to do with the theologian. It is the task of the former to pursue truth with complete freedom and spontaneity. The latter accepts something as true—mostly without sufficient reason—and works only within already prescribed limits. The quest of the philosopher remains an open one, guided only by reason. Its limit is the infinite, provided, that is, such a philosopher has not already accepted from his predecessors carefully laid down boundaries inside of which philosophy is a valid discipline. The theologian, on the other hand, and the philosopher who has accepted a revelation are concerned only with rehashing old concepts and must carefully refrain from questioning any dogmatically defined notions of man, God, or the universe.

The position is based on several assumptions. The first is, of course, that reason can be, and at times actually may be, in conflict with what is revealed. But the philosopher who has accepted a revelation has accepted it precisely because he is convinced that this revelation is not only reasonable, but that it is true. He is convinced, furthermore, that it contains a truth which he could never have arrived at merely through the use of his unaided human reason. Since he is convinced that such a revelation is true, he is equally certain that the truth it contains can never contradict, or be in opposition to, any truth he may discover in the purely philosophical area. The second assumption is that the only truth open to the human intellect is that which it can discover by its own unaided effort; that any acceptance of truth which cannot be adequately comprehended is an abdication of philosophy. Now it is true that such an acceptance of truth can no longer be considered philosophy, but neither can it be considered an abdication of intelligence and humanity. After all, it is man who philosophizes, and, while philosophy is the widest in scope of the human sciences, it is not the same to be a philosopher as it is to be a man. Philosophy is limited to the truth which can be discovered by unaided human reason, but man is not limited to such truth. And if the man in question also happens to be a philosopher, there is no reason in the world why he cannot accept as a man a truth which goes beyond the limits of philosophical investigation. Nor is such a man acting unphilosophically when he does so. Philosophy itself can provide him

with reasons for so doing. The human intellect is made to know
the real, to acquire truth. If it can acquire a greater and more
profound truth by an act of faith than it could otherwise acquire
on the purely natural level, then it becomes eminently reasonable
to make such an act of faith. The theologian does not scorn philosophical knowledge. He accepts it for all that it is worth and rises
above it only to make use of it again in seeking to comprehend
more perfectly the higher truth he has accepted. Modern philosophers have shown themselves more than willing to be corrected
by the natural sciences in some of their investigations. The biologist, the mathematician, the physicist, all of these are held in
veneration and their pronouncements carry great weight with
present day philosophers on what philosophy can or cannot accomplish. Why is it less reasonable for the science of revelation—
theology—to pronounce on whether philosophical conclusions
are valid or not, when seen in the eyes of a higher and more
perfect wisdom? It is a question of whether one is willing to face
reality as an integrated whole or not. The profundity of the real
exceeds our ability to grasp it adequately. Revelation is a manifestation of that profundity. It confronts us as a historical fact.
The rejection of it, or the ignoring of it, is more a limitation
placed on man's search for truth than the acceptance of it can
ever be.

RELATION OF PHILOSOPHY TO THEOLOGY

As a matter of historical fact it is appropriate to point out here
that all of the great systems of metaphysics written during the
Middle Ages were written by theologians in conjunction with
their theologizing. It was in union with their theology and under
the light of the revelation which they were explaining that they
achieved their success as philosophers. As great as were some
of the insights which were achieved by Plato and Aristotle, no
one can be merely a platonist or an aristotelian any more. It was
the concept of God as Being, which they took from the Scriptures,
which led Augustine, Aquinas, and Scotus to a fuller and more
perfect metaphysical knowledge of the Divinity.

One can add to all this the concept of the divine essence as an exemplar cause of all created things, an idea which in St. Augustine replaced the doctrine of the Platonic ideas. There is creation itself, which no Greek ever held; there is the immortality of the soul, which is vague, to say the least, in the writings of Aristotle; there is the substantial unity of man, which Plato never succeeded in establishing. All these notions are philosophical notions, yet we find them also in revelation. And it was the Christian philosophers who succeeded in establishing these truths philosophically after they read them in the Scriptures.

There is a richness and profundity in revelation itself which has succeeded in making better metaphysicians of those who accepted that revelation and philosophized under its light. And it is possible to do this without in any way confusing the two distinct disciplines of philosophy and theology. The one will never become identical with the other. Philosophy will always have for its object the reality which can be understood by man operating with the natural light of his reason. Theology will always look toward a revealed truth and seek to understand it better under the light of reason illuminated by faith. But two such disciplines can remain distinct without being completely separated from one another. Working in harmony there is no reason why one cannot aid the other. This aid, which will be supplied by the more perfect science, will then be twofold. It will in the first place consist of proposing new and more profound areas of truth to the consideration of the human intellect. And it will secondly be capable of exercising a negative control in so far as it can direct the intellect away from certain areas of investigation which it knows will lead nowhere but into darkness.

In this respect one need only consider again the knowledge which can be achieved about God from the viewpoint of natural reason. Philosophy can prove that God exists, and philosophers like Plato and Aristotle have done so. But as soon as philosophy begins to ask questions about the nature of this God, the answers are going to be inadequate at best. Is God one? Philosophy can truthfully answer: yes. But when one asks if this unity is possibly multiplicable within itself, philosophy must remain silent, if it is to avoid falling into error. The same inadequacy can be indicated about the philosophical question concerning the re-

lationship between nature and supposit. Philosophy could find
no reason to suggest that the former might possibly be different
from the latter. But should philosophy state that no distinction
between the two is in any way possible, then it stands convicted
by a revelation which points to the divine and human natures of
the one person, who is Christ.

It must be admitted, of course, that this approach is based on
the acceptance of a divinely revealed truth. That such truth,
furthermore, is able to be accepted only under the influence of
supernatural grace. Reason itself may dispose one to accept such
divinely given truth, but its actual acceptance is always due to
grace and not to reason. It is better to say, perhaps, that reasonable men have accepted such truth rather than to say that one
is led by reason to the threshold of revelation.

But just as reason can dispose man and at least negatively dispel
impediments to the acceptance of divinely revealed truth, so too
can it create impediments which stand between it and such acceptance. There are certainly many people today who are entirely
secularistic and materialistic in their outlook on life. There are
others who appear to be convinced that the human intellect can
only guess about what lies beyond the realm of sensible experience. Kantianism, Materialism, and Pragmatism have had a
lasting effect on the attitude of modern man about the capability
of the human mind to attain truth. Skepticism and doubt, a senti-
mental trust that, if there is anything beyond matter, it will all
work out all right, these have made drastic inroads on men's
confidence in their ability to discover truth. Philosophy is still
regarded by many as merely an attempt to correlate the conclusions of the various natural sciences. If it has any proper area of
its own, philosophy must settle for that region into which natural
science has not yet penetrated. But as science increases, so must
philosophy decrease, until finally it must disappear altogether.
Many who still speak of God have reduced Him to a meaningless
abstract projection of men's desires. And a heaven is nothing else
but the utopia which science will one day establish on earth.

There is very little hope that those with the attitude of mind
described above will be able to appreciate what is said in this
chapter. They can recognize that it is an attitude held by reason-

able men who have seen the reasonableness of accepting it and living according to it. The skeptic, the Agnostic, and the Relativist can at least be certain of this: there are those who accept with certainty the certainty of a truth which transcends the merely material and experiential order. Whether they themselves can ever hope to achieve such certainty and truth depends for the most part on a God Who wills that all men come to a knowledge of the truth.

REVELATION THROUGH CHRIST

Man is meant to achieve Being one day in all its fullness and perfection. He cannot do this merely as a philosopher or a scientist. For the Being toward which he is ordered is Itself beyond the reach of all natural science. Revelation is the necessary means objectively proposed to him which will lead him to a goal which is more than human. Man's own assent to that revelation and his practical living of it is the subjective means which is necessary for each individual man. Now if man is to achieve God in a special way, he must know something about the means and see this achievement as possible. That is why St. Thomas sees in the Incarnation of the Second Person of the Blessed Trinity the central fact in the history of creation. For the Incarnation shows man the possibility of such achievement and it is the Incarnate Son of God Himself who provides man with the necessary means. In the first place the Incarnation reveals that the ultimate union of man with God is not an impossibility, for God has united Himelf with man by assuming a human nature. Such a union of natures in the one person of Christ indicates at least the possibility of a union of man with God through knowledge. If the divinity has assumed a human nature into a substantial union with itself there is no reason why a less perfect union of men with Divinity in terms of knowledge is not possible.

Secondly, the Incarnation of the Second Person of the Blessed Trinity is itself an indication of the type of union with God which men may one day expect. Man is ordered to a union with God through knowledge. Now the Second Person proceeds from the Father by an intellectual generation. Hence the Word is akin to reason. The Word, then, is the intellectual image of God, and it is primarily because of his intellect that man is also called an image of God. Furthermore, in the Word is contained all the essences of all created things. Man's ascent to God is fittingly an ascent from a knowledge of created essences to the source of those essences in the Only-begotten Son of the Father. Now man cannot in his present state behold the Divinity, yet there has to be a certainty in the knowledge by which man is directed to his ultimate end. For this is the principle of everything ordered to that end. In the natural order the principles naturally known are most certain. But if man cannot yet know the Divinity but must accept by faith what Divinity has revealed about Itself, it is fitting that this revelation is made by One to Whom these things are already and immediately evident. Just as in the natural order, then, the certitude of a science is had by resolution into the first demonstrable principles, so, too, in the supernatural order the certitude about the truths of faith is founded in the instruction which has come from God Himself. Thus the Son, to whom the Father is clearly known, has declared to men what the Father is like.

There is no need, then, to conceive of a God so transcendent that no approach to Him is in any way possible. "Other" He may be, but not totally so. If philosophically we can never know the divine essence except by negation and analogy, at the same time we need not stop with a purely philosophical notion of God. In fact, we cannot. For philosophy, which necessarily leaves us with an inadequate and incomplete knowledge of divinity, has historically and as a matter of fact fallen into positive error about the nature of the Godhead. On the other hand, that philosophy which has been worked out in accord with a revelation has achieved an insight into divinity which was made possible only by the revelation with which it was joined. God is known in His Incarnate Son, and it is only that Son Who ultimately can lead man to a full and perfect knowledge of the triune God of revelation.

Thus it is that revelation and faith are seen as complements of natural reason itself. To the natural, indirect, and analogous knowledge of God which man is capable of attaining by reason, there is added a revealed truth to which man is to assent without fully understanding how it is true. That it is true, he knows, and he sees that the assent to it is reasonable and good. One of the truths so revealed is that man's destiny lies in a direct vision of the Godhead. In order to ascend to such perfect heights of knowing, God must descend first and raise man up to the possibility of that vision. This He has done, for the Incarnate Son of God has testified to the fact. Hence it is by submission to and faith in the Son that man is enabled to ascend to the destiny which he has been given. Knowledge must, for the time being, give way to faith, but only so that knowledge may one day come to full perfection in the vision of Him Who dwells in light inaccessible.

SUMMARY

1. The goal of knowledge is a grasp of being as the source and end of all things. This is God. Such knowledge of God as primary source and ultimate end is called wisdom.

2. This knowledge, however, is limited and imperfect. We can know *that* there is such a Being, but we cannot know *what* He is.

3. Some people, furthermore, are incapable of achieving many truths, which are open to natural reason, because of particular difficulties.

4. Since God wishes all men to come to a knowledge of the truth, it is fitting that He reveal truths, which otherwise would not be achieved by most men. It is also fitting that He reveal truths which are beyond the natural capacity of all men.

5. Truths which are revealed and which are beyond the natural capacity of all men can be accepted on faith. Such truths are not susceptible of being known, since the intellect is not moved necessarily to accept them by reason of their intrinsic evidence. Yet it is reasonable to accept them, although such acceptance is possible only under grace freely given.

6. It is obvious that such revealed truth cannot contradict truth naturally acquired, for the source of both is the same. Nor is such truth to be rejected because it is beyond philosophical reason.

For it is also reasonable to accept truth which reason left to itself could not achieve. Revelation and theology can be an indirect guide to keep philosophical reason from going astray.

7. This revelation made through Christ and accepted under the influence of grace will lead man to a knowledge of Being and Truth on a level which is truly proper to God Himself. Thus it is that man completes himself in terms of Divinity and thereby brings to full perfection his humanity.

SELECTED READINGS

Intrinsic Value of Scholasticism*

The intrinsic value of this Christian philosophy in the middle ages is a point for every philosopher to decide in the light of his own judgment. Most of them have their own opinion about it, but this opinion is not always founded upon a first-hand knowledge of the doctrines at stake. Now there is an excellent excuse, if not for judging what one does not sufficiently know, at least for not sufficiently knowing it. Life is short and the history of philosophy is growing longer every year. But if any Christian master felt the same indifference with respect to the history of scholasticism, he would be less easily excusable, because this is his own personal history or, at least, that of his own personal philosophical tradition. This tradition is not a dead thing; it is still alive and our own times bear witness to its enduring fecundity. There is no reason why this fecundity should come to an end. On the contrary, it can be expected to exhibit a new vitality every time it will re-establish contact with its authentic methods and its true principles, whose permanent truth is independent of time. The only object of the history of Christian philosophy, apart from being a history like all the others, is to facilitate access to the perennial sources of Christian speculation.

If, on the whole, this history has not completely misrepresented

* A *Gilson Reader*, Anton C. Pegis, ed. (Garden City, New York, Doubleday & Co., Inc., 1957), pp. 173-175.

its object, it can be said that the treasure of Christian philosophy in the middle ages exhibits an amazing wealth of still incompletely exploited ideas. But even leaving them aside, this history should convey to its readers an invitation to establish personal contact with at least three main schools of thought which no Christian philosopher can afford to ignore. Augustine will introduce him to a metaphysical method based upon the data of personal introspection; Duns Scotus will introduce him to a metaphysical universe of essences; Thomas Aquinas will tell him what happens to such a universe when existence is added to the essences as a further metaphysical dimension. Had they bequeathed to us nothing more than these three pure philosophical positions, the scholastics would still remain for all Christian philosophers the safest guides in their quest for a rationally valid interpretation of man and the world.

Scholastic Philosophy and Theology*

The adventures of philosophy in the seventeenth century should be a lesson for us on this point. In spite of what has been said, the evil then affecting scholastic philosophy was not its ignorance of the new science; the evil was the illusion that the task before it was to defend the antiquated science of Aristotle against the new science. Actually, the task for scholastic philosophy then was to locate this new science in its proper place, under the light of those very metaphysical principles whose meaning it had forgotten. Our task today is the same. It is not indeed to build up a new metaphysics and a new scholastic theology every time positive science invents a new world. The men of our generation have been born in the scientific universe of Newton; they have reached maturity in the universe of Einstein; they are entering old age in the universe of undulatory physics and, with luck, hope to die in a fourth universe, as different from Einstein's as his was from Newton's. Is it going to be said that we should have built up three new metaphysics and three new scholastic theologies in order to keep pace with the evolution of positive science during our own lifetime? Was not it better for them to remain unborn

* *Ibid.*, pp. 164-166.

than to be stillborn and straightway discarded? Our task today
is to recapture the true spirit of medieval metaphysics, to grasp
once more the genuine and profound meaning of its principles.
I should add that scholasticism, covered over by more than five
centuries of dust, is now experiencing its greatest evil—the ignorance of its own nature. To restore it to itself, let us listen to the
counsel of history: scholastic philosophy must return to theology!

In saying this, I am not in the least contesting the distinction
between faith and reason. Nor am I forgetting the formal distinction of objects, so dear to the dialecticians, between theology and
philosophy. I am not speaking of philosophy in general, but of
that kind of philosophy which we call "scholastic." I readily agree
that, without paying attention to theology, it is possible to be a
philosopher, but not a scholastic philosopher. The hackneyed objection that to philosophize as a Theologian is not to philosophize at
all, forgets that a formal distinction of objects is not a real separation in the order of exercise. One even wonders at times whether
this real separation is not responsible for the fact that, in certain
minds, the notion of scholastic theology, no less than that of
scholastic philosophy, has become obscured. If it were not obscured we should not have to stress the obvious fact that to
exercise the human intellect within the transcendent light of
faith means something else than to pretend to deduce philosophically demonstrated conclusions from an article of faith. The
philosophy we call scholastic is not distinguished from other philosophies by its essence; it is rather distinguished from them as
the best way of philosophizing. That is indeed how the encyclical
Aeterni Patris has described scholastic philosophy, and with perfect reason: *Qui philosophiae studium cum obsequio fidei Chris-
tianae conjungunt, ii optime philosophantur.* To philosophize
otherwise is assuredly to philosophize, but it is to philosophize
less well. At any rate, it is no longer to philosophize as did the
scholastics. There are certain fish that live only in warm water.
To say that they will die in cold water is not to deny that they
are fish. As for the fish that, as some insist at all costs, must be
made to live in cold water in order to maintain the purity of their
essences, they do not become true fish, but dead fish.

This is precisely what happened to metaphysics when, in order
to liberate it from the theology that had formerly liberated it

from Aristotelian physics, Descartes made it subservient to his own physics. Hence this paradoxical result, that in our own days, the only real defenders of metaphysics as an autonomous science are found to be the scholastic theologians. Now, let us be careful to observe, these theologians do not hold that metaphysics is necessary to sacred doctrine. The word of God is sufficient unto itself without any metaphysics. But if you make good use of metaphysics in theology, you will get a better theology, and you also will get a better metaphysics. This, at least, is what happened in the thirteenth century, and the truth of yesterday points out that of tomorrow. It is by restoring the several scholastic philosophies to their natural places—namely, their natal theologies— that history will better and better succeed in understanding them as they were. *Non erubesco evangelium* is a saying that we must know how to pronounce in all domains, even including that of scholarship. And it also is by returning to its natural place that scholastic philosophy can have the hope, or rather the certitude, that it will once more bring forth flowers and fruit. Only a prophet would be able to say what is to be the shape of its future. But the historian can safely state by whom scholastic philosophy will be given a true life in the future. The true scholastic philosophers will always be theologians.

What is Christian Philosophy?*

To the question: What is Christian philosophy? the shortest answer now is: If you read the encyclical letter *Aeterni Patris* you will find there the most highly authorized answer to your question. Reduced to its essentials, the answer is as follows.

In the first third of his encyclical Leo XIII recalls, along with the doctrinal function of the Church and the teaching office of the popes, the services rendered to theology by philosophy, but he does not forget to recall as well the benefits philosophy has always derived in the past from its close association with theology. In carefully weighted words, Leo XIII observes that "the human mind, being confined within certain limits, and these narrow enough, is exposed to many errors and is ignorant of many things. . . . Those, therefore, who to the study of philosophy unite

* *Ibid.*, pp. 186-187.

obedience to the Christian faith, are philosophizing in the best possible way; for the splendor of the divine truths, received into the mind, helps the understanding, and not only detracts in no wise from its dignity, but adds greatly to its nobility, keenness, and stability."

Obviously we are here returning, under a new name, to the very same situation occupied by philosophy with respect to Christian faith from the time of St. Justin up to the Cartesian philosophical reformation. Nor is it only a question for philosophy not to disagree with faith; a positive influence of faith over the human reason is here advocated not only as the best safeguard against error but also as a remedy to human ignorance.

It is no wonder, then, that instead of sketching a system of Christian philosophy, Leo XIII devotes the middle section of his encyclical to a truly admirable history of what happened to philosophy during the many centuries of its association with faith in the doctrines of the early Apologists, the Fathers of the Church, and the scholastic Doctors. Clearly, what Leo XIII calls Christian philosophy cannot be reduced to the content of any single philosophy; it is neither a system nor even a doctrine. Rather, it is a way of philosophizing; namely, the attitude of those who "to the study of philosophy unite obedience to the Christian faith." This philosophical method, or attitude—*philosophandi institutum* —is *Christian philosophy* itself.

It should now be clear that under the name of Christian philosophy Pope Leo XIII simply is sending us back to the method of handling philosophical problems traditional in the history of patristic and of scholastic theology; that is, to what the encyclical itself calls the "right use of that philosophy which the scholastic teachers have been accustomed carefully and prudently to make use of even in theological disputations." The panegyric of the "philosophy" of St. Thomas that fills up the last third of *Aeterni Patris*, not to the exclusion of other Doctors, but praising it as the very model and idea of the Christian way of philosophizing, is enough to assure us of what Christian philosophy truly was in the mind of Pope Leo XIII. Before anything else, it was the investigation, by means of philosophy, of the saving truth revealed by God and accessible to the light of natural reason.

Relation of Philosophy to Theology*

Before completing these pages I should like to propose a few further remarks. First of all, a few words about the relations of theology and philosophy. In my opinion, many an account of medieval philosophy has been impaired or vitiated by an insufficiently drawn distinction between these two disciplines: theology and philosophy.

Some seem to think that theology supplies cut and dried answers to the major philosophic questions, and in this way nullifies the endeavors of philosophy. Then there are those who fancy that in a Christian regime philosophy is subjugated to theology.

In real fact, theology possesses an object, a light, and a method that differ entirely from those of philosophy. Rooted in faith, it conducts its reasoning on the authority of the revealed word and proceeds *ex causa prima*; its object is the revealed datum itself, which it seeks to elucidate rationally.

When, therefore, a particular theological inquiry happens to provide an answer to a philosophic question, the answer is not given *philosophically*; the whole philosophic endeavor is to move along another plane. Philosophy, moreover, is not paralyzed but rather stimulated by this state of affairs. In fact, the mighty intellectual curiosity which stirred the Christian ages can only be explained against the background of the sublime mysteries propounded to them.

A word about the adage *philosophia ancilla theologiae*. Its origin, of course, is to be sought in St. Peter Damiani, who intended to silence philosophy with it. The Scholastic position is something entirely different. Therein philosophy is placed in the service of theology when, and only when, in its own workings theology employs philosophy as an *instrument* of truth in order to establish conclusions which are not philosophic but theological. *Ancilla*, then, it may be, but not *serva*, for theology handles philosophy in accordance with its own proper laws; a Minister of state yes, but a slave it can never be.

* J. Maritain, *An Essay of Christian Philosophy*, trans. by Edward H. Flannery (New York, Philosophical Library, Inc., 1955), pp. 34-36.

But in itself, or when engaged in its own pursuits, philosophy is not a handmaid; it is free, it enjoys the freedom to which as a form of wisdom it is entitled. I am fully aware that revelation *teaches* it certain truths, including philosophic. Even so, God alone is not subject to being taught, the angels themselves enlighten one another; being taught does not stifle the freedom of the mind, but merely attests that it is a created freedom. And for every created spirit truth holds primacy even over the quest for knowledge, however noble this quest may be. Some modern philosophers who disbelieve in Christian revelation presume to judge in terms of their own peculiar assumptions concerning this revelation the relationship established in the Christian system between philosophy and faith. Their method leaves something to be desired, for their assumptions are without validity save in a non-Christian system. Surely, if I did not believe that the primordial Truth itself is my teacher in the tenets of faith, if I believed that faith presents me with a mere code binding me to a human tradition, I would not accept the subordination of philosophy to faith. What I mean to say, in fine, is that no one will grant that philosophy should suffer durress: neither the non-Christian, in whose eyes faith would impose restraints on philosophy and obstruct its view; nor the Christian, for whom faith does not restrain philosophy but strengthens it and helps it to improve its vision.

BIBLIOGRAPHY

Aquinas, St. Thomas, *Summa Contra Gentiles*, Vol. I trans. by Anton C. Pegis. Garden City, N. Y., Doubleday & Co., Inc., 1955, chap. 1-8. *Cf.* also Vol. IV, trans. by Charles J. O'Neil, introduction and chaps. 27, 39, 42, 54.

Gilson, Etienne, *The Christian Philosophy of St. Thomas Aquinas.* New York, Random House, 1956, chap. 7.

———, *A Gilson Reader*, Anton C. Pegis, ed. Garden City, N .Y., Doubleday & Co., Inc., 1957, *cf.* esp. pp. 169-212.

Maritain, Jacques, *An Essay on Christian Philosophy*, trans. by Edward N. Flannery. (New York, Philosophical Library, Inc., 1955).

———, *Science and Wisdom*, trans. by Bernard Wall. New York, Charles Scribner's Sons, 1940.

GENERAL BIBLIOGRAPHY

Adamson, R., *Fichte*. Edinburgh, William Blackwood & Sons, Ltd., 1881.

A *Gilson Reader*, Anton C. Pegis, ed. Garden City, N. Y., Doubleday & Co., Inc., 1957.

Aquinas, St. Thomas, *Summa Contra Gentiles*, Vol. I, trans. by Anton C. Pegis. Garden City, N. Y., Doubleday & Co., Inc., 1955, Chap. 1-3. Vol. IV, trans. by C. O'Neil, Chap. 1, 27, 42, 54, *cf. Intro.*

———, *Summa Theologica*, trans. by Anton C. Pegis. New York, Random House, 1945, 2 Vols.

———, *De Potentia*, trans. by the English Dominican Fathers. Westminster, Md., Newman Press, 1952.

———, *De Veritate*, Vol. I, trans. by R. W. Mulligan. Chicago, Henry Regnery Co., 1949.

Ayer, A. J., *Philosophical Essays*. New York, St. Martin's Press, Inc., 1954.

Berdyaev, N., *The Origins of Russian Communism*. New York, Charles Scribner's Sons, 1937.

Bergman, Gustav, "Logical Positivism," in Vergilius Ferm, ed., *A History of Philosophical Systems*. New York, Philosophical Library, Inc., 1950.

Bergson, Henri, *Creative Mind: An Introduction to Metaphysics*, trans. by Mabel Andison. New York, Philosophical Library, Inc., 1946.

———, *Creative Evolution*. New York, Holt, Rinehart and Winston, Inc., 1911.

———, *Morality and Religion*, trans. by R. Ashley Andra and Cloudesley Brereton with the assistance of W. Horsfall Carter. New York, Holt, Rinehart and Winston, Inc., 1935.

———, *Matter and Memory*, trans. by Nancy Margaret Paul, and W. Scott Palmer. New York, The Macmillan Company, 1912.

———, *Time and Free Will*, trans. by R. L. Pogson. New York, The Macmillan Company, 1913.

Blau, J., *Men and Movements in American Philosophy*. Englewood Cliffs, N. J., Prentice-Hall, Inc., 1952.

Brennan, R. E., O.P., *Thomistic Psychology*. New York, The Macmillan Company, 1941.

Buechner, L., *Force and Matter*. New York, Truth Seeker Company, Inc., 1950.

Caird, E., *Hegel*. Edinburgh, William Blackwood & Sons, Ltd., 1883.

———, *The Critical Philosophy of Immanuel Kant*. New York, The Macmillan Company, 1909.

Calkins, M. W., *Berkeley: Essays, Principles, Dialogues, with Selections from Other Writings*. New York, Charles Scribner's Sons, 1929.

Carnap, R., *Philosophy and Logical Syntax*. London, Kegan Paul, Trench, Truebner & Co., Ltd., 1935.

Childs, J. L., *American Pragmatism and Education*. New York, Holt, Rinehart and Winston, Inc., 1952.

Cochrane, Arthur C., *The Existentialists and God*. Philadelphia, The Westminster Press, 1956.

Collins, James, *The Existentialists*. Chicago, Henry Regnery Co., 1952.

———, *A History of Modern European Philosophy*. Milwaukee, The Bruce Publishing Co., 1954.

———, *God in Modern Philosophy*. Chicago, Henry Regnery Co., 1959.

Comte, Auguste, *A General View of Positivism*, trans. by J. H. Bridges. London, Tribner, 1865.

Copleston, F., S.J., *Contemporary Philosophy*. Westminster, Md., The Newman Press, 1956.

Dempsey, Peter, O.F.M. Cap., *The Psychology of Sartre*. Cork, Cork University Press, 1950.

Desan, Wilfrid, *The Tragic Finale*. Cambridge, Mass., Harvard University Press, 1954.

Dewey, John, *The Quest for Certainty*. New York, Minton, Balch & Co., 1929.

———, *Philosophy and Civilization*. New York, Minton, Balch & Co., 1931.

———, *Logic: Theory of Inquiry*. New York, Holt, Rinehart and Winston, Inc., 1938.

———, *The Influence of Darwin on Philosophy*. New York, Holt, Rinehart and Winston, Inc., 1910.

———, *Essays in Experimental Logic*. Chicago, University of Chicago Press, 1916.

———, *How We Think*. Boston, D. C. Heath & Co., 1910.

———, *Psychology*, 3rd rev. ed. New York, American Book Company, 1891.

———, *A Common Faith*. New Haven, Conn., Yale University Press, 1934.

———, *Experience and Nature*. New York, W. W. Norton & Co., Inc., 1929.

———, *Reconstruction in Philosophy*. Boston, Beacon Press, 1948.

Edman, Irwin, *Four Ways in Philosophy*. New York, Holt, Rinehart and Winston, Inc., 1937, chap. 4.

Engels, F., *Ludwig Feuerbach*. New York, International Publishers Co., Inc., 1934.

——, *Herr Eugen Dühring's Revolution in Science (Anti-Dühring)*. New York, International Publishers Co., Inc., 1935.

——, *Socialism: Utopian and Scientific*. New York, International Publishers Co., Inc., 1935.

——, *The Origin of the Family, Private Property and the State*. Chicago, Charles H. Kerr Co., 1902.

England, F. E., *Kant's Conception of God*. London, George Allen & Unwin, Ltd., 1929.

Fichte, Johann Gottlieb, *The Popular Works of Johann Gottlieb Fichte*, 4th ed., W. Smith, ed. London, Tribner, 1889. 2 Vols.

Gilson, E., *The Spirit of Medieval Philosophy*. New York, Charles Scribner's Sons, 1936.

——, *Reason and Revelation in the Middle Ages*. New York, Charles Scribner's Sons, 1938.

——, *Réalisme Thomiste et Critique de la Connaissance*. Paris, J. Vrin, 1947.

——, *Being and Some Philosophers*. Toronto, Pontifical Institute of Medieval Studies, 1949, cf. esp. last chap., pp. 208-209.

Haeckel, Ernst, *The Riddle of the Universe*. New York, Harper & Brothers, 1899.

Hawkins, D. J. B., *Critical Problems of Modern Philosophy*. London and New York, Sheed & Ward, Ltd., 1957.

Hegel, G. W. F., *The Phenomenology of Mind*, 2nd ed., trans. by J. Baillie. New York, The Macmillan Company, 1931.

——, *Science of Logic*, trans. by W. H. Johnston and L. G. Struthers. New York, The Macmillan Company, 1929.

——, *Early Theological Writings*, trans. by T. M. Knox and R. Kroner. Chicago, University of Chicago Press, 1948.

——, *The Philosophy of Right and the Philosophy of History*, trans. by T. M. Knox and J. Sibree, Great Books of the Western World Series, Vol. 46. Chicago, Encyclopedia Britannica, Inc., 1952.

Heidegger, Martin, "On the Essence of Truth" and "What is Metaphysics," in W. Brock, ed., *Existence and Being*. Chicago, Henry Regnery Co., 1949.

Heineman, F. H., *Existentialism and the Modern Predicament*. New York, Harper & Brothers, 1953.

Henle, R. J., S.J., *Method in Metaphysics*, the Aquinas Lecture of the Aristotelian Society of Marquette University. Milwaukee, Marquette University Press, 1951.

Hocking, W. E., *Types of Philosophy*. New York, Charles Scribner's Sons, 1939.

Hoernle, R. F. A., *Idealism as a Philosophy*. New York, George H. Doran Co., 1927.

Höffding, H., *Modern Philosophers*. New York, The Macmillan Company, 1920.

Hook, S., *Marx and the Marxists*. Princeton, N. J., D. Van Nostrand Co., 1955.

Howison, G. H., *The Limits of Evolution*. New York, The Macmillan Company, 1904.

Huxley, T. H., *Lay Sermons*. New York, E. P. Dutton & Co., 1913.

James, William, *The Meaning of Truth*. New York, Longmans, Green & Co., 1909.

———, *A Pluralistic Universe*. New York, Longmans, Green & Co., 1909.

———, *Philosophy of William James, Drawn from His Own Works*, intro. by Horace M. Kallen. New York, the Modern Library, Inc., 1925.

———, *Pragmatism*. New York, Longmans, Green & Co., Inc., 1908.

———, *Selected Papers on Philosophy*. London and Toronto, J. M. Dent & Sons, Ltd., 1929.

———, *Some Problems of Philosophy*. New York, Longmans, Green & Co., 1911.

Jaspers, Karl, *The Way to Wisdom*, trans. by R. Manheim. New Haven, Conn., Yale University Press, 1951.

———, *Reason and Existenz*, trans. by W. Earle. New York, The Noonday Press, 1955.

Joad, C. E. M., *A Critique of Logical Positivism*. Chicago, University of Chicago Press, 1950.

———, *Guide to the Philosophy of Morals and Politics*. New York, Random House, 1938.

Jones, W. T., *Morality and Freedom in the Philosophy of Immanuel Kant*. New York, Oxford University Press, 1940.

Kant, Immanuel, *Critique of Practical Reason and Other Writings in Moral Philosophy*, trans. by L. W. Beck. Chicago, University of Chicago Press, 1949.

———, *Inaugural Dissertation and Early Writings on Space*, trans. by J. Handyside. Chicago, Open Court Publishing Company, 1929.

———, *Critique of Pure Reason*, trans. by N. K. Smith. London, Macmillan & Co., Ltd., 1933.

———, *The Critique of Pure Reason*, 2nd ed., trans. by J. M. D. Meiklejohn, Everyman's Library Series. New York, E. P. Dutton & Co., 1934.

———, *Fundamental Principles of the Metaphysics of Ethics*, trans. by Thomas Kingsmill Abbott. New York, Longmans, Green & Co., 1909.

————, *The Critique of Judgment*, trans. by James Creed Meredith. New York, Oxford University Press, 1911 and 1928. In two parts.

————, *Kant's Cosmogony*, W. Hastie, ed. Glasgow, Robert Mac-Lehose & Co., Ltd., 1900.

Kierkegaard, Soren, *Fear and Trembling*, trans. by Walter Lowrie. Princeton, N. J., Princeton University Press, 1941.

————, *Either/Or*, Vol. I, trans. by David F. and Lillian M. Swenson, Vol. II, trans. by Walter Lowrie. Princeton, N. J., Princeton University Press, 1944. 2 Vols.

————, *The Sickness Unto Death*. Princeton, N. J., Princeton University Press, 1946.

Klubertanz, G. P., S.J., *The Philosophy of Human Nature*. New York, Appleton-Century-Crofts, Inc., 1953.

Laky, J. J., *A Study of George Berkeley's Philosophy in the Light of the Philosophy of St. Thomas Aquinas*. Washington, Catholic University of America Press, 1950.

Lenin, V., *Materialism and Empirico-Criticism*. New York, International Publishers Co., Inc., 1927.

————, *Marx, Engels, Marxism*. New York, International Publishers Co., Inc., 1935.

Library of Living Philosophers, P. A. Schilpp, ed. Evanston, Ill., Northwestern University Press, 1939.

Luce, A. A., *Berkeley's Immaterialism: A Commentary on his "Treatise Concerning the Principles of Human Knowledge."* London, Thomas Nelson & Sons, Ltd., 1945.

McFadden, C., O.S.A., *The Philosophy of Communism*. New York, Benziger Brothers, Inc., 1939.

Marcel, Gabriel, *The Philosophy of Existence*. New York, Philosophical Library, Inc., 1949.

————, *Man Against Mass Society*. Chicago, Henry Regnery Co., 1952.

Maritain, Jacques, *An Essay on Christian Philosophy*, trans. by Edward H. Flannery. New York, Philosophical Library, Inc., 1955.

————, *Science and Wisdom*. New York, Charles Scribner's Sons, 1940.

————, *A Preface to Metaphysics*, trans. by E. I. Watkin. New York, Charles Scribner's Sons, 1940.

————, *The Degrees of Knowledge*, trans. under the supervision of Gerald B. Phelan. London, Geoffrey Bles, Ltd., 1959.

————, *Existence and the Existent*, trans. by L. Galantière and G. B. Phelan. New York, Pantheon Books, Inc., 1949.

————, *Bergsonian Philosophy and Thomism*, trans. by Mabelle Andison in collaboration with J. Gordon Andison. New York, Philosophical Library, Inc., 1955.

Marx, Karl, *Capital*, trans. by Eden and Cedar Paul, Everyman's Library Series. New York, E. P. Dutton & Co., 1934. 2 Vols.

————, *The Communist Manifesto.* Chicago, Henry Regnery Co., 1954.

Muirhead, J. H., *Idealism.* Chicago, Encyclopedia Britannica, Inc.

Murdoch, Iris, *Sartre.* New Haven, Conn., Yale University Press, 1953.

Mure, G. R. G., *An Introduction to Hegel.* Oxford, The Clarendon Press, 1940.

Ostwald, Wilhelm, *Natural Philosophy,* trans. by T. Seltzer. New York, Holt, Rinehart and Winston, Inc., 1910.

Paton, H. J., *The Categorical Imperative: A Study in Kant's Moral Philosophy.* Chicago, University of Chicago Press, 1948.

————, *Kant's Metaphysic of Experience.* New York, The Macmillan Company, 1936.

————, *The Moral Law; or, Kant's Groundwork of the Metaphysic of Morals.* New York, Barnes and Noble, Inc., 1950.

Paulsen, F., *Immanuel Kant: His Life and Doctrine.* New York, Charles Scribner's Sons, 1902.

Peirce, Charles Sanders, *Chance, Love and Logic,* ed. with intro. by Morris R. Cohen, and a supplementary essay by John Dewey. New York, George Braziller, Inc., 1956.

————, *Collected Papers of Charles Sanders Peirce,* Charles Hartshorne and Paul Weiss, eds. Cambridge, Mass., Harvard University Press, 1931.

————, *Philosophical Writings of Peirce,* J. Buchler, ed. New York, Dover Publications, Inc., 1955.

Perry, R. B., *Philosophy of the Recent Past.* New York, Charles Scribner's Sons, 1926.

————, *Present Philosophical Tendencies.* New York, Longmans, Green & Co., 1912.

Phelan, G. B., "The Existentialism of St. Thomas," *Proceedings of the American Catholic Philosophic Association,* Vol. 21. Washington, Catholic University of America Press, 1946, pp. 25-40.

Readings in Contemporary Philosophy, J. L. Jarrett and S. M. McMurrin, eds. New York, Holt, Rinehart and Winston, Inc., 1954.

Regis, L. M., O.P., *St. Thomas and Epistemology,* Aquinas Lecture of the Aristotelian Society of Marquette University. Milwaukee, Marquette University Press, 1946.

Reith, Herman, C.S.C., *An Introduction to Philosophical Psychology.* Englewood Cliffs, N.J., Prentice-Hall, Inc., 1957.

Royce, Josiah, *Lectures on Modern Idealism.* New Haven, Conn., Yale University Press, 1919.

Russell, Bertrand, *What I Believe.* New York, E. P. Dutton & Co., Inc., 1926.

Sartre, Jean Paul, *Existentialism,* trans. by B. Frechtman. New York, Philosophical Library, Inc., 1957.

————, *L'Être et le Néant.* Paris, Librairie Gallimard, 1938.

————, *La Nausée.* Paris, Librairie Gallimard, 1938.

Schelling, Joseph, *Of Human Freedom*, trans. by J. Gutman. Chicago, Open Court Publishing Company, 1936.
————, *The Ages of the World*, trans. by F. DeW. Bolman, Jr. New York, Columbia University Press, 1942.
Sellars, Roy Wood, *Evolutionary Naturalism*. Chicago, Open Court Publishing Company, 1922.
Sertillanges, A. D., O.P., *The Foundations of Thomistic Philosophy*, trans. by G. Anstruther. St. Louis, B. Herder Book Company, 1931.
Sheed, F., *Communism and Man*. London, Sheed & Ward, Ltd., 1938.
Smith, G., S.J., "A Date in the History of Epistemology," *The Thomist*, Vol. 5, the Maritain Volume. New York, Sheed & Ward, Inc., 1943.
Spencer, Herbert, *First Principles*. Akron, Ohio, Werner Company, 1864.
————, *Data of Ethics*. New York, D. Appleton and Company, 1884.
Stace, W. T., *The Philosophy of Hegel*. London, Macmillan & Co., Ltd., 1924.
The Philosophy of Communism, C. Boyer, S.J., ed. New York, Fordham University Press, 1952.
Urmson, J. O., *Philosophical Analysis*. Oxford, The Clarendon Press, 1958.
Ward, James, *Naturalism and Agnosticism*. New York, The Macmillan Company, 1903. 2 Vols.
Watson, J., *Schelling's Transcendental Idealism*, 2nd ed. Chicago, Griggs, 1892.
Watson, John, *Psychology from the Viewpoint of a Behaviorist*. Philadelphia, J. B. Lippincott Co., 1929.
Weldon, T. D., *Introduction to Kant's Critique of Pure Reason*. Oxford, The Clarendon Press, 1945.
Werkmeister, W. H., *A History of Philosophical Ideas in America*. New York, The Ronald Press Company, 1949.
Wetter, G., S.J., *Dialectical Materialism*, trans. by Peter Heath. New York, Frederick A. Praeger, Inc., 1958.
White, Morton, *The Age of Analysis*. Boston, Houghton Mifflin Co., 1955.
Whitney, G. T., and Bowers, D. F., *The Heritage of Kant*. Princeton, N.J., Princeton University Press, 1939.
Wilhelmsen, F., *Man's Knowledge of Reality*. Englewood Cliffs, N.J., Prentice-Hall, Inc., 1956.
Wild, John, *The Challenge of Existentialism*. Bloomington, Ind., Indiana University Press, 1955.

INDEX

315